CRACK OF THE BAT

Crack of the Bat

A History of Baseball on the Radio

JAMES R. WALKER

Foreword by Pat Hughes

UNIVERSITY OF NEBRASKA PRESS

Lincoln and London

This book is dedicated to the memory of Wynn C. Walker Jr. who taught me, among many other things, how to tie my shoes.

CONTENTS

FOREWORD

Pat Hughes

The radio voice of the Chicago Cubs since 1996, Pat Hughes has preserved and celebrated baseball's greatest announcers by producing, writing, and narrating his *Baseball Voices* series of CDs. Hughes created tributes to legendary announcers, including Mel Allen, Red Barber, Marty Brennaman, Jack Buck, Harry Caray, Milo Hamilton, Russ Hodges and Lon Simmons, Harry Kalas, Dave Niehaus, Bob Prince, Ron Santo, and Bob Uecker. The series is available at www.baseballvoices.com.

The 1979 hit single "Video Killed the Radio Star" by the Buggles is familiar to TV trivia fans as the first music video on MTV. While music videos have mostly departed MTV, for baseball fans, radio broadcasts remain a daily delight. It seems radio and its baseball "radio stars" were lowered into their graves a bit prematurely. Baseball on the radio is as healthy as ever, despite the televising of nearly every big league game. Millions of baseball fans make sure that one of the buttons on their car radio connects them to their team's radio voices. As a result, local broadcast rights contribute record revenues to MLB teams, and ratings remain strong despite many competing sound options. In fact, baseball has been a leader in packaging its radio broadcast for the information age media. MLB has been among the first to put games on the Internet and satellite radio. Over the nearly one hundred years of baseball broadcasts, the lure of the game for listeners has been a constant. In a world of unlimited channels, content is king, and baseball provides more than six months of engaging content every year.

In *Crack of the Bat*, Jim Walker has carefully documented how the great experience of the national pastime on the radio came to be. It was an arduous journey. Owners debated the value of baseball broadcasts for nearly twenty years. About half of them believed radio was a powerful tool for selling the game and bringing fans to the ballpark. The other half, as crazy as it sounds now, thought radio "gave the game away" and hurt attendance. While the outcome now seems a forgone conclusion, it was the proradio passion of the Cubs owner, William Wrigley Jr., and his president, Bill Veeck Sr., that saved baseball on the radio when other owners threatened to ban it. The management's belief in the promotional power of radio and later television is a major reason there are so many loyal Cubs fans today.

As the radio voice of the Chicago Cubs, I am proud to be part of this passionate proradio tradition. The Cubs welcomed radio, with as many as five Chicago stations carrying the games at the same time in the 1930s. I follow the brilliant legacy of wonderful Cubs announcers, including Quin Ryan, Hal Totten, Pat Flanagan, Charlie Grimm, Bert Wilson, Jack Quinlan, Lou Boudreau, Vince Lloyd, Jack Brickhouse, Harry Caray, and, of course, my longtime partner, Hall of Famer Ron Santo. Jim's book documents the contributions of many great announcers, including eight often-forgotten pioneers who helped invent the craft in the 1920s and 1930s. He also devotes a chapter to modern announcers and shows the massive influence of Red Barber and his most distinguished pupil, the incomparable Vin Scully. Barber was the first announcer to emphasize extensive daily preparation, to provide detailed, vivid accounts of the game, and to let the crowd's roar, not mere words, punctuate the great moments in the game.

While *Crack of the Bat* honors the great announcers of the past, it also shows how baseball broadcasts have adapted to changes in the broadcast media over the years. After the Second World War, the rapid increase in radio stations led to the development of vast team networks. Over the next three decades, as many teams limited the number of games broadcast on TV, radio was baseball's superhighway to fans across the nation. The book then brings readers right up to the present, by showing how MLB uses its backbone radio broadcasts to feed the newer media. It also shows that, despite technological change, the qualities of great announcing are timeless.

The effective baseball announcer exhibits at least eight exemplary skills. They are as useful today as they were forty years ago and will be forty years from today. The professional announcer

1. starts with solid, accurate reporting;
2. is fair to all, including players, managers, front-office executives, and umpires;
3. has a pleasing voice that wears well over the long season;
4. possesses a lively sense of humor and a distinctive personality and knows how to tell a good story;
5. draws on a rich vocabulary and command of the language;
6. creates a home run call that is distinctive and original;
7. senses the drama of the game and recognizes its crucial turning points; and
8. develops a thorough knowledge of all things baseball: the rules, the history of the game, and the facts and figures that come from extensive preparation on a daily basis.

Announcers also benefit from the good luck of calling the games of great teams, which elevates their own status. However, several Hall of Fame announcers, such as By Saam, Jack Brickhouse, and Bob Uecker, never covered a World Series winner. While the technologies that deliver the game to the fans have and will continue to evolve, the elements of announcing excellence remain constant.

Although *Crack of the Bat* carefully documents the history of baseball on the radio, it does not wallow in nostalgia. The "good old days" of baseball on radio are in many ways the present. Perhaps the best evidence that baseball broadcasts today are better than ever is the number of outstanding announcers currently calling the game. At no time in the history of the game have so many Hall of Fame announcers been active, including Marty Brennaman, Jaime Jarrin, Denny Matthews, Tim McCarver, Jon Miller, Eric Nadel, Vin Scully, Dave Van Horne, and Bob Uecker. While *Crack of the Bat* is a uniquely comprehensive and valuable account of baseball's radio history, it also reminds us just how compelling baseball broadcasts can be in the hands of its skilled announcers. Video may have killed other radio celebrities, but today's fans of the national pastime can listen to more "radio stars" than ever before.

ACKNOWLEDGMENTS

I am hardly the first author to report that no one writes a book alone. Many colleagues and friends have helped in this project. For the past twenty years, Joel Sternberg, my generous colleague at Saint Xavier University, provided me with valuable references in broadcast history; his sustained interest and support made this a better book. I had the time needed to complete the research and writing because of the sabbatical awarded to me by Saint Xavier University for the 2012–13 academic year. That essential support made this book possible. In addition, a faculty research grant from sxu's College of Arts & Sciences paid for most of the photographs included in this volume. My great friend and frequent coauthor, Rob Bellamy of Duquesne University, provided many keen insights into the development of the media industries in the United States. This volume is much richer as a result. Research resources provided by the National Baseball Hall of Fame and Museum's A. Bartlett Giamatti Research Center, the Library of American Broadcasting at the University of Maryland, the Wisconsin Historical Society, the Oral History Collection at Columbia University, the Joyce Sports Research Collection at the University of Notre Dame Hesburgh Libraries, the George A. Smathers Libraries at the University of Florida, and the Recorded Sound Reference Center at the Library of Congress yielded much of the primary source material employed extensively in this volume. My thanks to the many fine staff members at those institutions who assisted me in my searches. This book, especially chapter 11, gained firsthand wisdom from personal interviews with the award-winning broadcasters Pat Hughes of the Chicago Cubs and Charley Steiner of the Los Angeles Dodgers. My special thanks to these models of radio professionalism. Professionalism also is the call word for the many fine publishing experts that work at and with the University of Nebraska Press. I offer them my deepest gratitude for their hard work.

Finally, I want to acknowledge the most valuable assistance of my wife, Judith R. Hiltner, who provided constant support, kind criticism, and superior copyediting throughout this project. Her insights touched nearly every page of this volume. The reader will not be aware of her many contributions, but they will benefit greatly from them.

CRACK OF THE BAT

Introduction

A Game in Words and Sound

Radio is a writerly medium. It privileges the power of words. Reading and listening nurture the mind's eye. Film and television hit you in the eyes. Writers love radio because of its rich use of language, which they treasure more than most listeners do. During the baseball broadcast, this language is enriched by the announcer's resonant voice, the ballpark's ambient clatter, the distinctive exhortations of players at play, and the "crack of the bat." But baseball on the radio is language first and foremost. Writers appreciate, and perhaps are a little jealous of, the artful prose of the gifted announcer, composed in an instant, while the serious writer takes hours, days, or sometime years to match it. What the Dodgers' Vin Scully invents in the moment, the *New Yorker*'s baseball writer Roger Angell might top, but only in fortnight.

In the early days of the radio game, newspapermen ridiculed baseball announcers. But after television began stealing radio's thunder, journalists began praising the former pariah, lamenting the declining audience for the radio gamecast. Television exposed the often dull reality of a late-August game, providing little action and an even less impact on the final standings. The players were small and all too human. On the radio, the game could become whatever the listener, encouraged by the announcers, wanted to see. Players became larger-than-life figures. A vivid example hangs at the Fenimore Art Muesum in Cooperstown, New York. Folk artist Malcah Zeldis's painting *Homage to Hank Greenberg* captures a spellbound young Jewish girl and her family as they listen to the radio gamecast, seeing the Tigers' Hall of Fame slugger as a superhero.

While a generation of fans treasured the experience of baseball on the radio and even argued elegantly for its superiority to television (see chapter 10), the video medium long ago surpassed radio as the medium of choice for most baseball fans. Billion-dollar contracts are signed by television networks, not radio webs.

This book rightfully celebrates the beauty and craft of baseball on the radio, but consistently within the context of its role in the modern media environment. There are certainly many paths through any history, and this book offers only one. Much of the prior historical work on baseball on the radio has focused on the personal contributions of announcers to our celebration of the national pastime. Works by Curt Smith, Eldon L. Ham, and Tony Silvia, as well as dozens of individual announcer biographies and autobiographies, provide a rich personalized history of the game's greatest voices.[1] Although this volume examines the development of the announcer's craft in chapters 3 and 11, the primary focus is the evolution of radio's coverage of the game from 1920 to the present and baseball's reaction to it. The interplay among baseball owners, broadcast stations and networks, and baseball's sponsors receives most of the attention. Announcers helped create many cherished fan memories, and their calls are repeated in any telling of the Major League Baseball's story. What has been slighted or even completely overlooked in previous studies of baseball on the radio are the political, social, and economic forces that enabled those historic calls by the memorable "voices of the game."

While some early studies have covered this history, they have relied mostly on oral histories or newspaper and website accounts. This volume makes use of these sources but also enriches our understanding of baseball's radio history through the use of major archival resources. In particular, the archives at the National Baseball Hall of Fame, the National Broadcasting Company Records, 1921–69, at the Wisconsin Historical Society, the Library of Congress, the Walter Lanier "Red" Barber Papers and Book Collection at the University of Florida, the New York Yankee business records at the New York Public Library, and the holdings of the Library of American Broadcasting were examined. These archives yielded thousands of pages of primary source material, including letters, memos, and baseball owners' meeting minutes. The archives also yielded rare newspaper and magazine accounts of radio's early coverage of baseball. While some of the history examined in this volume has been referenced elsewhere, much of it has never been uncovered or documented extensively from primary sources.

The book follows the chronology of baseball on the radio over three distinct periods: the formative years, the age of acceptance, and the television era. During the formative period from 1920 to 1936, baseball owners struggled over how to use the new medium. During this period, the professional baseball announcer emerged from the ranks of sports reporters, radio staff announcers, and baseball public-address announcers. Franchise owners were sharply divided over the benefits or liabilities of the new medium. Major national advertisers aggressively pushed reluctant team owners into the radio age. Significantly for the development of radio, the World Series broadcasts became a major national phenomenon.

In the next age from 1937 to 1960, owners finally accepted radio as full partner. During this age of acceptance, the airing of all regular-season Major League games live from the ballpark became the standard and teams solidified their ownership of radio rights. Re-creations of road games from telegraph reports gave way to live broadcasts. Thus, each Major League game was actually covered by two broadcast teams. The addition of a color commentator, usually an ex-player, also became the status quo. Taking advantage of the explosive growth in radio stations after World War II, teams developed extensive regional networks. In the early 1950s, two national radio networks offered daily games, but by the early 1960s well-established team networks made the remaining national broadcast obsolete. The limited number of television channels in the precable era made baseball on the radio a defining experience for a generation of fans. National network broadcasts even had a rebirth, first on CBS and later on ESPN.

The final period, 1961 to the present digital age, is the television era. Team broadcast networks continued to expand during most of this period, but alternatives to local radio stations developed as well. The Internet became a major distributor of out-of-market broadcasts. Audio distribution came first, providing the model for MLB's very successful video service. Satellite radio supplied MLB with another audio revenue stream. Despite a decline in ratings, traditional radio stations paid teams record rights fees to gain access to baseball fans. In an era when distribution channels seem endless, content is king. Baseball wears that crown every summer.

While this book is structured chronologically, it does not give all eras equal attention. The preponderance of the analysis falls during the formative period when the structure that continues into the twenty-first century developed. This is the most historically interesting epoch, when the relationship between Major League Baseball and the nascent radio industry was in flux. The resolutions from this conflicted time endured throughout the next two eras. The remainder of this introduction examines some of the key themes that are more fully examined in the book. We begin with a question that has a seemingly self-evident answer.

Theme 1: What Is a Baseball Broadcast?

At first this appears to be an odd question. Is a baseball broadcast not simply an announcer with a microphone at a ballpark describing the action in front of him or her? Of course the call must be transmitted next to the public through some means: a flagship broadcast station or a team's broadcast network, perhaps a national radio network such as ESPN Radio or the Sirius XM satellite network or through the Internet as part of MLB's Gameday package. The announcer speaks, crowd noises are mixed in, and almost instantly listeners hear the result. That is all there is to it. But the history of radio's presentation of the game, particularly its early history, is a bit more complex.

Designated hitters aside, baseball is a game with nine players on a side, played over nine innings. It has also been broadcast at least nine different ways. The following list, moving from the most common to the more obscure, provides examples of each approach:

1. *Standard broadcast*: The live voice of the observer at the field is linked to a station transmitter, networked broadcast transmitters, a satellite radio service, or the Internet.
   Examples: all contemporary radio broadcasts.
2. *Wire service re-creation*: Play-by-play descriptions in telegraph code are received by a station. The announcer re-creates the game action on the basis of the telegraphed account.
   Examples: virtually all Major League road-game broadcasts until 1946; MLB coverage on the Liberty Broadcasting System from 1949 to 1952.
3. *Delayed wire service re-creation*: After-game re-creations are broadcast from telegraphed reports.
   Example: Chicago Cubs re-creations sponsored by the team in 1930s to promote the team during the evening, when listening levels were highest.
4. *Inning-by-inning summary*: Summaries of the game action in telegraph code are transmitted to a station and read by a station announcer.
   Examples: Coverage of the 1920 World Series on Detroit News radio-telephone station (later WWJ); flash broadcast of Washington Senators' opening-day game in 1922.
5. *Pirated broadcasts*: The call heard on the originating station doing a live broadcast of the game is repeated.
   Examples: Gordon McLendon using Mel Allen's call of Yankee games as the basis of some re-creations on the Liberty Broadcasting System; KQV using KDKA's re-creations of Pirates road games as the source for its own re-creations; General Mills sponsoring broadcasts on WMCA in New York in 1936.
6. *Voice-relay broadcast*: A live observer at the game is linked by phone to an announcer at a radio station who relays word for word what the observer tells him.
   Example: the first radio broadcast of a World Series in 1921 on WBZ in Newark, New Jersey.

7. *Out-of-park observer*: Observers are stationed outside the ballpark telephoning results to a station for re-creation.

Example: in 1938 KQV in Pittsburgh observing Pirates games from vantage points outside Forbes Field.

8. *In-park observer*: Observers are stationed in the ballpark and report results by portable radio transmitter or telephone to a station for re-creation.

Example: discussed by American League owners at their 1936 meeting.

9. *Newspaper-station broadcast*: A wire-service reporter writes descriptions of the play-by-play action that are transmitted by telegraph to radio stations and read by a station announcer.

Example: AP network of newspaper-owned radio stations covering the 1925 World Series.

The simple question has at least nine, not so obvious answers. The reasons for these varied approaches were technological, economic, and legal. The standard broadcast is the most expensive, especially for road games. It requires teams, stations, or sponsors to pay for announcers' travel and substantial line fees. Re-creations greatly reduced the cost of producing road games by eliminating announcers' travel expenses and AT&T line charges. In addition, teams only gradually realized they must maintain full legal control of their radio rights. Until they did, some stations created their own unsanctioned gamecasts, using a variety of now discarded techniques.

Newspaper-station broadcasts were part of that industry's attempt to compete with developing radio networks in the mid-1920s. Since many newspapers had their own local radio stations and were connected to the Associated Press wire service, the AP reports could be wired and read locally throughout the country. Radio companies received exclusive broadcast rights for the 1926 World Series, effectively eliminating the newspapers' competing radio coverage. Stations poaching MLB radio rights used several other approaches. By listening to authorized broadcasts, observing the game from nearby rooftops, or receiving reports from ballpark spies, stations could obtain play-by-play information without the team's consent and at a minimal cost. These nefarious baseball broadcasts were ended after federal court action in 1938 (see chapter 8).

Theme 2: Team Differences

I examine how owners gradually embraced radio from the first radio World Series in 1921 until the New York franchises finally allowed regular-season home-game broadcasts in 1939. Acceptance was slow in coming but not because owners were mindless Luddites. Despite the commonality of owning a Major League team, owners were located in very different markets and had very different economic resources.

In 1922 the U.S Supreme Court upheld a court of appeals ruling that made Major League Baseball exempt from U.S. antitrust laws. Baseball owners could now legally act as a cartel, working together to secure the best radio deals possible. For the World Series and All-Star Game, MLB would, through the commissioner's office, offer a united front. But the local situations were varied at best and chaotic at worst.

Chicago Cubs owner William K. Wrigley Jr. experienced in the power of advertising to sell chewing gum, immediately recognized the value of the felicitous spring-to-fall marriage of youthful radio and the baseball establishment. The radio game offered owners a two-hour daily commercial for their teams. Weekday daylight games could reach women, children, and some men, while weekend contests could add most of the rest of the male population to baseball's radio audience. Added to increasingly engaged local fans were hundreds of thousands listening in outlying regions, who could use increasingly available automobiles and paved roads to come to the ballpark on weekends. The few paying customers lost to the radio version of the game would be more than made up for by newly minted fans.

To benefit from the new medium, the team on the field needed to be good. Advertising rarely sells a bad product for long. However, a successful team could use radio to expand its fan base dramatically. But what if the team was very bad, and what if the market was pinned in by other teams or simply so large that weekend customers were superfluous? Radio worked for Wrigley's powerhouse Cubs team located in the Midwest "capital" Chicago, but what about the hapless St. Louis Browns, stuck with a bad team to shill? What about the New York Yankees, with a great team in a big market but little reason to risk losing any paying customers to the new medium? Two stations affiliated with major daily newspapers broadcast the Cubs' games, solidifying the media-sport bond that benefited both businesses. But what about broadcasting games on stations with no newspaper connections? What about franchises that needed the steady support of local newspapers to promote their teams and risked alienating the "fourth estate" by allowing daily broadcasts? Given teams' different circumstances, it is not surprising that owners differed considerably in the way they approached the emerging medium.

While baseball's antitrust exemption made it possible for teams to work cooperatively, it certainly did not require it. The baseball cartel's cooperation was forthcoming when it could produce a common benefit, such as restricting players' salaries through the reserve clause or limiting competition for Minor League players by developing farm systems. Controlling labor costs by eliminating competition among owners for that scarce resource helped keep most franchises profitable. When times got tough, as during the Great Depression of the 1930s, cooperative owners could even enforce mandatory wage cuts. Players had nowhere else to go if they wanted to play "big league" ball. But the antitrust exemption also allowed owners to ignore social and economic change. Their stagnation had social and economic consequences.

Owners could enforce spoken or unspoken "gentlemen's agreements," such as removing African Americans and dark-skinned Hispanics from their game. Despite the outstanding talent in these groups demonstrated in many head-to-head competitions with whites-only barnstorming teams stocked with Major League players, owners refused until 1947 to tap that player pool. The Major League cartel could also resist technological innovation. In the early 1930s, ignoring clear evidence of the positive effect of night baseball on attendance, owners refused to light their ballparks. Their intransience provoked one major American industrialist to offer to install lights so that he could use the ballparks for nighttime skeet-shooting competitions (see chapter 8). Radio was just another technology that owners could thwart if they chose to do so; and about half of them did just that, while the others embraced it enthusiastically.

Theme 3: A Geographic Divide

But radio was different from night baseball. The cost of putting up lights and the potential bump in attendance from playing games when most fans could actually attend was similar for each team. The benefit of radio was very different depending on a team's location. The big split between eastern and western (at the time really midwestern) franchises over the broadcasting of regular-season games was partly driven by geography. Eastern teams were pinned in by nearby franchises. In the 1920s and 1930s, Washington, Philadelphia, and New York had six of the sixteen Major League clubs clustered along a 225-mile stretch of the East Coast. Using radio to reach distant listeners with the hope of bringing new fans to the park was less appealing when those fans were already in another team's geographic territory. Owners in these markets knew their fans were local. Good streetcar or subway access was essential, not radio broadcasts. Not surprisingly, the major eastern exception was the Boston market, where the radio entrepreneur John Shepherd III exploited the geographic isolation and poor radio reception of the region to build the very successful Yankee and Colonial Networks (see chapter 8). He used regional sports, including baseball, as a major audience draw. This early development of regional baseball broadcasts helped make the Red Sox a large-market franchise with baseball's second-highest payrolls in the first decade of the twenty-first century.

Out west things were different. Pittsburgh was somewhat isolated by mountainous terrain and a doggedly antiradio ownership, but most of the other franchises saw the promotional benefits of radio. With considerable distances between franchises, Midwest teams could reach out by radio to regional fans in what has been dubbed the "hinterlands" model.[2] Cleveland could covert northern Ohio into Indians fans. Cincinnati could reach southern Ohio, West Virginia, and Kentucky. Chicago had Illinois, southern Wisconsin, and northern Indiana within reach of its powerful AM stations. The Detroit Tigers could form a Michigan network and draw weekend fans from throughout that state. St. Louis was in the best geographic position of all: the most western franchise, with all of the Mid-South and Great Plains states at its beck and call. Only the range of St. Louis–based AM stations limited its influence. However, in the early 1930s, St. Louis teams, especially the Browns, resisted radio because of territorial conflicts over the radio broadcast of more successful Chicago teams.

As MLB's antiradio feelings faded and regional networking became more common, the Cardinals in the 1940s and 1950s used radio to turn a smaller-local-market team into giant regional baseball power, becoming the model for how hinterlands teams could exploit radio. New regional franchises were added in Milwaukee (1953), Minneapolis (1961), Houston (1962), Atlanta (1966), and Kansas City (1969). These teams followed the Cardinals model by building expansive team radio networks, enlarging their teams' markets.

The antitrust exemption gave owners the power to resist radio initially, but Major League Baseball was not isolated from outside influence. In the 1930s, General Mills and other major advertisers pushed owners to accept radio, even offering training for their announcers. In baseball, daytime sponsors such as General Mills saw a direct route into the American home, persuading a generation of children and their moms that Wheaties was "the breakfast of champions." When owners banned radio from their parks, as they did in New York, General Mills would sponsor re-creations of games or bring in out-of-market broadcasts (see chapter 6). Sponsors also offered a new revenue stream. In the 1920s, radio rights were often free; many teams saw radio only as a promotional tool. The sponsor push made radio rights a piece of a team's money pie, however small at first. Coming at a time when owners' resistance to radio was fading, the sponsor push of the 1930s ended owners' resistance to regular-season broadcasts, making home-game coverage, and later all game coverage, the standard for all Major League teams.

Theme 4: Newspapers and Radio

Newspapers had a very mixed reaction to radio's coverage of baseball from the very beginning. Coverage of the first two World Series broadcasts in 1921 and 1922 was produced in cooperation with daily newspapers. In 1921 the *Newark Call*'s sports editor, Sandy Hunt, described the action between the New York Yankees and Giants from the Polo Grounds. His descriptions were related word for word by Thomas Cowan at station WJZ. By the next year, the radio call came directly from the field, with the legendary *New York Tribune* sportswriter Grantland Rice at the mike or, in this case, the telephone mouthpiece. Both the *Tribune* and the *New York Times* gave the broadcasts considerable coverage, lauding radio's power to bring baseball's crown jewel directly to the people. In several other markets, newspaper-owned stations, such as WMAQ and WGN in Chicago, WWJ in Detroit, and WCPI in Cincinnati, provided early coverage of regular-season games. Newspapermen such as Hal Totten and Quin Ryan were among the earliest baseball announcers (see chapter 3).

The initial newspaper infatuation with radio faded quickly. In the early 1920s, the Baseball Writers Association fought even the announcing of scores on the radio, fearing it would harm the sale of evening papers that carried the day's Major League results. Live play-by-play from the ballpark was unthinkable. Radio listeners would know the outcome of each play just as quickly as fans in the stands did. Newspapers could never hope to keep up with the speed or depth of game coverage, if radio were allowed in the ballpark. But radio did invade. First, announcers worked in the stands, constantly distracted by fans and the summer sun. The voices of the game then secured a spot at the edge of the press box, as far from the writers as possible, so their ceaseless chatter would not interfere with the ruminations of the fourth estate. Finally, in Chicago's Wrigley Field in 1929, the radio-friendly Cubs ownership built them their own space, the first broadcast booth.

Newspapers never could match radio's speed, but they still tried. For the 1923 World Series, one paper linked the game's radio broadcast to a linotype operator, who would set the announcer's call in lead slugs. The print version would follow. Two years later at the 1925 Series, newspapers built their own version of a radio network. Associated Press reports written on the fly at ballparks were transmitted by wire to seventy-three newspapers that also owned radio stations. The reports were read word for word by local announcers. But the AP and national network of papers still could not report the play-by-play as fast as RCA's radio network could. The next year the project was abandoned when radio networks insisted on exclusive rights to the World Series radio transmissions. Newspapers continued to fight radio by limiting its ability to report the news in what came to be known as the Press-Radio War. But the fourth estate was fighting a losing battle with the fifth.

Newspapers gradually ceded detailed game descriptions to radio and later to television, focusing on in-depth analysis and postgame interviews. The electronic media won the immediacy race in reporting sports events, but print media dominated the interpretation of those events for another two generations. In the 1990s, the rise of sports cable networks and the Internet weakened the dominant role that newspapers and magazines had long played in educating fans about the national pastime. Sportswriters, however, had one lasting advantage over broadcasters. Only baseball writers were given the honor and responsibility of electing the game's greatest players to the Hall of Fame. Despite the tireless scrutiny of the lifetime careers of baseball's elite provided by radio and television broadcasters, they never won suffrage.

Theme 5: Commercialization

The relentless commodification of baseball on the radio is another consistent theme that emerges in this volume. Although commercialization was resisted throughout the 1920s and 1930s, this study traces how advertising and promotion became inextricably woven into the coverage of baseball. The advertising-supported commercial model for the U.S. radio industry emerged gradually in the 1920s. By the end of the decade, advertising supported most stations, but a substantial portion of the programming on commercial stations was broadcast unsponsored, or what the industry called "sustaining programming."

The Communications Act of 1934 required all broadcast stations to serve "the public interest, convenience, and necessity." Stations would retain the right to use the publicly owned airwaves only if the Federal Communications Commission (FCC) believed they were meeting this vague public-service standard. In an era when the commercial model was not full accepted, networks and stations saw sports, and especially baseball, as public-service programming. It served the public interest, and the public was very much interested in it. The World Series was unsponsored from 1921 until 1934, when the Ford Motor Company convinced Commissioner Kenesaw Mountain Landis, in the fifth year of the Great Depression, to accept $100,000 for commercial rights to the Series. In keeping with the public-service tradition of World Series radio coverage, the games were carried on all four national radio networks: NBC Red, NBC Blue, CBS, and Mutual. The games continued on multiple networks until 1939, when Mutual gained exclusive rights. Even after that, the games were offered to any station willing to pay the line charges to connect to Mutual. Throughout radio's golden age of the 1930s and 1940s, the World Series dominated the medium on multiple networks.

Sponsorship of regular-season games started earlier but was not the primary motivation for owners to allow broadcasts of their home games. Proradio owners wanted radio to promote their product. Chicago Cubs owner William K. Wrigley Jr. gave access to Cubs homes games to all interested stations, hoping to dominate daytime radio ratings in the Windy City. The strategy worked. In the 1930s, Cubs coverage often reached more than half of all Chicago listeners.

In this early promotion-first model, sponsorship was only a means for radio stations to recoup their production costs and a make modest profit. Like the Cubs, most teams did not charge for rights until the mid-1930s. As noted earlier, starting in the early 1930s, major advertisers, especially General Mills, began pushing owners to allow more coverage of Major League games. The breakfast-food maker courted owners, teaching announcers how to promote attendance at home games and to incorporate advertising messages into their broadcasts. Many announcers actually worked for the sponsor with their team's approval. While announcers prided themselves on accurate coverage of the live action, they knew who paid their checks. Radio broadcasts were there to sell the sponsors' products and the home team's on-field product. As the current Cubs play-by-play announcer Pat Hughes tells young broadcasters, "If you want to be a true journalist, then baseball play-by-play is probably not the career avenue for you." If you plan to be the voice of a team, "you really are an extension of the public relations department of the ball club."[3]

As the commercial mode became more entrenched, product plugs proliferated. In 1953 Commissioner Ford Frick, previously a baseball announcer himself, complained to the *Sporting News* about the over-commercialization in baseball broadcasts.[4] But advertising's presence continued to expand over the decades. In 2006, Entercom, owner of the Boston Red Sox radio rights, even sold naming rights to its own radio network. Current baseball announcers Pat Hughes of the Chicago Cubs and Charley Steiner of the Los Angeles Dodgers have both noted in interviews with the author the increasing number of in-game commercial announcements that they are required to read. As Steiner put it, announcers are being asked to "jam more stuff into the thimble." He recalled that when he was with the Yankees, even the announcer disclaimer— "Any rebroadcast, retransmission, or account of this game, without the express written consent of Major League Baseball, is prohibited"—was sponsored by a legal firm.[5] Certainly baseball provides a welcoming context for promotional pitches, the frequent pauses in game play begging for commercial appropriation. Audiences often do not notice the additional plugs squeezed around the sporadic action.

But baseball broadcasts sold more than their sponsors products and services; they sold radio, itself. Baseball, especially the World Series, nurtured the infant medium of radio in the early 1920s. Starting with the 1921 Series, which launched WJZ—one of the nation's most important early stations—the Fall Classic brought hundreds of thousands, then millions, then tens of millions of new listeners to radio. Other sports, particularly heavyweight title fights, sold the new medium, but the World Series, spread over a week or more, created sustained interest. In the early 1920s, when receivers were still scarce in American homes, thousands would gather around radio-connected loudspeakers in public spaces to hear play-by-play coverage by Graham McNamee on RCA's WEAF and Major J. Andrew White on Westinghouse's WJZ (see chapter 1). Initially, the broadcasts covered the New York area, then the East Coast, spreading to the Midwest and beyond. By 1926 much of the nation was receiving the games live. The following year both NBC and CBS carried the World Series between the Pittsburgh Pirates and the New York Yankees coast to coast.

Theme 6: Nationalizing Major League Baseball

Radio dramatically expanded the footprint of Major League Baseball. It began with World Series coverage in the 1920s but expanded rapidly in the 1930s, as most and then all teams began broadcasting their games on high-powered AM radio stations. The daily ritual of listening to the Cubs or the Cardinals, the Red Sox or the Yankees, the Tigers or the Reds, became a fixture in millions of American homes. After World War II, team networks rapidly expanded the influence of Major League franchises. Local amateur teams and Minor League teams faced daily big league competition for the attention of baseball fans. While some critics blamed televised baseball for the decline in game attendance that led to a dramatic contraction of the Minor Leagues in the 1950s, the media culprit was more likely radio. While television's rapid growth in the decade affected all competing entertainment options, including Minor League Baseball, very few Major League games were telecast into Minor League markets. Other than national TV games of the week on Saturday and later Sunday, fans outside of New York and Chicago received few MLB games. The limited number of stations in most markets meant there were no outlets for baseball after the three national networks acquired their local affiliates. But radio had plenty of shelf space for MLB's product.

The number of radio stations grew dramatically after the Second World War (see chapter 9), just as national radio networks began to reduce their programming, especially in prime time. As weekday baseball shifted to the evening hours, it became big-time programming for thousands of local radio stations. In the early 1950s, two national networks, the upstart Liberty Broadcasting System (LBS) and the established Mutual Broadcasting System, offered competing daily national games. Poorly capitalized and overextended, LBS folded by 1952. MLB sped the demise by denying LBS access to most of its teams' games. But Mutual's *Game of the Day* continued until 1960. By that time, every team in baseball had its own team network, and Major League Baseball was an evening and weekend staple on thousands of U.S. radio stations.

The decline of the Minor Leagues helped codify the Major Leagues as the dominant baseball brand in America. That process had been ongoing since the turn of the century, but Major League broadcasts daily reminded Minor League fans that they were watching an inferior product. Except for those youngsters still playing the game, Major League Baseball came to be baseball for the large majority of fans. The Minor Leagues began to recover only in the 1980s, when they rebranded themselves as a local, family-oriented, low-cost entertainment alternative to the big league game. The Minor Leagues were a pleasant summer night's family outing; the baseball that mattered was played in mostly publicly funded Major League ballparks. Urban governments supported those projects in order to keep Major League Baseball in their communities. Without "big league" baseball, how could an urban center be a "big league" city?

Further evidence of MLB's dominance came with the invention and growth of fantasy baseball. When the fantasy version of the national pastime exploded on the scene in the 1990s, it spawned a variety of games: rotisserie, head-to-head, daily, and others. But each had at least one thing in common: they all used statistics from Major League players. Fantasy baseball meant fantasy Major League Baseball.

The elevation of one brand of professional baseball, MLB, over all others has had profound economic consequences. This is most evident in the disparity among team revenues and player salaries. The elevation of the MLB brand first by radio and then by broadcast and cable television helped the Major Leagues generate $7.5 billion in revenue by 2012. The average MLB player salary in 2012 was $3.44 million, while Minor League players earned only a tiny fraction of that amount. Many independent-league players face the grind of a full season for a few hundred dollars a month.[6] Sadly the income disparity between Major and Minor League players mirrors the concentration of wealth in the top 20 percent of the U.S. population. Excluding the value of family homes in 1983, the top 20 percent owned 91.3 percent of the country's wealth. In 2010 the figure stood at 95.7 percent. The top 1 percent owned 42.1 percent of the nation's wealth.[7] While stadium and television revenues supply most of funds to support these "Major League" salaries, the establishment of team owner-ship of broadcast rights and the structures put in place during radio's golden age provided the financial mechanisms that ensure today's bounty for MLB players and owners.

Radio set the stage for the modern media-sport empires. Chapter 1 begins the story of baseball on the radio long before owners discovered the immense contribution that electronic media would make to their bottom lines. The story of baseball on the radio begins in the early 1920s. The medium of radio was just becoming something more than a hobby, while Major League Baseball was starting to recover from its greatest scandal.

Part I

The Formative Years, 1920–36

1   Early World Series Coverage

In the early 1920s, commercial radio was born, and Major League Baseball was reborn. KDKA's broadcast of the presidential election returns on November 2, 1920, from Pittsburgh is often seen as the birth of commercial broadcasting in the United States. As with many firsts, it was preceded by considerable activity, but this date provides a convenient starting point for radio's journey. Nine months later on August 5, 1921, KDKA broadcast an MLB game between the hometown Pirates and cross-state rival Phillies was broadcast from Forbes Field. Meanwhile, baseball was reinventing itself in the wake of the 1919 Black Sox scandal. Major changes to the grand old game included the installation of its first commissioner, Kenesaw Mountain Landis, a federal judge; a jacked-up ball that produced an avalanche of home runs; and rule changes that stripped pitchers of their most deceptive tools. Radio waves moved at the speed of light, while Babe Ruth's homers zipped almost as quickly over the new Yankee Stadium's short right-field fence. Radio and baseball were entering the postwar Jazz Age, destined to exploit baseball's most compelling story: the World Series.

Although a public-relations nightmare, the 1919 Series scandal had shown just how ingrained this competition between two formally independent leagues had become in less than two decades. If the kingpin gambler Arnold Rothstein could compromise the "faith of fifty million"[1] by fixing the World Series, it was because October baseball had utterly captivated them in the first place. Anticipating the efforts of television a generation later, the first radio broadcasters exploited two high-stakes sports events, heavyweight boxing and the World Series, to sell radio to the public. In the process they invented station networks, producing what the radio historian Erik Barnouw dubbed the "Golden Web," the era of radio history dominated by national radio networks.[2]

The 1921 World Series: Radio's First?

The received history traces the first broadcasts of a World Series game to October 5, 1921, with separate broadcasts from WJZ in Newark, New Jersey, and KDKA in Pittsburgh, Pennsylvania. The Series was the first of three consecutive World Series matchups between two New York clubs, John McGraw's Giants and Babe Ruth's Yankees. Although many chroniclers of the game's history consider this the first broadcast of the World Series, there is some question about its primacy. The 1921 WJZ broadcast actually was an instant re-creation of the game from reports circuitously related from the Polo Grounds by telegraph to the *Newark Call*'s newspaper office and then by phone to WJZ's announcer Thomas Cowan for broadcast.[3] The station followed a plan similar to the one used by RCA to provide live reports of the Jack Dempsey–Georges Carpentier heavyweight fight on July 2, 1921. At that fight, J. O. Smith, speaking by telephone to the ringside announcer, J. Andrew White, repeated White's call of the fight word by word into a microphone at the RCA transmitter stationed in Hoboken, New Jersey. The Dempsey-Carpentier broadcast is considered the first major sports event broadcast to a regional audience, which was spread over an estimated 125,000 square miles.[4]

Although WJZ had broadcast musical recordings during the previous week, the World Series' broadcast was part of the *Call*'s launch of the station, and the staff always considered it the station's "opening day." Like many newspapers in the 1920s, the *Newark Call* saw radio as an inexpensive way of promoting the newspaper and establishing a beachhead in the new medium. Covering the World Series was a sure way to gather public attention for the new radio venture.

Thomas Cowan, WJZ's first World Series voice, in his contribution to Columbia University's oral history collection on early broadcasting, described his station's first home. The station was located in a shack at the top of the Edison plant in Newark, New Jersey. The facility was primitive at best, with not even a staircase leading up to the shack. Employees had to climb a fifteen-foot metal ladder and then work their way through a hatch in the roof. Once inside, they encountered an interior of a fifteen-by-twenty-foot "contractor's shack" anchored to the building. The room was ringed by windows and contained a radio transmitter, a bench, and a telephone. There were no draperies and no heat. Cowan reported that the shack was nothing like a modern radio studio, "because we hadn't as yet imagined anything of the kind."[5]

From this primal radio perch, Cowan "parroted" every word spoken to him on the phone by the *Sunday Call*'s sports editor, who was receiving telegraph reports from the ballpark: "We couldn't use telephone lines to broadcast, as we do today, on the remote. We solved that problem by putting a telephone in the box . . . where the game was played. The Sports Editor of the *Sunday Call*, Sandy Hunt, called me in Newark and for the first game I held that infernal receiver to my ear until my arm was nearly paralyzed and my ear was sore."

The next day a telephone headset relieved Cowan's arm "paralysis." By the third game, he "actually grew into the personality of Sandy Hunt." Cowan reported that the assignment made him so "fagged out" that he "couldn't even collect [his] thoughts enough to tell who had won": "The pools down in the shop would say, 'Who won, Cow?' and I'd say, 'I don't know, I just work here.'" Cowan concluded that he "was just a parrot all the time on this first World Series."[6]

It is clear from Cowan's description that there was no announcer at the ballpark, only an observer who related the game action. If we define "radio broadcast" as the transmission of the voice of an announcer directly observing the contest, the 1921 World Series was not the first broadcast, since there is no evidence that the games' observer reported what he saw directly to the audience. Indeed, this was not the first time that detailed radio reports on a World Series had been related by wireless (as radio was known at the time). Although the information may have been relayed more quickly in the 1921 contest, the *Detroit News*' station, later given the call letters wwj, reported on the 1920 Series. In addition, the U.S. Navy cleared its frequencies so amateurs could relay 1920 Cleveland Indians–Brooklyn Robins World Series action to ships at sea. According to the *Boston Globe*, the navy's "reports of the games, play by play, will be received at the Charlestown station by telegraph and they will instantly be relayed by wireless."[7]

At least one other radio description of the 1921 Series originated from the New York area. During the New York Electrical Show in October 1921, the National Amateur Wireless Association also broadcast play-by-play coverage of the World Series. J. O. Smith, apparently using telegraph reports of the game, offered "play by play, by voice" as well as an evening summary of each game. At one point the coverage was interrupted by the message "Ku Kux, Ku Kux." Smith thought that the Ku Klux Klan was offering a secret radio code, but the signal turned out to be code used by two Japanese ships outside the three-mile limit.[8]

Another issue with the 1921 Series coverage concerns the alleged participation of KDKA as a second originator of broadcasts direct from the ballpark. In *Voices of the Game*, author Curt Smith reported that the legendary sportswriter Grantland Rice, "fedora-topped" with "earphones clamped over his head," was "linked by direct line to KDKA" with two other stations—WJZ in Newark, New Jersey, and WBZ in Springfield, Massachusetts—connected to a Westinghouse network.[9] The same three-station hookup reported by Smith also is mentioned in the *Sporting News* on October 28, 1972. This account has Rice on a telephone at the Polo Grounds reporting the action to Cowan, who then broadcast it on WJZ.[10] Other secondary sources report that the Pittsburgh station covered the game on the basis of information coming by "wire" or "direct line" from the Polo Grounds, but none of the sources, including Smith and the *Sporting News*, identifies how they learned of KDKA's broadcast or provides detailed descriptions of the coverage.[11] It appears that the 1921 KDKA Series broadcast advocates may have combined information about the 1921 and 1922 World Series' radio coverage.

There is little evidence to support the assertion that Grantland Rice had anything to do with the radio coverage of the 1921 Series. In the preface to his autobiography, Rice claims that his first of many "radio outbursts" was during the 1922 Series. His most recent biographies also identify his World Series premiere as the 1922 Fall Classic.[12] In contrast to the paucity of documentation of KDKA's reporting on the 1921 Series, several sources provide detailed explanations of how WJZ in Newark used the 1921 Series coverage as a coming-out party for this new station. Cowan's own first-person account also makes the case compelling. In addition, although WJZ coverage received modest attention in the press, no contemporary newspaper accounts have been found documenting KDKA's "phantom" coverage. In addition, summaries of the station's early activities published in *Wireless Age* in 1922 and the *New York Times* in 1924 do not mention any World Series coverage in 1921.[13] On the other hand, the 1924 *Times* article does reference WJZ's 1921 World Series coverage.

The best historical evidence supports WJZ as the lone station broadcasting play-by-play reports of the 1921 World Series. Although the announcer was not live on the scene, he was in real-time telephone communication with a *Newark Call* sports reporter, Sandy Hunt, who was receiving telegraph reports from the game. But if the game's announcer is required to be on the scene, the most reasonable candidate for first radio World Series is the 1922 Fall Classic. The coverage of these games on WJZ was reported extensively in both the *New York Times* and the *New York Tribune*.

The 1922 World Series: The First Live Broadcast

The *Tribune*'s coverage was clearly self-serving, as Grantland Rice, one of the paper's two great sportswriters, was the 1922 Series' announcer. The Series featured a rematch between the Giants and Yankees and resulted in a Giants repeat victory. Three stations, WJZ, WGY in Schenectady, New York, and WBZ in Springfield, Massachusetts, were linked for the broadcasts.[14] Just as in 1921, all of the games were played at the Polo Grounds, eliminating the need for setups from different stadiums. Rice spoke from a press box not far from home plate, into a telephone-receiver microphone connected to Newark station WJZ. He assumed the rigors of a live broadcast with little to prepare him for a very new communication challenge. Although probably the most famous and poetic sportswriter of the first half of the twentieth century, Rice found the immediacy of radio challenging, later telling Red Barber, one World Series radio at bat "was enough for me for all of my life."[15] He also complained that radio required all of his focus, forcing him to sacrifice extra income from writing about the Series in magazines or syndicated articles.[16] However, at the time in the pages of his own paper, Rice wrote about the experience as if it were no more challenging than a walk in the park. He describes the ease of talking "to a million people, scattered over two hundred thousands square miles, in a single address." After "the pleasant shock" of realizing no one could interrupt him, this job was "as simple as talking to one man, a dumb man who isn't deaf; as simple as asking for a cigarette or ordering a peck of potatoes from the grocer over the phone."[17]

Rice's performance was reviewed in *Wireless Age*, an enthusiastic supporter of the emerging medium's presentation of the World Series live from the ballpark. "Play by play, ball by ball, strike by strike the report came from Grantland Rice. We listeners could tell from the volume of cheering whether it was an out or hit. . . . And wonder upon wonders, we could even hear the boys going about the stands crying their hot dogs and cold drinks! . . . Several times we even heard the crack of the bat on the nose of the ball—or was it just our imagination? We all but saw!" *Wireless Age* did note that Rice would "rest his throat" from time to time. This meant he went off the air and simply relayed what he saw to a WJZ announcer, who broadcast the description. *Wireless Age* also observed that Rice's occasional errors were sometimes prophetic flaws. When the Giant outfielder Irish Meusel scored from third on a hit, Rice barked, "Meusel scares. Beg pardon, scores." While Rice's call was factually wrong, it was emotionally true. Meusel did scare the Yankees fans. The magazine concluded that the WJZ broadcast had transported them to the ballpark. "We heard it all. Almost literally, we were really at the Polo Grounds."[18] As an aid to listeners, *Wireless Age* published a sample "radio player board" that fans could use to record the moves of each player while listening to the broadcasts.

Aided by an all-Gotham encounter, New Yorkers embraced WJZ's 1922 World Series coverage. Crowds gathered around radio shops throughout the city to hear the broadcasts. While the tradition of watching the Series results displayed on boards outside newspaper offices and other public locations was a well-established practice, radio brought the results to the crowd even faster, scooping the newspapers. *Wireless Age* reported, "radio dealers with their simple equipment of an antenna, ground, receiving set and loud speaker were able to beat the newspapers, beat them consistently by about half a minute."[19] Many radio dealers stayed open on Sunday so potential customers could enjoy the Series' final game. *Wireless Age* speculated that such public displays accelerated the growth of radio. While most everyday radio listening was in the home and private, radio broadcasts of the World Series brought many new listeners to publicly located speakers. The spectacle of large crowds listening to the World Series sent the message that radio had arrived as a serious medium. In broadcasting the World Series, WJZ was lauded by *Wireless Age* for providing a public service to "homes and offices," "ships at sea," "keepers of lonely lighthouses," "the sick, the shut-in, the farmer." But the station faced some technical challenges in presenting the Series.[20]

Maintaining the connection between Rice's stadium phone and WJZ in Newark required considerable effort. A growing feud between WJZ's owner, Westinghouse, and AT&T, owner of New York's most important station, WEAF, prompted AT&T to forbid the use of its phone lines to carry Rice's voice from the Polo Grounds to Newark. As the early radio historian Gleason Archer noted, "it was natural for [AT&T] to regard the Westinghouse Company and other radio station owners as trespassers on its special domain [networked radio stations]."[21] AT&T was extremely comfortable with its near monopoly status in telephone and wanted the same domination of the infant radio industry. This conflict between the "Radio Group" (Westinghouse, RCA, General Electric, and others) and the "Telephone Group" (AT&T) erupted into a full-fledged war in the 1920s that was ultimately settled in 1926 with intervention by the Department of Justice. For the 1922 Series, Westinghouse's WJZ had to make do with refitted Western Union telegraph wires that added a noticeable hum to the transmission. The station reduced the line distortion by creating resistance coils and a transformers line filter for the Series.[22]

Despite Rice's inexperience and less than optimal transmission from ballpark to station, the coverage was a major boost for radio; the *Tribune* estimated that the broadcast could be heard over a "300 mile area" by an audience of three million, including "fans far out at sea."[23] The *Tribune* issued reports on each day's Series broadcast. For Game Four, the paper reported, despite a rainstorm, "Grantland Rice's Voice Distinctly Audible to Fans as He Tells Every Move of Baseball Game."[24] According to the *Tribune*, crowds began to gather at noon at one store to secure a spot by the radio loudspeaker. The *Tribune* reported large crowds of listeners, while "some of the hotels in the city have even had special invitation cards printed inviting guests to listen to the series."[25] Those guests heard Rice's narrative of the game, vividly punctuated by the "the crack of the bat," "cries of soda venders," "the Star Spangled Banner," and "umpire's announcements.'"[26] The *Tribune* also reported that in deference to the Series' importance "all of the metropolitan stations have voluntarily agreed to forego their own periods of operation in order that WJZ can have full sway in the ether."[27]

RCA ran a quarter-page ad in the *Tribune* urging fans to "hear the crowd roar! at the World Series' games with the Radiola" and to ask their nearest dealer for the "Radiola score sheet" so they could "mark up every move on a convenient chart of the field."[28] DeForest Radio's ad told radio's early adopters, "Never Mind those World Series Tickets— You're Going to All of the Games—You're Going to Thrill with Every Big Play That Is Made—At Home!"[29] Yoking World Series broadcasts and receiver sales became established practice for radio manufacturers and distributors in the 1920s and beyond.

Although the *Tribune*'s hype may have been in its self-interest, even the rival *New York Times* was impressed by WJZ's efforts, estimating an audience of five million when the connected stations WGY in Schenectady, New York, and WBZ in Springfield, Massachusetts, were added to WJZ's listeners. The *Times* reported that "the voice of the umpire on the field announcing the batteries of the day mingled with the voice of a boy selling ice cream cones," while "the cheers which greeted Babe Ruth when he stepped to the plate could be heard throughout the land, and as he struck at the ball the shouts that followed indicated whether the Babe had fanned or got a hit even before the radio announcer could tell what had happened."[30]

While the WJZ live broadcast captured considerable attention, other stations continued the practice of announcing World Series action from wire-service reports. Radio gradually replaced the public scoreboard display as the source of instant World Series results.

The 1923 World Series: Newspaperman Takes a Powder

The 1922 World Series broadcasts were a blessing for radio but a threat to established interests. The Baseball Writers Association requested that the owners ban radio from the 1923 games because the broadcasts might harm the sale of evening papers that carried the game results. Worried owners even voted to deny WEAF's request to cover the Series, but Commissioner Landis overruled both the owners and the press. Permission was given to two stations, RCA's WEAF and Westinghouse's WBZ, to broadcast the games. It was WBZ's third World Series radio at bat.

On WBZ, Major J. Andrew White, the nation's most experienced sports announcer at this early date, took the Series' mike. White was also the editor of *Wireless Age*. When that publication printed an extensive account of radio's coverage of the 1923 Series, it reminded readers that its editor was "probably the greatest word-picture painter of sporting events today."[31]

WEAF offered another new voice for the Series, now broadcast from both the Polo Grounds and the new Yankee Stadium. By the start of the 1923 World Series, Grantland Rice had decided that his talents were not suited to the rapid pace of radio. His position at the microphone for the third consecutive matchup between the Giants and the Yankees was taken by his *New York Tribune* colleague W. O. McGeehan. Rice was the chief promoter of the "Gee Whiz!" school of sports writing that romanticized athletic accomplishments and overlooked most failings. For Rice, Babe Ruth was the great American hero who saved dying children with his magical home runs, not the bordello regular. W. O. McGeehan, on the other hand, focused a critical eye on the sport. As one journalism historian put it, "Rice was a kindly writer" who excelled at "rhythm and euphony," while McGeehan was a "cynic" who preferred "ironic twists that made ordinary sentences interesting."[32]

Perhaps the cynic is better suited to words written deliberately than those spoken in the heat of action. What is certain is that McGeehan was not suited to radio; a different kind of talent was needed for success as a big-game announcer. In the fourth inning of the third game at the Polo Grounds, McGeehan decided he had had enough of his adventure in radio and turned over the mike to his radio coach, a relative newcomer himself, Graham McNamee. McNamee had trained to be a classical singer but saw more opportunity as an announcer at AT&T's flagship station WEAF in New York. Although he had apprenticed at his first sports event, a middleweight championship fight, only a few weeks before the Series, he seized the opportunity on radio's biggest stage to become the medium's first announcing star.

The game featured rival coverage by WEAF and WJZ, but WEAF had a clear advantage. AT&T provided high-quality phone lines for transmission of the signal not only to WEAF and its audience in the New York area but to WGY in Schenectady, WJAR in Providence, Rhode Island, and WCAP in Washington DC, effectively giving it coverage over much of the eastern United States and beyond.[33] The coverage apparently made it as far west as St. Joseph, Missouri, where "Al Robinson, proprietor of a barber shop," planned to install "a radio set at the establishment about Oct 10 to receive world series broadcasts."[34] According to McNamee, the coverage included two field microphones to catch crowd reactions, one for the announcer, and a spare mike in reserve. The mikes fed into a makeshift control room, and McNamee had headphones so he could hear instructions from the control-room engineer. McNamee could switch his mike on or off but had to direct the engineer to switch the field microphones on or off.[35]

As in 1922, WBZ had to make do with lower-quality telegraphy lines to carry the signal back to its station. But it did have a new RCA-built portable amplifier created for sports remotes. However, WBZ's most significant addition was human. For the first time in a baseball broadcast, Major White worked the game with a spotter, someone to help him identify the players. This was especially helpful during fast-moving plays. The spotter, J. O. Smith, used a special diamond mounted on a board. Smith shifted "little pieces of cardboard labeled with the player's names around the diamond" to remind White which players were involved in the action.[36] Smith's spotting helped White call a more accurate game and was especially important for an announcer who had not covered either team before the Series. White also invited celebrity guests to share his mike, including the pitching great Christy Mathewson and the newspaper writers Grantland Rice, Hugh Fullerton, and Fred Lieb, president of the Baseball Writers Association. While still wary of radio, the writers at least were willing to talk on it.

According to *Wireless Age*, WEAF's accounts of the games were shared with WGY in Schenectady, New York, WCAP in Washington DC, and WJAR in Providence. WJZ's coverage was not networked. However, the radio program listing in the *New York Times* also includes WNCA in Boston, WBZ in Springfield, Massachusetts, and KYW in Chicago as covering the World Series, although whether these were simply reports on the games or retransmissions is not clear.[37] WJAR reported that in Providence a crowd of thirty-five hundred listened to a public-address system carrying the games. One Washington DC newspaper linked WCAP's radio descriptions of the game directly to a linotype operator. The worker then "immortalized" the announcer's words by turning them into "a hot slug, waiting to be gathered up and taken to the press room."[38] The radio account rapidly achieved the permanence of print. The World Series was making news while becoming a regional, if not national, radio event.

The 1924 World Series: The Expanding Web

The all–New York stranglehold on the World Series finally weakened in 1924, when the Washington Senators won their only championship at the expense of McGraw's Giants. Networked RCA stations, using AT&T

lines, provided exclusive coverage of the Series; Westinghouse's WBZ withdrew after three pioneering years. Coverage came from two parks, from which WEAF in New York broadcast for six of the seven contests. Game One was originated by WNYC, the city's municipal station, because the game conflicted with WEAF's religious programming. The WEAF network of stations had grown to include at least six others: WCAP in Washington, WJAR in Providence, WEEI in Boston, WCAE in Pittsburgh, WGY in Schenectady, and WMAF in South Dartmouth, Massachusetts.[39] A later *New York Times* story indicated that eight stations were linked by telephone lines for the Series.[40] The Series network was growing, but the supply of network stations had not yet caught up with the nationwide demand for this premium programming.

The number of U.S. radio stations had expanded from 30 on January 1, 1922, to 530 on the same date in 1924.[41] Most of these stations produced all of their own programming and as a result had limited hours of operation. For the World Series, stations would often receive play-by-play wire-service reports and relay to the public over the air. While these were not the fully developed re-creations of later years, the broadcast did supply fans at homes, at offices, and assembled at a loud speaker in front of a newspaper office or radio store with nearly real-time accounts of the action. If a local newspaper had a radio station, it could synergize its coverage of the World Series. As the telegraph reports of each play were received, the newspaper's radio director would announce the plays while a scoreboard operator would flash them on the paper's World Series display board outside the newspaper office. The waiting public could watch the board and hear the call at the same moment.[42] But these local reports lacked the drama and verisimilitude of Graham McNamee's on-the-scene call from the ballpark. Without better station networking, unreliable long-distance signals or locally broadcast "re-creations" would have to do.

Secretary of Commerce, and later president, Herbert Hoover was particularly supportive of expanding the reach of radio networks. In an October 1924 address broadcast over eighteen stations scattered from Boston to Oakland, he recommended the development of a "nationwide radiophone system so that the broadcasting of an event of national importance could be heard by any one of the 20,000,000 listeners in the United States."[43] Since AT&T controlled the long-distance lines that could support such a system, other radio interests looked to short-wave retransmissions or high-power "superstations" as an alternative to AT&T's domination of networking. Shortwaves would be used to relay broadcasts internationally, and fifty-thousand-watt stations appeared in major cities in the coming years; but the "golden web" that would sustain the "Golden Age of Radio" was spun by AT&T. The desire to share live World Series broadcasts to the nation was one of many forces pushing the development of that golden web. *Wireless Age* declared the national primacy of baseball and its World Series: "Baseball is a National Institution, and the broadcasting of the World Series was one of the most truly National Services which this country has ever seen."[44]

Graham McNamee, after his solid 1923 pinch-hit performance, entered the starting lineup as the 1924 Series' lead announcer. Radio fans of McNamee's reporting included Mrs. Calvin Coolidge, who listened to games she could not attend in person.[45] But not all fans applauded McNamee's call. The *Boston Globe* reported that those who disapproved of McNamee's "broadcasting and treatment of their favorite team were not slow in saying so. New York and Washington alike pilloried him." McNamee put a positive spin on the complaints. "It showed that the old fan spirit had not passed from baseball and that everyone was still convinced that his home team ought to win. It is a healthy condition and I hope it continues."[46]

The 1925 World Series: Newspapers Fight Back

By the October 1925 classic between the Senators and the Pirates, the web was expanded to include stations in Providence; Boston; Hartford; Philadelphia; Pittsburgh (two); Washington DC; Worcester, Massachusetts; Schenectady; and Chicago. AT&T produced the broadcast, but Commissioner Landis controlled the access, waiting until late September to grant AT&T approval to cover the games.[47] In the New York area, the Series was carried by five stations: WEAF, WNYC, WJZ, WGBS, and

WOR—an amazing index of interest considering the absence of a Gotham team for the first time in half a decade.[48] The out-of-stadium audience, including radio listeners and player-board viewers, was estimated at ten million. Among those was, once again, Mrs. Coolidge, this time joined by "Silent Cal."[49] In New York, the *Times* noticed a difference between how Gotham's listeners and player-board watchers reacted to the games: "Thousands may cheer the weird gyrations of the little white ball on the player-scoreboard as lustily as they would at the game itself. But radio audiences must take their dramatic moments in silence or else something important from the announcer is drowned out."[50]

For Graham McNamee, his third World Series would be remembered as a wet one. At one Pittsburgh game, he suffered through a driving rainstorm while he worked the games from the stands, rather than from the comfort of a press box. He informed listeners of the rain streaming "down his neck" and a few of them let him know it did not matter. "What do we care whether you are cold or hot, wet or dry; or what's the state of your health? All we want is to hear about the game."[51] Outside of a few exasperated critics, McNamee's mail was appreciative and overwhelming; he received fifty thousand letters after the 1925 Series.[52] That kind of response made it clear that the World Series on the radio was fast becoming an American institution. McNamee was joined in the Series call by Quin Ryan of WGN in Chicago, one of few stations in the country that broadcast regular-season games.

But the "old media," in this case newspapers, were fighting back. Responding to the popularity of radio coverage of the World Series, the Associated Press organized a major coordinated effort among seventy-three newspapers with radio stations to "saturate" the "ether" with "Play-by-Play Broadcasts of Games." The AP stationed specially trained reporters at the games with "telegraphers who have made reputations for speed" to write and send descriptions of the games with minimal delay. At the seventy-three newspaper offices, "as the story appears word by word from the telegraph wires . . . it will be repeated into microphones and thus instantaneously made audible to radio fans everywhere."[53] No longer reporting from the field, Westinghouse radio station WJZ, as well as WRC in Washington DC, also took the wired AP copy and verbalized it for its listeners. The AP attempted to beat radio at its own game by writing the story nearly as quickly as an announcer could describe it orally and then networking that story over telegraph wires. The strategy had the advantage of achieving geographic breadth, covering virtually the entire nation, but it lacked the immediacy and emotional power of the spoken word. The Associated Press was stretching the boundaries of the written word by maximizing the speed of its creation. But because words still had to be written and then telegraphed, the newspaper network could not keep pace with live radio. Writing can produce expressions that are timeless, but radio can always communicate them in less time. The AP's newspaper network was a valiant attempt to compete with radio, but it did not endure. The interconnection of radio stations for the World Series continued to expand each year.

In addition to AP's network, the 1925 World Series produced what is perhaps the strangest radio re-creation ever staged. As reported extensively in *Publishers Weekly*, the "radiogame," produced by the Louisville station WHAS, was an original. The station hired players from two semipro teams to impersonate the Pirates and Senators by acting out each play of the game on the basis of instructions radioed to players in the field. "Each [defensive] player was equipped with a complete wire device by which he received each play as called."[54] The batters and runners were told what to do by the fielders. At the end of each inning, the equipment was exchanged, and an electrician checked connections as needed. The exhibition drew two thousand fans to Parkway Field in Louisville, "despite cold raw wind and overcast skies."[55] The re-creation was high fidelity; photos of the action from Pittsburgh and the Louisville re-creation "were similar in nearly all respects."[56]

The 1926 World Series: The Healing Power of Ruthian Radio

The Yankee-Cardinals contest of 1926 continued the pattern of yearly coverage expansion both westward and to stations in the contesting teams' cities. RCA's Broadcasting Company of America used AT&T's lines to expand network coverage to twenty-two stations. RCA's deal with Commissioner Landis eliminated the AP feed used by newspapers to broadcast play-by-play reports of the Series over their radio stations.[57] The "newspaper network" was dead. RCA had the aural coverage to itself. The RCA network moved dramatically westward with stations in Pittsburgh, Cincinnati, Detroit, Chicago, Minneapolis, St. Louis, and Kansas City. WEAF announcers Graham McNamee and Phillips Carlin described the Series over RCA's network to an estimated fifteen million listeners.

The *New York Times* voiced concern about radio's negative effect on the World Series gate, noting the popularity of radio in the city and the failure to sell out Yankee Stadium.[58] Radio was also converting scoreboard watchers into radio listeners, as some fans who had gathered to watch returns posted in Park Row were now drawn to the speakers in front of the shops on New York's radio row.[59] The *Times* also acknowledged the growing legitimacy of the radio version of the Series by transcribing and publishing Graham McNamee and partner Phillips Carlin's call of all seven games, replacing the AP game summaries that had been a newspaper staple for years. The radio version was becoming the official version. This is how fans heard McNamee's call of the climactic play of the Series, Ruth's failed attempt to steal second: "One strike on Bob Meusel. Going down to second—the game is over. Babe tried to steal second and is put out, catcher to second. The world series of 1926—we will never say it again—is over. It has come to a close, and the championship goes west, southwest, down to the sovereign State of Missouri."[60]

While the Babe's base-running blunder ended the Series, his earlier exploits, reported by radio, were said to revive the near dead, adding to his heroic shine. John Dale Sylvester, an eleven-year-old Yankees fan, recovered from blood poisoning after receiving messages of encouragement from Ruth and other World Series participants. According to the *New York Times*, "The boy's return to health began when he learned the news of Ruth's three home runs in the fourth game of the series. His fever began to abate at once, and the favorable course was hastened . . . after he had listened to the radio returns, clutching the autographed baseballs which he received by air mail."[61] The boy's condition improved to the point that he could leave his room to listen to Game Six of the World Series.[62]

The year 1926 was a watershed in the history of U.S. radio. Under pressure from the Justice Department and disillusioned with the broadcasting business, AT&T began the process of transferring ownership of its broadcast radio holdings to RCA. On September 9, RCA incorporated the National Broadcasting Company to handle chain broadcasting for AT&T's old network and WJZ's weaker network. The original networks became known as NBC Red and NBC Blue and soon provided a nationwide interconnection of radio stations. A month after the 1926 World Series, NBC made a spectacular debut at the Grand Ballroom of the Waldorf-Astoria, launching the golden age of network radio. The feud between the radio group and the telephone group was over. Through the two networks, RCA assumed a dominant position in the radio industry, while AT&T quietly made millions connecting stations to RCA's webs. In July 1927, NBC linked at least forty-eight stations together for its coverage of the Dempsey-Sharkey heavyweight championship fight, featuring McNamee and Carlin at the mike. That fall the World Series broadcast performed on its first truly national stage.[63]

1927–33 World Series: Two National Broadcasts

Although NBC's position was dominant, the growing CBS network, under the direction of William S. Paley, joined NBC in 1927 to provide coast-to-coast Series coverage. McNamee and Carlin handled announcing duties for NBC, while Major J. Andrew White, veteran of the 1922 and 1923 Series broadcast on WJZ, took the mike for CBS. The NBC chain included forty-three stations from "Maine to California and from Canada to the Gulf of Mexico," while the more modest CBS network had signed up ten stations to carry the Series by October 4, 1927.[64] NBC estimated that twenty million people tuned into the broadcast of the first game. WGY in Schenectady and KDKA in Pittsburgh offered descriptions of the game on shortwave broadcasts to listeners outside the United States.[65]

The *New York Times* reported that two fans in Greenland "Munch Salted Peanuts, Sitting on Snowclad Mountain, and Hear Bats Crack over Radio" while listening to WGY's Series reports.[66] The fear that radio coverage might hurt attendance persisted. By September 13, NBC officials still had not been given permission to cover the Series, but they expected to "do the job," noting that "advance notice is not given of the broadcasting of ball games because some of the baseball people are afraid that attendance will be reduced."[67]

While Graham McNamee's fame spread with each additional station carrying his voice, so did his critics. The *New York Sun* offered pointed criticism of his 1927 efforts: "M'Namee's Eye Not on the Ball: Radio Announcer Mixes Up World Series Fans." The *Sun* accused the man whom *Radio Digest* dubbed the "world's most popular announcer" of embellishing on the "spectacle about him while players hit safely or retired to the dugouts," making "right handed batters left handed and announc[ing] triumphantly on occasion that the Giants were leading— which must have been rather a surprise to McGraw [since the Series matched the Yankees and Pirates]. He put players on bases where they weren't and left them off of bases where they were."[68] The *Sun* was not alone in its barbs. The *Boston Globe* also offered pointed and detailed criticism of McNamee. The paper had at least eight other issues with McNamee's call of the opening game:

1. In the first inning, he ignored the game to rant about the success of someone named "One-Eyed Connolly" in crashing the gate.
2. McNamee's reporting of balls and strikes from the field was slow, with the telegraph reports to the *Boston Globe* beating the announcer's call twelve times in the second inning alone.
3. He completely forgot to report balls and strikes on several occasions.
4. He missed players coming to bat while focused on telling a story about another player.
5. While reading a letter during the game, he suddenly told the fans. "It is now two strikes, Combs struck out."

6. While offering his opinion on night baseball, he suddenly told listeners that "Gehrig is out" but had not yet announced he had come to the plate.
7. He read a telegram sent to him telling him "to cut out the extras and stick to a play-by-play report of the baseball game."
8. Perhaps most damningly, he left the microphone for several minutes in the seventh inning to get a soft drink, and "as far as the audience was concerned, the game had been temporarily halted." When he returned, he did not report what had happened while he was away from the mike.[69]

While McNamee was still seen by many people as the world's most popular announcer, his fame triggered closer scrutiny. He was clearly no longer the most critically acclaimed baseball announcer. The radio announcer's job was changing, as the novelty of radio coverage faded. Fans expected an accurate call from a professional who focused on the sport. Regular-season announcers with the experience of hundreds of games under their belts eventually replaced the once-a-year celebrity announcer at the World Series. But this change was not immediate. Despite the critics, McNamee was the World Series for millions of Americans. With a variety of partners, including the future baseball commissioner Ford Frick, McNamee continued to call the games for NBC each year through 1931.

In 1932 Commissioner Landis assigned McNamee to cover the pregame festivities. Landis shifted the NBC play-by-play duties to two of baseball's first regular-season announcers, Hal Totten of the Cubs and Tom Manning of the Indians. Both were employed by NBC stations: Totten by WMAQ in Chicago and Manning by WTAM in Cleveland. CBS also continued to cover the Series each year. Starting in 1929, Ted Husing replaced Major J. Andrew White as lead announcer. Husing continued his assignment until his frank evaluation of the umpiring during the 1933 World Series raised the wrath of Judge Landis (see chapter 5).

The 1927 World Series established a pattern for World Series broadcast that continued through the 1933 season. Both NBC's Red Network and

Blue Network stations carried the games using the same network feed. CBS also broadcast the games to a smaller but still substantial national network. Commissioner Landis also insisted that any nonaffiliated station willing to pay the line charges be allowed to take one of the two network feeds. The number of stations taking the World Series grew steadily from at least 67 in 1928 to 102 in 1931, and the two network radio broadcasts reached over twenty million listeners. Shortwave transmitters located in Pittsburgh (KDKA) and Schenectady (WGY) shared the broadcasts with an international audience.[70]

Toward the end of the 1920s, the announcer was beginning to move from the press box for the postgame celebration. In 1929 Graham McNamee announced to the national audience, "This is Graham McNamee down under the stands again, a little bit out of breath, as we came down pretty fast. I'm going to ask some of the boys if they won't say just a word to tell you how they feel in regard to winning this series." Slugger Jimmy Foxx told NBC's national audience, "Hello friends. I hope you got as big a thrill as we did. Quite a finish, I think."[71] By now, even the infant medium of television was offering sketchy coverage of the Series. In 1932 CBS's New York experimental television station W2XAB aired game scores inning by inning.[72]

In a little over a decade, radio's coverage of the World Series had grown from one, possibly two, stations to a nationwide institution with rival networks offering competing coverage. The World Series and heavyweight title fights were the two most popular attractions the budding webs had to offer. Audiences grew from a few thousand to an estimated twenty million plus, as radio replaced the public scoreboard as the major venue for the out-of-stadium experience. The MLB commissioner was now in charge of access to games to help ensure that radio broadcasts would not be too attractive and thus discourage fans from coming to the ballpark. Graham McNamee's modest singing career had ended, but his fame and the accompanying criticism of his work were becoming legendary.

Baseball's Fall Classic helped sell the new medium of radio, which expanded from less than 1 percent of American homes in 1922 to 62.5

percent by 1933.[73] In October 1930, the popular humorist Will Rogers captured the wonder of many far-flung Americans at the World Series on the radio. "We cuss the radio for a lot of things that come over it, but when something like the world's series comes along and you can be away out here in the irrigated belt, 3,000 miles away, and can hear the crack of the bat, you got to admit it's quite an invention."[74] Just as later in the age of television, the World Series gave the new medium of radio an electromagnetic jump-start. At the same time, radio aided baseball in its recovery from the 1919 Black Sox scandal. The symbiotic bond between broadcasting and baseball was sealed.

2 The Local Game Begins

While the World Series broadcasts by NBC and CBS brought national attention to baseball on the radio and created the first generation of star announcers in Graham McNamee and Ted Husing, the development of local station coverage of the national pastime proceeded at a much more leisurely pace. KDKA in Pittsburgh began broadcasting baseball scores at regular intervals with the start of the 1921 season.[1] Major League Baseball game broadcasts followed with KDKA's broadcast of an August 5, 1921, Pirates-Phillies game and WJZ Newark's coverage of the first radio World Series in 1921. However, local stations did not broadcast much baseball in the early 1920s. It took several years for stations to establish advertising as the basis for the financial support of radio programming. Until steady advertising income flowed into most stations, programming costs were kept to a minimum. Stations depended on a few staff announcers, in-house musicians and singers, and low-cost or no-cost entertainers and public figures seeking publicity or simply some experience with the new medium. Radio was just beginning, and it was for beginners. The federal government gave licenses to virtually every applicant but required many stations to share the few scarce frequencies set aside for broadcasting.

In this embryonic stage of radio, there was little money to attract established entertainments, including Major League teams, to the new medium. The national pastime was already dominating newspaper sports pages during the spring, summer, and early fall. Postwar attendance was riding a strong economy and the home run boom initiated by Babe

Ruth. Attendance climbed from 6.5 million in 1919 to 8.8 million in 1922 to 10.1 million in 1930.[2] Network radio, with some promotional help from newspapers, grew the World Series, boosting national interest in and local attendance at the postseason contests. But regular-season games were strictly local matters in MLB's ten markets: New York, Chicago, Philadelphia, Boston, St. Louis, Detroit, Washington DC, Cleveland, Cincinnati, and Pittsburgh. Most owners were convinced that any promotional bump from the aural medium would be lost in reduced attendance. Announcing scores, providing game summaries, or having players shill the game on air was all to the good, but play-by-play coverage of a live game would only bind the fans more tightly to their radios instead of bringing them to the park. Who wants to buy the cow when they can get the milk for free?

In April 1922, the *Sporting News* (TSN), the game's nearly official spokesman, saw little hope in the precocious newcomer. In a section of the editorial page titled "This Our Latest Problem," the "baseball bible" expressed concern that even giving the scores over the radio would harm attendance. "Mr. Radio is going to butt into the business of telling the world all about the ball game without the world having to go to the ball park to find out." But the worst was yet to come. "Next, we presume, it will be play-by-play that is sent out into the ether and to those who merely care for what happens rather than seeing how it happens, the radio will fill the bill." With radio now a reality, the distant video future offered even greater peril. "And next we will have the whole works shot to pieces because instead of mere sounds the radio will be reproducing in every home that has a ten-dollar equipment the picture of the play. . . . Then what will become of baseball?" With only one World Series and a handful of other games broadcast, TSN's editors saw a new threat to baseball as "this new radio craze is already crimping attendance at anything where the feast is for the ear rather than the eye."[3] But such opinions on radio, even in TSN, were not unanimous. While the editors saw a threat, at least one columnist saw radio as an opportunity to tap into a new fan base.

In the August 1922 "Back of Home Plate: Observations of a Veteran Scribe" column, John B. Sheridan predicted that the concomitant emergence of better cars, better highways, and better radio would accelerate profits for baseball owners. While *TSN* editors and MLB owners saw radio sabotaging local attendance, Sheridan saw radio turning rural listeners into baseball fans.

"The radio brings the big league game very close to the country folks. It seems to me that radio will be about the greatest boost that baseball has ever got." Once enticed, the new fans could hop into their more powerful, more comfortable cars and take advantage of publicly funded highways. "Now couple up the good road and motor car with the radio, which creates and whets the appetite for baseball, and what do you get? Week-end games, and certainly Sunday and holiday games, which will draw from a territory 200 miles in every direction from the locale of play."[4]

Radio should help that gate, not harm it. In two columns, a few months apart, the *Sporting News* outlined the essential arguments advanced by the antiradio and proradio positions, arguments that were repeated throughout the next decade and a half. Radio would give away the product, hurting attendance. Radio would expand the game beyond its urban, adult male core to include rural listeners, and later daytime games would covert women and children into baseball fans. By the end of the decade, baseball owners themselves split into two radio camps: radio hurts versus radio promotes.

While the *Sporting News* seemed divided on the benefits of radio game broadcasts, it consistently defended broadcasts of baseball scores and other information about the national pastime. The broadcasting of scores at the conclusion of a baseball day benefited ball clubs by promoting the game, but it did represent a challenge to one part of the baseball establishment: the sporting press. When the Baseball Writers' Association protested to the commissioner and the two league presidents the reporting of game results from ballparks using owner-provided facilities, the *TSN* columnist Francis C. Richter saw the writers' reaction as "excessive and not warranted by the facts."[5] Echoing earlier comments by *TSN*'s editors,[6] Richter argued that those who did not have time to go to the game would not have time to listen to scores from the game; they would still need the evening paper to keep informed. In addition, increased coverage by radio would increase interest in the game and thus newspaper coverage of baseball. While not endorsing play-by-play broadcasts of the games, TSN was at least letting radio through the press-box door.

The First Game

The first documented call of a baseball game from inside the ballpark was also the first regular-season game broadcast. On Friday, August 5, 1921, Harold Arlin, a twenty-six-year-old time-study foreman for Westinghouse transitioning to radio announcer on the nation's first commercially licensed radio station, KDKA, brought a few hundred listeners in the Pittsburgh area a play-by-play description of an afternoon Forbes Field contest between the hometown Pirates and the visiting cross-state rivals, the Phillies of Philadelphia.[7] Two days earlier, Arlin had re-created a Pirate-Phillies game at KDKA's studio from information transmitted from Forbes Field.[8] Now Arlin would experience the sights and sounds of baseball in person.

Arlin called the one-hour-and-fifty-seven-minute game from a ground-level box, first-base-side seat using a converted telephone receiver as a microphone. The "mike" sat on a board that Arlin placed on the box seat's arms to create a makeshift desk. Transmission equipment was nearby in the stands behind home plate. The Bucco fans went home happy that day as the Pirates broke up a 5–5 tie with three runs in the bottom of the eighth for an 8–5 victory. For Arlin, it was another day at his office, the city of Pittsburgh.

On a lark, Arlin, trained as an electrical engineer at the University of Kansas, auditioned and won the position of commercial radio's first staff announcer. He also served as the station's program director. Arlin's KDKA commercial radio firsts included the first broadcasts of a college football game (a Pitt victory over West Virginia), a tennis match, and a baseball scoreboard show. Major League Baseball was just another experiment. "Our guys at KDKA didn't even think that baseball would last on radio. I did it sort of as a one-shot project, a kind of addendum to the events we'd already done." Planning for the broadcast was minimal, as Arlin recalled decades later. "I went out to Forbes Field and set up shop." With little audience and less expectation, production quality was low. "Sometimes the transmitter worked and sometimes it didn't. Sometimes the crowd noise would drown us out and sometimes it wouldn't. . . . No one told me I had to talk between pitches."[9]

While Arlin struggled with baseball play-by-play, his performance was spellbinding compared to the radio premiere of America's new baseball superstar, Babe Ruth. After a Pirates-Yankees exhibition game in Pittsburgh, the Bambino got his first taste of radio, a written speech he was to read over KDKA. But like a snapping curve over the outside corner of the plate, the microphone "froze" the Babe. While Ruth leaned against the wall smoking a stogy and recovering from mike fright, Arlin pinch-hit for him. Later KDKA received "several letters commenting on 'what a wonderful voice Babe Ruth had.'"[10]

Arlin's career in radio lasted only five years, but the baseball pioneer lasted to his ninetieth year. Forty-five years after his landmark broadcast, the Pirates honored Arlin with a day at the park. In August 1972, Arlin called a few innings of a Pirates game featuring his grandson Steve Arlin pitching for the visiting San Diego Padres. Grandson Steve remembered that his grandfather was at a loss for words. "I was pitching against Pittsburgh, and the long-time Pirates radio broadcaster Bob Prince asked Granddad to call an inning of the game. He was pretty excited about that, although his turn in front of the microphone turned out to be not much more than saying 'strike' or 'ball.' He sort of froze."[11] Arlin never anticipated the significance of radio for baseball. "No one had the foggiest idea, the slightest hint of an inkling, that what we'd started would take off like it did."[12] At the time, KDKA's contribution to baseball history received no notice in the *Sporting News*.

Pioneering Efforts

Arlin's opening volley in Pittsburgh did not inspire immediate imitation. There were no regular-season broadcasts for the chaotic first couple of years of broadcast radio. By the end of 1921, there were only 30 licensed radio stations, but by the end of 1922, the 30 had become more than 550.[13] Stations were focused on starting their operations and putting some kind of programming on the air. The hours were filled with bedtime stories, local singers, radio talks, and piano music. Location broadcasts were anticipated but seldom executed. While World Series broadcast had begun in 1921 and became a national sensation by 1926, other baseball coverage was limited and unreliable. As early as opening day 1922, the *Washington Herald* reported that it "flash broadcast" the inning-by-inning results of the Washington Nationals' home opener against the Yankees from the press box at the Florida Avenue ballpark. According to the *Herald*, "the idea made a big hit with those who are unable to get out to see every game." The paper then planned to expand coverage to "broadcast play-by-play from the press box . . . for the eager followers of the Nationals."[14]

However, expanded coverage would have to wait. The generator provided by Doubleday-Hill Electric Company broke down, delaying coverage until about 5 p.m. The following Monday, the newspaper tried for a second time.[15] The columnist Kirk Miller of the rival *Washington Times* scorned these early attempts at baseball broadcasts. He playfully ridiculed this "new brand of serial nuisance twinkling through space which has amateur radio addicts throwing corrugated spasms at varying wave lengths. Baseball-o-gram darting through nocturnal acoustics is breaking up nightly concerts, market reports, bedtime stories and sober citizens' sleep."[16]

Gradually, stories on radio's foray into baseball began popping up in the press. In Chicago, high schools planned to bring baseball and football games to the radio.[17] While it is unknown if the high schools ever followed through with their plans, coverage of a Chicago big league club began with the Cubs' opener, a 3–2 loss to the Pirates on April 17, 1923. Westinghouse's Chicago station, KYW, transmitted a game description provided by the baseball editor of the *Pittsburgh Post* and a second writer from the *Pittsburgh Gazette-Times*.[18] It is not clear from the *Chicago Tribune* account if the commentators were actually reporting from Cubs Park (now Wrigley Field). But the lack of any reference to a ballpark location suggests that this account was created in studio. While experiments such as these are likely to have occurred at other stations as well, there is little documentation of these early attempts at baseball on the radio.

In early October 1924, WGN covered the postseason city series between the White Sox and the Cubs. The WGN announcer "Sen" Kaney made the call from Cubs Park. While one reviewer, Elmer Douglas, thought Kaney's baseball knowledge "equals the sum of the Sox runs at the close of the sixth inning" (0), his and Kaney's enthusiasm "was equal to the Cubs' lead of nine runs." Douglas felt that, through radio, fans could experience the press box's vantage point, including "yelling by the crowds, the flying pigeons," and "the whistles, the chug-chug of railroad engines and passing trains a block or so to the west—also the 'high wind.'" A few days later, KYW covered the fifth game of the postseason city series with WGN's Kaney at the mike.[19]

Occasional pioneering broadcasts followed in other Major League markets. In *The Broadcasters*, Red Barber credits Tom Manning with sporadic broadcasts of Cleveland Indians games from League Park starting in 1925. Another source, *Who's Who in Major League Baseball*, published in 1933, puts the date at 1926.[20] Manning began regular coverage of the Tribe on WTAM in 1928. He continued through 1931, when WTAM lost rights to the games to WHK and Manning was replaced by the former Indians left fielder Jack Graney.[21] In Boston, Fred Hoey provided broadcasts of Boston Braves games starting in 1925 and Red Sox games in 1927 on WNAC.[22]

But it was two Chicago stations—WMAQ and WGN—that were the most precocious in covering big league ball. Both began airing home-game broadcasts of Cubs games in 1925. WMAQ offered coverage of all regular-season home games from the start, while WGN expanded its coverage to all home games by 1927.

WMAQ's pioneering effort was led by Chicago's "First Lady of Radio," Judith Waller. Initially hired by the *Chicago Daily News* to put its new radio station, WMAQ, on the air, Waller brought many educational programs to radio (e.g., *University of Chicago Roundtable*), but her successful efforts to recruit the Cubs to radio in 1924 formed the foundation for baseball's regular-season broadcasts. A quarter century later, Waller recalled the moment:

> I went to see Mr. William Wrigley, Jr. the fall before that the World Series had been broadcast, but never had there been a play by play baseball broadcast from a home park [in Chicago]. I wanted to ask Mr. Wrigley if he would consent to our broadcasting the home games of the Chicago Cubs. Whether he was intrigued by the fact that a woman was asking him for this privilege, or just because the whole venture was so new, I don't know. I remember he called in his manager [actually Cubs president] Bill Veeck and said that the *Daily News* wanted to broadcast the home games of the Chicago Cubs. They gave us permission to do that, and so the first broadcast of play-by-play baseball out of the home park was done by WMAQ.

Both Waller and the Cubs were convinced that radio coverage did not hurt but actually improved attendance: "At the end of the first year the Cubs finished in fourth place, but their financial receipts were the highest of any club in the National League. I have a letter which they sent me stating this fact, and noting broadcasting had not in any way reduced the gate receipts of the Cubs. Actually, it had so stimulated interest, especially among women, that before another year had passed they had established a Women's Day at the park."[23]

Waller's memory was in error, but her conclusion appears reasonable. The Cubs actually finished last in 1925 but were fourth, not first, in attendance. However, after a season of radio exposure, the Cubs' 1926 fourth-place team finished first in attendance and led the National League every year until 1933.[24] Certainly, the team's on-field success—two first-, one second-, two third-, and two fourth-place finishes—contributed to the seven-year first-in-attendance run, but exposure on radio also helped.

To call the games, WMAQ tapped not a radio voice but the *Chicago Daily News* sportswriter Hal Totten. Not surprisingly, newspapers favored knowledgeable sports reporters over smooth-toned staff announcers. On April 23, 1924, Totten broadcast his first Cubs game and home opener, a 12–1 shellacking of the visiting St. Louis Cardinals. After this "spring training" debut, Totten really started his baseball announcing career a season later. In a 1931 station history, WMAQ said Totten "does not present the meaningless ranting of the casual fan, but the cool reporting of the experienced sportsman."[25] WMAQ's home broadcasts of the Cubs were immediately popular, and Totten became a fixture on Cubs broadcasts, covering the team during the regular season from 1925 to 1935 on WMAQ and from 1936 to 1943 on WCFL. He finished his radio career in the early 1950s as an announcer for Mutual's "Game of the Day." He also received national exposure on the World Series broadcasts. But almost immediately, Totten faced competition from WGN, the station of the *Daily News*'s rival the *Chicago Tribune*.

In 1924 WGN made its first big sports splashes covering the Indianapolis 500 on Decoration Day and the University of Illinois homecoming football game against Michigan. For the Michigan game, the station engineer used two mikes, one for announcer Quin Ryan and a second placed on the scoreboard to pick up crowd sounds and the band. The two microphones could be mixed to blend the crowd sounds with the announcer's voice, making sure that Ryan would be heard "except on [Red] Grange's runs."[26]

The following spring, WGN's Major League coverage began with Quin Ryan's broadcast of the Cubs' opening-day game from Cubs Park. Ryan called the game from "the roof of the grand stand," and the *Tribune* predicted that listeners would "hear the crack of the bats, the roar of the crowd, and a play by play story of the game." WGN followed with a second broadcast—a game against the Cardinals the following Saturday—and then with "numerous baseball games including every game of the world series" during the 1925 season.[27]

For the 1926 season, WGN committed to broadcasting the Cubs' home opener and every Saturday home game. Sunday home games were added as the season progressed. Once again Quin Ryan, now off the roof in the grandstand, manned the mike, "giving those graphic word pictures and humorous interludes that have made him the greatest radio reporter in the country," according WGN's owner, the *Chicago Tribune*. The paper also lauded Ryan's World Series work with Graham McNamee the previous fall. Joining Ryan for every game were WGN's rising stars "Sam 'n' Henry," later made famous on NBC radio as Amos 'n' Andy, adding "their humorous comment to [Ryan's] story of the contest."[28] Employing a strategy now known as cross promotion, WGN used baseball to promote one of its most popular programs, while adding unique value to its competing broadcasts of Cubs games. In 1926 rival WMAQ offered more extensive Cubs coverage, all regular-season home games, but WGN had "Sam 'n' Henry." In early July, WGN broadcast a baseball-boxing doubleheader, with an afternoon Cubs game followed by an evening lightweight championship bout between Rocky Kansas and Sammy Mandell from White Sox Park.[29]

But it was the 1927 season that made WGN a "full-time" baseball station. In early April, the station announced it would offer home-game coverage of both the Cubs and the heretofore radio-silent White Sox. Chicago baseball fans could listen to Major League Baseball almost every day during the regular season. Broadcasting of the White Sox games was made possible by the American League lifting its ban on radio broadcast during the previous winter. The *Tribune* claimed that both team presidents, William E. Veeck and Charles A. Comiskey, believed radio would "stimulate interest in the national pastime."[30] WMAQ kept pace by offering the home games of both teams. Its three-year run of complete home coverage of the Cubs made it, arguably, the stronger baseball station.

In 1927 Quin Ryan reported that listeners' letters offered evidence that WGN's baseball broadcasts were drawing new fans to the park. Baseball was making fans "eat up the radio" and write "letters in droves." Ryan also claimed that "crowds of listeners daily grouped in wayside 'gas' stations, in hotel lobbies, in cigar, and radio shops," and "hundreds of them who've never seen a big league game vow that they are going to make special excursions to the city to attend a contest at the Cubs or Sox parks." The new fans were absorbed in the games. One woman working as a bookkeeper became so involved in a broadcast that she wrote in the middle of one column of numbers, "Two strikes on Hartnett," the Cubs catcher. An equally engaged grandma barked, "Come on, Hack," when the Cubs slugger came to bat. A disabled Michigan boy wrote Ryan claiming that he had "found a new game, the game of make-believe baseball announcing. He sits beside the vacant lot while the other lads play ball and reports the game into an imaginary microphone!"[31]

Baseball on the radio seemed to be selling the national pastime and radio itself. The *Tribune* argued that baseball, including WMAQ's full schedule of games and the paper's own game coverage and daily announcing of scores, "has done more to popularize daylight radio than almost anything else" and had "become an established radio feature almost everywhere."[32] Decades later, the retired baseball commissioner Ford Frick reflected in his autobiography on the boost radio gave to Cubs attendance in the 1920s and 1930s: "Attendance at home games soared; public interest in the Cubs spread beyond Chicago into Indiana, Wisconsin, Iowa, southern Michigan, and lower Illinois. . . . In fact one of the first indications of the power of radio in those days was the increase in out-of-town patrons, and the number of out-of-state license plates in the ball park parking lots on weekends."[33]

New York Broadcast Blues

While radio baseball boomed in the Windy City, Gotham teams offered slim pickings to Yankee, Giant, and Dodger fans. New York teams had little incentive to offer broadcasts. Rights fees were minimal or nil, so radio added little to their revenues. In addition, their attendance came primarily from local fans who took mass transit or walked to the park. Weekend out-of-town fans were a small part of the gate, so there was no urgency to promote their teams beyond Gotham. As radio was developing in the United States, two of the New York City franchises, the Yankees and the Giants, had outstanding teams. Between 1921 and 1927, the Yankees averaged ninety-three wins per season, claiming five AL pennants; the Giants averaged ninety wins and copped four NL pennants. Except for 1925, the Bronx Bombers, housed in spacious Yankee Stadium, led the league in attendance every year during the 1920s, often by a wide margin. The Giants led the NL in attendance from 1920 to

1924 and finished in at least the top three every year during the decade. While the lowly Dodgers averaged only seventy-five wins during this period, they were the most "local" of the New York teams, with fans primarily from Brooklyn. They also tended to follow the lead of the two stronger Gotham franchises. In this sea of success, radio was a threat to the comfortable status quo.

Owners did not even want radio stations broadcasting game results, let alone play-by-play, from their parks. In July 1923, the National League owners discussed RCA's efforts to interest the National League in broadcasting the World Series and the results of regular-season games from the ballpark. National League president John Heydler reviewed the history of the requests and the league's past deference to newspaper interests in limiting radio:

> Gentlemen, we have had here several requests from the Radio Corporation of America to broadcast ball game results direct from the ball park. First they took it up here. They wanted permission of the New York Club. I took it up with Mr. Stoneham, and decided it was not the right thing to do; that the newspapers objected to that broadcasting, the evening papers. In fact later on the Base Ball Writers Association filed a protest with me about allowing the Radio Corporation to radio the ball results. They come in now and ask for permission to radio the World Series Games.

Finally, Heydler also reported that seven of the eight AL franchises were "emphatically against this proposition of broadcasting stuff out of the park."[34] The NL owners then voted unanimously to deny RCA the right to broadcast the World Series. But that fall, Commissioner Landis took command of World Series radio rights, granting RCA permission to cover the fall classic.

While New York City franchises made frequent appearances on the radio coverage of the World Series during the 1920s, regular-season games were limited primarily to opening day. For example, the Yankees' opening game of the 1927 season, against the Philadelphia Athletics, was broadcast on WEAF and WJZ with Graham McNamee calling the game.[35] A year later, WEAF and WOR aired the Giants' opening game against the Boston Braves. McNamee called the game for WEAF and Major J. Andrew White for WOR. In 1931 and 1932, New York's NBC stations covered the home openers of both the Yankees and the Giants with McNamee as the feature announcer.[36] Stations WEAF and WJZ, and others no doubt, offered listeners daily summaries, usually about five minutes in length, of the baseball scores.

There were occasional exceptions to the New York baseball broadcast boycott. The Dodgers allowed four different stations—WEAF, WABC, WMCA, and WOR—to broadcast on a single day in 1931. The future baseball commissioner Ford Frick was one of the day's mike men and recalled that the game produced a "flood of fan mail" from the gamecast-deprived New Yorkers. On the season's final weekend, the Dodgers played the visiting Cardinals, and the home club allowed radio into the stadium. Frick called the games but acknowledged his limitations: "it was a hit-or-miss production entirely lacking the professional touch of today's presentations."[37] Even re-creations based on wire reports were sparse on New York City stations. In October 1935, the Giants sued to end the practice entirely, seeking an injunction to stop Teleflash from providing information to stations during the games. Without a steady flow of game information from the parks, stations could offer only delayed re-creations, after the game results were known. With few marquee games, city stations made due with high school championships and contests between the police and firefighters. In 1933 station WINS, having been rebuffed by the three Major League clubs, persuaded the nearby Newark Bears to allow broadcasts. After a positive impact on attendance at Bears games, the broadcasts continued.[38]

The Broadcast Game Rises in the West

The New York teams' broadcast reticence was shared by most eastern franchises and for some of the same reasons. While no teams in the 1920s could duplicate the Yankees' success, most eastern franchises were tightly aligned on the Atlantic coast, with little room to grow their markets beyond their metro areas. Most fans still came to the ballparks in streetcars, buses, and subways. Radio's documented ability to draw in the hinterland fans was of limited value in these geographic settings. While most eastern franchises ignored radio or openly fought it, western teams, led by the Chicago clubs, embraced radio as the game's new fan maker. Of course, at the time, Major League Baseball's "west" ended at the west bank of the Mississippi River in St. Louis.

A November 1929 article in *Baseball Magazine* reviewed the sectional split. "Western Magnets View the Microphone as a Friend and Booster for Baseball. Eastern Magnates Look upon It as a Dangerous Interloper," announced baseball's monthly magazine. *Baseball Magazine* placed the New York City (Yankees, Giants, and Dodgers), Philadelphia (Athletics and Phillies), Boston (Red Sox and Braves), Washington DC, and Pittsburgh franchises firmly in the "nay" radio column.[39] Only the Pirates represented an exception to the East Coast cluster. The magazine acknowledged Chicago as the spark plug for the western radio engine. In 1925 Chicago stations began regular broadcasts, overcoming telegraph-company restrictions that limited communication from the ballpark to telegraph transmissions. The next year, radio play-by-play spread to the Motor City with the *Detroit News*'s WWJ broadcasting the Tigers. WWJ broadcast all of the Tiger home games, with the station's chief announcer, Ty Tyson, working from a "place in the press stand." Microphones were assigned to Tyson and also concealed "in various parts of the field" to pick up "crowd noises to lend realistic atmosphere to the game heard by listeners in their homes."[40] Tyson began his first Tiger broadcast simply: "Good afternoon, boys and girls, this is Ty Tyson speaking to you from Navin Field."[41] In 1927 Garnett Marks called the first St. Louis game from Sportsman's Park.[42] The next year, the St. Louis teams broadcast games regularly on three stations: KMOX, KWK, and WIL. At the same time, WTAM in Cleveland began offering Indians home broadcasts.

Cincinnati was the last of the western franchises to allow radio. WLW entered Redland Field (later Crosley Field) in 1929. Bob Brudette called first season of the Reds games from a booth on the ballpark roof, only to be replaced by the much more flamboyant Harry Hartman a year later.[43] *Baseball Magazine* concluded that all the western teams, with the exception of the Reds, saw radio as a "pronounced success in filling the park." The Reds withheld judgment due to the newness of radio's coverage and the poor performance of the team in 1929.[44]

While the Reds were assessing radio's benefits, the Cubs and Tigers were sold. After three years of regular radio, the Cubs set a National League record for attendance in 1928. Despite a sharp economic downturn in the city's bread-and-butter auto industry, the Detroit Tigers saw a $50,000 increase in gate receipts the year they added radio. According to *Baseball Magazine*, the eastern magnates' question "why should anyone lay between fifty cents and a dollar and a half for the entertainment that one could receive comfortably seated in an easy chair at home?" was "illogical." For the fan, the radio experience was no substitute for seeing "a good ball game with the two eyes that providence gave him. . . . So don't for a moment labor under the hallucination that you can sit home and enjoy a game as it is broadcast, and receive the same thrill and reaction that you would if you were at the scene of battle." Radio was merely a fill-in for the times when the "rabid" fan could not make it to the diamond. It was not driving current fans away; it was enlarging the pool of fans by converting women to the game. Radio coverage, not "Ladies' Day," drew "women as steady customers at the turnstiles." Their presence made "men more careful of their speech" and civilized the ballpark crowd.[45] While the radio debate was settled for *Baseball Magazine*, it was just beginning for organized baseball.

Minimal Rights Fees

By the end of the 1920s, baseball was an established radio product in many markets, but owners were not profiting much from the broadcast of their games. Owners first saw radio profit from the hyping of their on-field products, rather than from rights fees. William Wrigley offered the games for free, and his son Philip K. Wrigley extended the offer to just about any station willing to carry the games. The appeal of rights-free programming was strong, and as many as five stations were carrying Cubs games in the 1930s. Only gradually did other teams begin to demand rights fees from radio stations. Even then, the fees were relatively modest.

WTAM, a powerful Cleveland station owned by the even more powerful NBC, paid the Indians only $3,000 (about $43,000 in 2014 dollars) for the rights to the Tribe's 1930 home games, except for Sunday contests. The team wanted no Sunday radio at all, because "if the fans got a taste of a Sunday broadcast at the more important games, it would make them feel that they should have the same right throughout the season."[46] Niles Trammell, NBC's president, questioned the practice of paying teams for radio rights at all, seeing it as "a very, very dangerous precedent" that had spread to the St. Louis market and station KWK.[47] John F. Royal, the former WTAM general manager and now NBC's programming manager, responded that WTAM was forced to pay rights or lose the games to CBS, but the situation had changed now that the Indians' owners had a stake in CBS-owned WHK and had shifted the games to the Columbia affiliate.[48] For the 1931 season, the Indians continued to prohibit Sunday broadcasts, but rights fees more than doubled to $7,000 for all home games.[49]

The Cleveland Indians' situation shows the conflicted disposition of proradio teams at the end of the 1920s. While owners saw some promotional value in the medium and revenue from modest rights fees, they were still protective of the home gate, especially for the typically well-attended games on Sunday afternoon. Even radio's baseball supporters saw the medium as a potential attendance drain. For owners to exploit radio's promotional potential, while protecting the home gate, the best approach was to broadcast all road games and limit the number and scheduling of home-game broadcasts. However, the cost of broadcasting road games was more than the still-developing local radio advertising market could bear. Re-creating the games cost much less, but teams could not easily control information about the games. Any station with that information and an announcer could create its own version of either home or road games. As re-creations improved over time, they were sometimes preferred to live broadcasts from the ballpark (see chapter 8).

In its first decade, local coverage of Major League Baseball evolved from an opening-day novelty to a source of sustained tension among the baseball owners, split along regional lines. Like the owners, baseball's unofficial voice, the *Sporting News*, was divided on the benefits of radio to baseball. For the first half of the decade, radio-station revenues were limited and networks fragmentary; only in the second half did advertising become the established means of funding radio. The earliest game broadcasts were unsponsored, primarily promoting only newly formed radio stations or the newspapers that owned them. Opening day was broadcast in the first year, typically followed by occasional games throughout the season. By the second half of the 1920s, some teams, especially in the Midwest, committed to coverage of all home games. In Cleveland, Sunday home games were excluded to limit any harmful effects on attendance. For proradio owners, radio's major benefit was promoting the team, especially to distant listeners and women in hopes of luring them through the ballpark turnstiles. Some owners invited multiple stations to cover their home games, seeking to "to tie up the entire city" with the coverage of their team.[50] The newspaper industry was concerned that the broadcast of baseball scores would harm sales of its evening sports extras. While some newspaper-owned stations broadcast games, most did not and saw any information transmitted by radio as a threat to their hold on the news. In the 1930s, the newspaper industry even tried to force radio to restrict its news coverage (see chapter 4). Meanwhile, baseball's first generation of announcers was learning its craft. These pioneers are the focus of the next chapter.

3   Inventing a New Craft

In the beginning, there were no baseball announcers, only a few men willing, and sometimes eager, to voice a new expression of the national pastime. As noted in chapter 2, a variety of newspapermen and radio announcers called a handful of games from KDKA's first Major League contest through the 1923 season. Starting in 1924, more regular coverage of Major League Baseball developed in the Midwest. The first Major League markets with full coverage of home games were Chicago, Detroit, Boston, St. Louis, Cleveland, and Cincinnati. In Chicago, Boston and, St. Louis, the two-team markets, broadcasts of home games meant a summer full of radio baseball for fans, since stations covered both teams and one of the two teams would play most every day.

Regular exposure helped build a strong bond between listeners and the first generation of baseball announcers. While the quality and style of announcing certainly varied, most fans seemed content or even enthusiastic about their hometown guys. In Chicago, Cubs and White Sox fans could choose from as many as five competing broadcasts, with each announcer developing his own clientele. At various times, multiple station broadcasts of the same game aired in Boston, St. Louis, Detroit, and Cincinnati. Beyond the local voice(s), fans heard only network (NBC, CBS, MBS) World Series and later All-Star Game announcers. Although distant AM stations could be heard at night on sky waves, during the day, only local broadcasts came in clearly. Since baseball was a daytime game in the 1920s and 1930s, fans rarely heard anyone other than their own local voices of the game.

Those voices came from mainly three sources: newspapers that owned radio stations, all-purpose radio announcers, and team public-address announcers. This chapter profiles the first eight announcers of the earliest sustained regular-season broadcasts. This gang of eight includes three newspaper men (Hal Totten, Quin Ryan, and Fred Hoey), three radio men (Ty Tyson, Pat Flanagan, and France Laux), and two public-address announcers (Tom Manning and Harry Hartman). Later, the chapter examines the primitive conditions under which these pioneers honed their skills during the first decade of regular-season baseball on the radio.

Newspaper Converts

Daily coverage of baseball by newspapers was well established by the dawn of the radio age. Newspapers had been writing about baseball since the game's gestation in the first half of the nineteenth century. By 1900 major metropolitan dailies had separate sports sections. Coverage of sports expanded significantly after the First World War, and baseball, as the country's preeminent sport, received intense coverage. Many of the earliest radio stations were established by newspapers. The daily press owned 5 percent of all stations in the mid-1920s with ownership growing to about 13 percent by 1933.[1] Newspapers saw radio ownership as a promotional tool, using news bulletins to promote paper sales.[2] Radio also was market protection in a world of changing media.

Three early newspaper stations included pioneering regular-season baseball broadcasters: WMAQ (*Chicago Daily News*), WGN (*Chicago Tribune*), and WWJ (*Detroit News*). When stations needed someone to announce football and baseball games, they often turned to reporters. The most famous early example was the *New York Tribune*'s use of the legendary sports writers Grantland Rice and W. O. McGeehan for the World Series broadcasts of 1922 and 1923. But these print veterans found the aural medium a daunting challenge. Rice lasted for only one World Series, 1922, and McGeehan took a powder during Game Three of the 1923 World Series, leaving the Fall Classic call in the hands of the newcomer Graham McNamee.

As the new company "toy," the radio station offered fresh opportunity for less established staff. For example, Judith Waller moved from a minor position at the *Chicago Daily News* to become manager at WMAQ and the first significant female figure in U.S. radio. The same was true for sports broadcasts. Anyone with an interest in, and preferably some experience in, writing about sports could become the newspaper-owned station's football and/or baseball announcer. The very first regular-season baseball play-by-play broadcaster came with that background.

Hal Totten: Chicago

In Chicago, Hal Totten had worked full-time on the rewrite staff of the *Daily News* for only about a year when he first broadcast football over WMAQ in 1923. But Totten wanted to cover baseball.[3] The next year he got his start with an occasional Chicago Cubs game over WMAQ. Starting in 1925 with the Cubs and in 1927 with the White Sox, Totten broadcast Chicago team games until 1944, moving from WMAQ to WCFL in 1936. Curt Smith, author of several books on baseball announcers, rated Totten as a ten on baseball knowledge but a six on voice quality (high, gentle) on his one-to-ten announcer-rating scale. Such an assessment might be expected for an announcer coming from a print background.[4] Decades after Totten left broadcasting, Jim Bowman of the *Chicago Tribune* characterized his style as "so low-key that his trademark was a simple 'G'bye now' delivered at the end of each broadcast."[5] As a young man in Florida, Red Barber remembered listening to Totten's "pleasant, calm voice, . . . a business-type broadcaster.[6] One listener, writing to NBC in 1934, lauded Totten's laidback style: "Hal never gets so excited that he loses control of his voice. . . . He is your best baseball announcer."[7] With the reporter's need to know, Totten overcame manager resistance to conducting pregame interviews while players warmed up on the field.[8] After announcing for Mutual's "Game of the Day" in the early 1950s, Totten became a league executive, serving as president of the Three-I League for ten years and then of the Southern Association starting in 1960.[9]

Quin Ryan: Chicago

Competing with Totten of the *Daily News*'s WMAQ was Quin Ryan at the rival *Chicago Tribune*'s WGN ("World Greatest Newspaper"). Ryan, the son of a Chicago judge, was educated at Loyola Academy and North-western University. While WGN's entry into baseball broadcasting was gradual, Ryan was a jack-of-all-trades at the *Tribune*. He was a sports writer, an advertising writer, and a book reviewer, and he edited the paper's employee newsletter.[10] Ryan transferred from the *Tribune* to WGN in August 1924. By 1925 *Wireless Age* proclaimed Ryan "as much a fixture in Chicago as the Chicago river or the Wrigley Building."[11] A radio general-ist, Ryan worked Notre Dame football games, Kentucky Derbies, Indianapolis 500s, national political conventions, the Dempsey-Tunney fights, Red Grange's four-touchdown Illinois-Michigan game, and the 1925 Scopes trial in Dayton, Tennessee. He was also the voice of "Uncle Walt" on the radio comedy *Gasoline Alley*.[12] Later he became manager of WGN, turning his baseball-announcing duties over to Bob Elson in 1931.

Ryan continued throughout his career to contribute columns to the *Tribune*. In a 1927 column, Ryan provided rare, and somewhat embel-lished, insights into the announcer's mind during a ball game.

> Gosh, one hour is gone and it's only the fourth inning; wonder if they drag games out in order to sell more hot peanuts in the grand-stands? . . . This Tiger fielder, Fothergill, has a neck as wide as a chimney. . . . He runs as though he were pulling a sleigh. . . . There are evidently three things in the world you can't argue with—a radio horn, a woman, an umpire. . . . Wonder what the people unacquainted with baseball think when they hear "Kamm flies out to left field—Hunnefield rolls to short and is thrown out at first—and two men die on the sacks." . . . Wish we could have a microphone in the bleachers; we'd pick up some rare remarks. . . . Funny to think that this stuff is being listened to in front of cigar shops and radio stores, as the letters say it is.[13]

Ryan had studied acting at Northwestern, and his work as a WGN announcer gave him some advantages over the newspaper-bred Totten, who "had a gentle voice that delivered a dry, unemotional broadcast."[14] Ryan's style was more similar to the theatrical Graham McNamee's. In October 1925, after Ryan broadcast his first Cubs games on WGN, he joined forces with McNamee to broadcast the Pirates-Senators World Series on RCA's network flagship station WEAF. In 1929 Ryan covered the Cubs' first World Series of the radio era, inaugurating a newly installed glassed-in broadcasting booth at Wrigley Field.[15]

By the 1935 World Series, Ryan left regular-season WGN baseball broadcasts to Bob Elson but still had enough pull to become part of the new Mutual Broadcasting System's coverage of the 1935 World Series between the Cubs and the Yankees. Ryan's last World Series was the broadcasting icon Red Barber's first. According to Barber, Ryan's radio work was less than optimal. "Ryan was primarily a WGN executive who never bothered to improve as a broadcaster. He did not prepare himself. He thought, there in 1935, on the World Series, on a network heard in New York, Chicago, Detroit, and Cincinnati, that he was still talking to the boys in the barbershop back in 1925." After Game Two, when the Series moved to Chicago, Barber took over for Ryan, ending the broadcast pioneer's baseball career.[16] But Ryan had a long career with WGN and contributed to the *Chicago Tribune* into the 1970s.

Fred Hoey: Boston

The first announcer of Boston Red Sox and Boston Braves (or Bees) games was already an established Beantown baseball writer by the time of his first broadcast. Fred Hoey worked for the *Boston Journal* and the *Boston American* before he joined forces with John Shepard III, the owner of the New England–based Yankee Network, perhaps the strongest regional radio network in America. Shepard pursued "a policy of neglecting no major sporting event in New England," hiring announcers to cover four sports on radio: baseball, football, boxing, and wrestling.[17] With sports as a key part of the network's regional identity, Hoey's Beantown roots, as a fan, amateur player, usher, official scorer, and baseball writer, were a virtue. Hoey's newspaper background also gave him a privileged perch in the Boston ballpark press boxes. In his first year, Hoey faced competition at Red Sox games from Ted Husing, soon to be one the country's best-known sports announcers. But according to Hoey, Husing sat in the press box just above the Boston writers, who had to endure his constant chatter at every game. In contrast, Hoey positioned himself at the end of the press box out of voice range. He endured cold wind but earned the scribes' gratitude. The writers rewarded Hoey by feeding him information on out-of-town games that only they could access. Soon Hoey was the only voice of the Red Sox. The Boston writers were also helping one of their alumni. Hoey admitted, "We held favor with the writers because we belonged to the gang, having written baseball in Boston for the old *Boston Journal* and later for the *American*."[18]

With a good reporter's commitment to accuracy, Hoey compiled detailed charts of American League players, including information on age, height, weight, home, previous-season record, and "pertinent facts of his career that might be of interest to the fans." This was much of the information that radio-TV-press guides came to encompass. Hoey used his "dope charts" to make sure his "ad-libbing" was on the mark. On one occasion, having misplaced a chart, Hoey relied on memory and told his audience that Lou Gehrig's batting average the previous season was .338. Dozens of letters soon corrected Hoey, who was three points off, providing a lesson on the how knowledgeable fans were and how closely they listened.[19]

By 1936 Hoey was covering Red Sox / Bees home games over the twelve-station Yankee network. Shepard claimed the broadcasts reached over five million listeners. The *Sporting News* celebrated Hoey's deliberate style and focus on accuracy. "He never calls a base runner out or safe until the umpire has signaled his decision, with the result that he never has to correct himself or accuse the umpire of faulty judgment. He endeavors to report the game from the newspaperman's angle." TSN noted Hoey's popularity with fans, evidenced by his reception of "25 telegrams and a score of letters from listeners each day."[20] He also led the TSN poll for fans' favorite baseball announcer in September 1936, although he eventually finished fourth that year.[21] In 1931 the Fred Hoey Day sponsored by the Boston Braves drew to the park thirty thousand fans, who showed their love for their favorite announcer with a $3,000 gift.[22] One fan wrote *TSN* praising Hoey as an announcer "who sticks right to the facts of the game and no blarney."[23] Having grown up listening to Hoey, Til Ferdenzi, a *New York Journal-American* reporter and later NBC-TV director of sports publicity, recounted his virtues: "Fred was a home-town boy and he became a hero, a regional giant. . . . He was excitable—not trained. He had a dry, biting sort of voice. But very much local. And *very much* applauded."[24] But Hoey seemed more popular with fans than with his sponsors, General Mills and Socony-Vacuum Oil.

At the conclusion of the 1936 season, Hoey's tenth on the air, General Mills decided not to renew his contract for 1937. According to the *Sporting News*, fan and press reaction was swift and certain:

> A storm of protest throughout New England has poured into the radio offices and newspaper rooms over the announcement that Fred Hoey, for the past 11 seasons broadcaster of the Boston American and National League games, would be relieved of the job on the Yankee network. It is said by the sponsor that Fred, a former newspaper man, does not talk with enough fluency and a more voluble chatterer is to be placed at the mike.
>
> Newspaper writers have taken cognizance of the situation and columns have been devoted to defense of Hoey, presenting the unusual spectacle of baseball scribes going to bat for a radio announcer.[25]

According to Ferdenzi, Hoey's dismissal was front-page news, and fan protests led to picketing at the two Boston ballparks.[26] The protests were successful. Hoey's sponsors renewed his contract, "following a deluge of protests against his dismissal." Fans of the Boston teams listening on the Yankee Network would hear the familiar "Hello, everybody—this is Fred Hoey broadcasting today's ball game" during the 1937 season.[27] Socony-Vacuum Oil even took out several ads in the *Boston Globe* announcing the continuing call of "Fred Hoey, favorite local baseball announcer."[28]

But Hoey also had a problem with "demon rum." He reportedly had to withdraw from announcing Game One of the 1933 World Series after four and a half innings because of a "bad cold" that some critics claimed was a bad hangover.[29] According to Ferdenzi, "Poor old Fred had a bit of a drinking problem, and eventually his love for the sauce greased the skids for him as a baseball announcer."[30] In March 1939, Hoey was fired a second time and replaced by the retired Giants and Cardinals star Frankie Frisch. John Shepard said that Hoey was "released" because he asked for a raise and because the addition of a new sponsor made it "the right time to change our broadcaster."[31] Hoey denied demanding more money, claiming he merely had asked to be released from his contract for an after-game show. Although Frisch had been interviewed frequently on the radio, he had no play-by-play experience. Perhaps underestimating the challenges of the job, he predicted, "For the first few days I'll probably be a little nervous, something like a rookie player coming into the big leagues for the first time."[32] Unlike Hoey, the "Fordham Flash" had no connection to Boston or New England and lasted only one year in the booth, moving on to manage the Pirates in 1940. Frisch got a second chance to broadcast with the Giants from 1947 to 1949. Despite a second rallying of fans, with a petition from the "Fred Hoey Boosters Headquarters" calling for his rehiring, Hoey was done as a play-by-play announcer.[33] However, he was hired quickly by WBZ for a daily ten-minute baseball-scoreboard show. Boston's first baseball voice died on November 17, 1949, of what was ruled an accidental asphyxiation from a gas leak at his home, although some people suggested it was a suicide. In Hoey's obituary, the *Boston Globe* avowed that he "was generally credited with building up baseball broadcasting to the lofty spot it holds in the American sports scene today."[34]

The Radio Announcers

While stations affiliated with newspapers turned to a reporter with radio ambitions to brave the elements during broadcasts from the ballpark, several of the founding gang of eight made their way to the ballpark by way of the radio studio. Early stations had few employees, primarily engineers and announcers: those who set up the mikes and those who stood behind them.

Ty Tyson: Detroit

In a 1922 booklet on WWJ, the *Detroit News* claimed that it was "the first newspaper in the world to install a radio broadcasting station, and the first to increase its social usefulness by furnishing such a service to the public."[35] Indeed, the station began transmitting on August 20, 1920, and the paper publicized the station's coverage of primary election returns on August 31, more than two months before KDKA's more celebrated reporting of the 1920 presidential election returns. In October 1920, the station made its first foray into baseball, and "the man in the street, traditionally skeptical, was much impressed when . . . the results of the World Series base ball contest between Cleveland and Brooklyn were instantly sent out to the waiting base ball enthusiasts."[36] From the beginning, the *Detroit News* saw the station as an extension of its public-service responsibility to the community. This spirit was channeled into the station's broadcasting of regular-season home games of the Detroit Tigers, beginning April 20, 1927. For the first seven years, until 1934, WWJ offered the games unsponsored, despite their demonstrated popularity.[37] Even when WWJ began accepting Mobil Oil's sponsorship, the commercialization was tepid. According to Ernie Harwell, all the announcer said was, at the start of the broadcast, "this game is brought to you by Mobil Oil" and, after the contest concluded, "this game has been brought to you by Mobil Oil."[38]

Taking on WWJ's inaugural Tiger broadcast was WWJ's chief announcer, Edward Lloyd "Ty" Tyson. The Tigers provided Tyson a place in the Navin Field press box, and WWJ added field microphones to capture crowd sounds.[39] The crowd sounds surely included considerable cheering as the Tigers thumped the visiting St. Louis Browns 7–0.

Tyson grew up in Tyrone, Pennsylvania, the origin of his nickname, and attended the Pennsylvania State College, where he developed a strong interest in sports. During World War I, he served in the army before joining WWJ in 1922. The bandleader Fred Warning, a hometown friend, recommended Tyson to WWJ's station manager. In a 1932 station anniversary program, WWJ described Tyson as "a wiry, energetic chap of slightly more than average height."[40] In 1924 Tyson got his first taste of sports broadcasting when the University of Michigan allowed wwj to broadcast only because its game with Wisconsin was sold out. The broadcast is credited with increasing ticket demand for Michigan's next game. Tyson became the voice of Wolverine football. But baseball became his announcing focus after his first Tigers game in 1927. Tyson covered the team for wwj until retiring from covering the Tigers in 1942. He returned in 1947 to call the Tigers' first televised game. After cancer took the life of the Tigers radio announcer Harry Heilmann, Tyson rejoined Tigers' radio for two additional years, 1951–52.

Tyson liked nicknames and coined several for Tigers stars. Hank Greenberg was "Hankus Pancus"; Charlie Gehringer was simply "Mr. Tiger"; while Lynwood "Schoolboy" Rowe had nicknames for his nickname: "Schoolhouse," "Schoolie," or "the guy who's playing hooky today." Tyson was noted for his quick wit and unhurried approach. "His technique is deliberate and sure, flavored with a dry humor which has made him a favorite with listeners and players alike."[41] In *Voices of Summer*, Curt Smith rates Tyson a ten out of ten on popularity on the basis of his wide acclaim as a broadcaster in Detroit. According to Bob Latshaw of the *Detroit Free Press*, by the late 1920s, there was not an afternoon the Tigers played that anyone could escape Tyson. Passing open windows on the way home, "it was possible for a youngster to leave school, walk a half-mile, and never miss a pitch."[42] When Judge Landis refused to consider him as an announcer during the Tigers' 1934 World Series with the Cardinals, because Landis believed that Tyson's coverage would be partisan, the *Detroit News* rounded up six hundred thousand signatures on a petition asking the commissioner to put Tyson on the broadcasts. Although Landis continued to deny Tyson access to a national audience on NBC or CBS, the commissioner did allow Tyson to cover the games for wwj and its Ty Tyson fans.

Pat Flanagan: Chicago

William Wrigley's open park policy brought wbbm and its new announcer, Pat Flanagan, to the park in 1929. Flanagan had a curious résumé for a baseball announcer. While an ad salesman at WOC in Davenport, Iowa, owned by the Palmer College of Chiropractic, he had actually practiced the therapy briefly. He joined WBBM in 1928 as a farm expert and then developed a morning show focusing on exercise and weight control. But a career in sports broadcasting came quickly.[43] While Hal Totten's connections to NBC through WMAQ brought him opportunities to broadcast the World Series and All-Star Games to the nation, Flanagan's work at CBS-owned WBBM opened the door for him to call baseball's crown jewels. He called his first World Series in 1929, when his hometown Cubs lost to Connie Mack's A's in five games. He covered home Cubs and White Sox contests though 1943, when a bout with cancer forced his retirement to Catalina Island, the Cubs' longtime spring training site.[44] But his retirement was only temporary. His final radio job was as sports director for a Phoenix radio station. He died in 1963.[45]

"A nervous fellow who normally weigh[ed] about 150 pounds with his microphone in his hand," Flanagan was also "gabby."[46] He claimed to use 37,800 words during an average two-hour-and-seventeen-minute baseball broadcast, the same number of words in half of an average-length novel. His verbal speed and vocal intensity took their toll: Flanagan would lose four to nine pounds during a broadcast. He once lost eleven and a half pounds during a Cubs-Phillies doubleheader, while talking continuously for six and a half hours.[47]

In a 1934 *Broadcasting* profile, F. P. Wagener—the advertising manager of Flanagan's Cubs sponsor, Prima beer—lauded his skill as a radio announcer and pitchman. Flanagan's "clear-cut and simple explanations of the game, made and still continue to make baseball fans of women who had previously thought of baseball only as a man's game, and of men who were only vaguely interested in the game." Wagener credited Flanagan with contributing to Prima's 600 percent sales increase and convincing sixty-five thousand women to order the brew over the phone while listening to the Cubs broadcasts.[48]

While game accounts from wire-service feeds had been practiced since the mid-1920s, Flanagan was remembered for his re-creations. More than just recounting the facts of the game, Flanagan offered play-by-play coverage that imitated the call of a live game from the ballpark. The longtime Cubs broadcaster Jack Brickhouse put it simply, although not entirely accurately, when he asserted, "Harold Arlin invented baseball on radio. Pat invented re-creations."[49] Prima's Wagener reported that Flanagan simply went on the air one day, unannounced, and began to give play-by-play descriptions of an away game. At the conclusion of the game, he told his listeners, "If you want these out-of-town games regularly, write and tell us." After the station received over nine thousand letters requesting the games, Prima beer made sponsorship of away games "a permanent part of [its] broadcasting."[50] Flanagan, however, was not the first re-creator of baseball. The Washington Senators authorized WRC to broadcast play-by-play descriptions from wire reports in 1925 and 1926. Still, Flanagan was the first announcer to get an enthusiastic endorsement from his sponsor, and he established regular-season baseball re-creations in the Windy City.

France Laux: St. Louis

Like Pat Flanagan, the St. Louis baseball broadcaster France Laux started his career at a medium-market station (KVOO in Tulsa, the Voice of Oklahoma) and then moved to a CBS-owned-and-operated station, KMOX. In Oklahoma, Laux had an extensive sports résumé, playing college football, coaching baseball and basketball, and refereeing football. He was also part owner of the Bristow Oklahoma State League team featuring the future "Gashouse Gang" leader Pepper Martin. While working for a Tulsa station early in his career, Laux also did a re-creation of the 1927 Yankees-Pirates World Series. It was his first announcing job. He was pressed into service after the scheduled announcer became incapacitated. KMOX called in the spring of 1929 offering him thirty days to prove his worth as a baseball announcer. The thirty days became thirty years at the station, including coverage of the Cardinals and Browns from 1929 to 1946. Laux's CBS connection afforded him the opportunity to cover five World Series and four All-Star Games for the network by the end of 1937.[51]

In a 1937 national CBS broadcast, the *Sporting News* awarded Laux a trophy "in recognition of his service in broadcasting more World Series and All-Star games than any other radio announcer."[52] The publication was always a strong supporter of its hometown announcer. In 1934 *TSN* wrote that, in contrast to Tom Manning, who "inclined more to the dramatic," Laux "has earned a reputation for his complete accounts mirroring succinctly, as they do, every play that comes up in the game."[53] Early in his career, Laux frequently received critiques from his father, J. Francis Laux Sr. According to Laux, his father "was a stickler for correct pronunciation": "When I made a bungle, I heard from him."[54] Laux brought his own children before the mike on several occasions, and one of them called one inning of a Cardinals game during a 1934 "Wheaties Baseball Party" sponsored by General Mills at Sportsman's Park.[55]

While supported by the *Sporting News*, Laux faced stiff competition in the St. Louis market when Dizzy Dean, baseball's most flamboyant player, became its most flamboyant announcer in 1941. Later, Harry Caray, nearly Dean's equal in colorfulness, joined the St. Louis fray. The longtime *St. Louis Post-Dispatch* writer Bob Broeg thought Laux's deliberate style and rural speech worked against him. Laux "always spoke in a flat, metallic southern type of accent. It was accepted in the thirties, but later on, when competition hit him during the war years . . . it was really quite a drawback." Although Laux was popular with players and managers, his announcing was restrained and terse. Broeg recalled Laux as "a quiet, low-key guy, which worked for him *away* from the mike, and worked against him *behind* the mike."[56] In 1947 Cardinals owner Sam Breadon tired of sharing the mike with the Browns and wanted his team's road games covered live. He gave exclusive rights to Cardinals broadcasts to WTMV, with announcers Harry Caray and Gabby Street, a former Cardinals manager. Laux did a few more Browns games, but according to Broeg, "France wasn't just old-timey, he was done."[57]

Organization Men: The Public-Address Announcers

In the 1920s, radio was a new medium, but stadium announcers had been part of Major League Baseball for many years. Field announcers used simple, but heavy, megaphones, running up and down the foul lines to inform fans about lineup changes, the batter, defensive adjustments, and special events of the day. Announcers could lose six to eight pounds on a hot summer day.[58] The New York Giants introduced the first amplified system in 1926, and announcers gradually moved from the field to the booth.[59] For the Ohio teams, Cleveland and Cincinnati, the man who daily announced and could reasonably pronounce the players' names seemed a logical choice to call the game through the ether as well.

Tom Manning: Cleveland

The Cleveland Indians' first baseball announcer started with station WTAM in 1923, but his connection to the Tribe was long-standing. Tom "Red' Manning started as a batboy and in 1918 became field announcer, announcing line ups, until picking up a microphone in 1926. He was offered a scoreboard show, primarily because he could pronounce correctly all of the players' names. Manning continued his work as a public-address announcer while picking up an additional three bucks per day from his radio work. As he told it, when he first confronted a microphone, he thought he had been hired for that booming voice. When he blasted away, he blew out the WTAM transmitter, knocking the station off the air for an hour.[60]

As a boy, Manning sold newspapers, winning a contest as the newsboy with the loudest voice.[61] He also had success in Cleveland as a manager of amateur teams. Long before most other teams, the Indians management required approval of all announcers, and Manning was General Manager Billy Evans's choice. According to Manning, his first Indians broadcast, on June 26, 1928, was a complete surprise. He arrived that day a public-address announcer but was led by Evans to a broadcast setup in the League Park press box and told that his new job was to call the games on radio.[62] Evans applauded Manning's work in a 1930 letter to WTAM. Manning "has proved to be very satisfactory, not only to the Station but the Ball Club as well."[63] Manning called the Indians' regular-season games until 1932, when a change in team ownership resulted in radio rights switching from WTAM to WHK, a CBS affiliate. WHK replaced

Manning with the retired Indians outfielder Jack Graney, the first former player to switch to announcing. Manning continued to broadcast baseball for NBC, which owned WTAM, calling the World Series nine times for the network. This sustained national exposure helped him win the 1938 *Sporting News* award for outstanding baseball announcer. *TSN* lauded Manning's ability "to describe the actual happenings on the diamond so vividly that his hearers, many of whom were novice fans at the beginning, always thoroughly understand his broadcasts."[64] Curt Smith said Manning's "tones rasped; he was jocular, effusive."[65]

Red Barber remembered Manning as an early influence and as an "announcer in sports who went the highest from the lowest start." Barber described Manning as "a trim, smallish man with flaming red hair. His eyes were bright blue. He bounced when he walked. He exuded confidence."[66] A 1932 letter to the *Sporting News* touted Manning as the nation's best baseball announcer. "If you don't believe this, ask anyone in Cleveland."[67] In reviewing coverage of the 1932 World Series, the *Sporting News* wrote that Manning "was on the top of every play with a terse, slangy style that went over big."[68] But Manning's animated style did not please all. In 1934 one listener wrote NBC, "In the All Star [game] a person could not understand your Tom Manning" because "he loses control of his voice."[69] In his later life, Manning suffered from deafness in his right ear but returned to the Indians radio booth for the 1956 and 1957 seasons with Jimmy Dudley.

Harry Hartman: Cincinnati

Although Harry Hartman was not the first Reds announcer, he was the first to establish himself as the voice of the Reds, covering the team over WFBE (later WCPO). When Red Barber came to Cincinnati in 1934 to call the Reds games for WLW, Hartman was already entering his fifth year, having been recognized by the *Sporting News* in 1932 as the nation's top Major League announcer. Hartman won the award again in 1936. In *The Broadcasters*, Barber claims his success in Cincinnati cost Hartman his job, but Barber had moved to Brooklyn two years before Hartman left radio announcing to sell advertising. Hartman's marriage in early

1939, not competition from Barber, may have been the stimulus for his midlife career shift.[70] The two broadcasters offered competing play-by-play accounts of Reds games from 1934 through 1938.

In 1928 Hartman started at WFBE by selling advertising time, calling fights and hosting a daily, quarter-hour sports interview program. According the *Sporting News*, he also called some Reds games in 1928.[71] In 1930 Hartman, now an established Cincinnati radio personality, replaced the Reds' first regular radio announcer, Bob Burdette. According to Curt Smith, Hartman "convinced Sid Weil, then the franchise owner, that his team needed a more exciting Voice."[72] Hartman also saved money, serving as both the Reds' radio and public-address announcer. According to Barber, Hartman would sit behind home plate with two mikes, one for radio and one for public address, with the PA mike off while he called the game and the radio mike off when he made announcements to the crowd. "When the afternoon sun got real hot, as it did most every summer afternoon in Cincinnati, Harry simply took off his shirt. Harry was a beautifully simple man."[73] The rotund, three-hundred-pound Hartman had a limited education but a great gift for coining active verbs, including "bammo," "whammo," and "socko." The Baseball Hall of Fame historian Lee Allen, who grew up in Cincinnati, avowed, "Harry was sort of rough around the edges, it's true, and his dictionary wasn't too thick, but he was earthy and people liked him."[74] Hartman followed the team to spring training and even worked out with the club on occasion. A 1935 *TSN* photo showed the rounded Hartman, baseball glove on hand, filling out every inch of a large Reds uniform. "He became an extension of the team," according to Allen.[75] While never achieving Barber's national fame, Hartman was a lovable Cincinnati institution during the first seasons of baseball broadcasts in the Queen City.

From Box Seat to Broadcast Booth

Hartman's experience sitting behind home plate while he called the game on radio and handled the public address reflects the experience of the first of first baseball announcers. Since the first games were experiments, little thought was given to the announcer's location. He had to be close enough to the game to see the action and close enough to a phone line for his voice to be transmitted to the originating station. Photos and descriptions of the first regular-season game call by Harold Arlin in 1921 and the first World Series announced from the home park by Grantland Rice in 1922 locate the announcer in the first row of seats, calling the game from a fan's perspective while exposed to the elements. During this first two years of calling Cardinals and Browns games, France Laux remembered reporting from the stands: "I sat downstairs in the stands behind the screen and then, to escape inquisitive fans, moved to the edge of the upper deck."[76] One can only imagine how many inappropriate comments made their way from fans' mouths through the announcer's mike to the home speaker. There were no "seven-second delays" in the mid-1920s. From-the-stands announcing continued through the 1925 World Series between the Pirates and the Senators, Graham McNamee complained about the driving rain at one Pittsburgh game as he called the game from the stands.

By the 1927 World Series, McNamee had moved to the press box, and it was time for the writers to complain. Ring Lardner's famous comment, "I attended a double-header, the game Mac was describing and the game I was watching," was partially provoked by McNamee's location just behind the writer.[77] For the next game, Lardner was relocated away from the rising star of radio.[78]

McNamee's repositioning to the press box illustrated the next advance in the announcer's progression. A 1927 photo of WMAQ's Hal Totten shows the announcer located with his telephone-receiver "mike" and transmission equipment in the first row of the upper deck at Wrigley Field. A photo of Totten taken two years later shows him, bundled in an overcoat, in the front row of the press box. While both locations provided protection from the rain, wind and cold were other matters. Other announcers were positioned behind the working writers, and their relentless narration caused considerable consternation. In Boston, Fred Hoey positioned himself at the end of the press box as a favor to his colleagues of the fourth estate, despite exposure to the elements during New England's often challenging early season weather. Ty Tyson, who worked for WWJ, owned by the *Detroit News*, skipped the in-the-stands stage and broadcast his first game from the press box.

The ever proradio William Wrigley is credited with installing the first broadcast booth in time for the 1929 Cubs-Athletics World Series. The glassed-in booth was "in the most advantageous position possible," with "constant telephone connection to the score board."[79] The booth provided space for the multiple stations covering the Cubs. The creation of a permanent space for radio symbolized its acceptance by the team as an enduring part of the baseball world. As more teams began granting stations the right to cover home games, Wrigley's innovation became, ever so gradually, the norm in baseball. The radio booth would become part of the national pastime's architecture.

Critiquing the Announcer: Writers Take Their Shots

While noisy announcers could be shifted to the end of the press box or eventually their own sound-insulated booth, writers still resented the intrusion of the aural medium into their baseball world. The most famous criticism was Lardner's lampooning of McNamee's 1927 World Series call, but other newspapermen also ridiculed the amateurish radio coverage of games. An instructive example comes from a *Baseball Magazine* piece in which the newspaperman James M. Gould recounted how a broken leg forced him to stay at home and hear the broadcast of the Detroit Tigers–St. Louis Browns game during the summer of 1930. Gould claimed that the following came from his "transcript" of the Browns announcer, possibly France Laux, who was calling Browns games in 1930:

> Detroit's at bat and Harry Rice is the first Tiger up. Crowder is pitching for the Browns. He is looking to check signals with Clyde Manion, the Brownie catcher. He has the signal, up comes his right arm and here's the pitch. Looks like a pretty strike. No, it's a ball, low and inside. And by the way, that's not Harry Rice at bat at all, it's Marty McManus. Knew he used to play with the Browns? Ha, ha! Crowder winds up, here's the pitch and—o-o-h, he sure hit that one. It looks

like a sure triple—no, he'll only make two bases on it. Well, what-dyeknowabout that? Gullic caught the ball.

Gould continues his transcription of the Browns announcer's adventures in baseball, noting with considerable irony that after watching "baseball for some 22 years," he finally learned what "a good willing worker could do in the way of frills of description to a perfectly good baseball game. It was marvelous and almost worth breaking a leg to listen to."[80]

Gould focused on the weaknesses of early baseball announcers in simply reporting the game accurately. Compared to their print brethren, their reporting seemed riddled with mistakes. However, announcers must observe the action, identify the players, and compose their verbal account in a split second. And they must repeat the process for a game that can last several hours. In this early period, they also did it alone. There were no color commentators, just one man creating a vision of baseball for his listeners. The baseball writer needs only to note accurately the action and actors, while composing his far-briefer report at what to the radio announcer seems a leisurely pace.

While most members of the Baseball Writers Association probably maintained a similar distain for the voices of the game, Edward Burns, writing in the *Chicago Tribune* in 1930, focused on how radio coverage was changing the baseball writer's job. In a Robert Benchley–style, tongue-in-cheek column, Burns picked no direct quarrel with the game's voices, having "never met a baseball announcer" who he "didn't think was a nice, smart fellow and very much into his job." What concerned Burns was just how difficult radio broadcasters doing their jobs were making his job:

In the days before baseball broadcasting an author could write his stuff with a happy leisure. If he managed to set down the correct score he had earned his wage. If he didn't have time to record some of the main features of the game, his bosses and most of his public, save the few hundreds who actually saw the contest, never were the wiser. It was indeed a happy life.

These days, when a poor overworked baseball writer comes into his desk to do his piece, he finds that everybody in the office knows everything that happened at the ball park, and, on occasion, things that didn't happen at the ball park. They've heard the game from their broadcast. You may not realize it, but this widespread, detailed knowledge makes it very tough on the author and frequently causes him to miss his supper.[81]

Burns jealously observed that the broadcaster gets "5,000,000 words to tell his story," but "the baseball writer has 1,000 words." Reflecting the separation between listeners and ballpark, in an era before portable radios, Burns surmised that the broadcaster must also "think how reassuring it is to his dramatic talents to know that not one of his customers is seeing the game. He can speak freely." Burns concluded that radio broadcasters were here to stay: "We're all just one happy family and my motto is: 'Live and let live.'"[82]

Writers gradually began to accept the new reality of a radio rival for the public's attention. Newspaper coverage began to shift from game descriptions to postgame interviews, player and manager profiles, and analyses of the game action. But the divide between the talkers and the scribes never disappeared. Indeed, it was soon codified. When the National Baseball Hall of Fame established its rules for induction, only members of the Baseball Writers Association were given a vote.

Educating the Announcer: The Floyd Gibbons School of Broadcasting

By the early 1930s, radio sports were an established and growing part of the radio menu, and a new generation of announcers wanted to specialize in sports. The Floyd Gibbons School of Broadcasting devoted lesson number 26 of its "Complete Course in the Technique of Broadcasting" to training the next generation of announcers. Gibbons was a noted radio commentator, newsreel narrator, and adventurer who served as the *Chicago Tribune*'s war correspondent during the Great War. In France, he lost an eye while attempting to rescue an American soldier. From then on, he wore his signature eye patch over his left eye. While more of a celebrity than a radio mainstay, Gibbons was known for his rapid-fire on-air delivery. He was once clocked at an average of 217 words per minute.[83] However, by the early 1930s, he was famous enough for his radio work to lend his name to a home-study course for fledgling broadcasters.

The Gibbons lesson on sports broadcasting did not focus specifically on baseball but on principles that could be applied to all sports. Most of the examples focused on football coverage but could easily be used in baseball coverage. The lesson covered a variety of topics: the importance of foreknowledge (research and preparation), types of descriptive broadcasts, the difficulty of presenting an unbiased report, setting the scene, describing the action, the use of present-tense verbs, the primacy of accurate description, variation in voice volume and pitch, the use of short sentences and dramatic pauses, ways to handle crowd noise, and the need to repeat descriptions of important plays.

The Gibbons school reviewed two types of descriptive broadcasts: technical and dramatic. The appropriate approach varied depending on the announcer's perception of the audience. An audience of devoted fans should prefer a technical broadcast that focuses on detailed, objective description of the game "set forth in a swift-moving narrative form."[84] The announcer supplies few personal stories about the players or the teams. The dramatic broadcast assumes a much broader audience that must be attracted to the contest. The announcer works to have "the audience actually attend the contest through him, rather than to tell the audience what is going on."[85] The announcer feels the crowd's emotions and expresses them. He allows time for "sidelights" on players and events surrounding the actual contest. In this early lesson, Gibbons is anticipating the eventual split among baseball announcers into reporters, like Red Barber, and unabashed dramatists, like Gordon McLendon. The balance between fact and fiction remained a central tension for baseball announcers. In the lesson, the Gibbons school recommends a middle ground, arguing, "Proponents of both schools yield much to advocates of the other. Our most popular observers do not carry either theory to the extreme."[86]

The Gibbons school also addressed the problem of partisanship. Should the announcer try to appear neutral at all times, or can he be a "homer" that openly roots for his team? Except when covering the World Series or other national sports events, announcers are usually speaking to a local/regional audience made up of the team's fans. The Gibbons school argues that avoiding partisanship is very difficult and, ultimately, counterproductive. In sports, one team often dominates the action, so the neutral observer will appear partisan simply because he will have much more positive commentary for the winning team. Instead, "one of America's leading observers" offers this advice: "Do not be partisan to either side," but "try to be partisan to both sides!" By hyping the actions of both teams, the announcer is free to bring his full emotions to bear. He no longer worries that he might be offending one side or the other. Instead, he becomes "a violent friend of everybody in the game" and "a well-wisher of every man on every team."[87]

While we do not know how many, if any, future baseball announcers used Gibbons's sportscasting course, the text of the home-study guide covers many of the issues that announcers confronted throughout the game's history. The need for journalism versus the need to dramatize and the problem of partisanship were issues navigated by announcers from the beginning of sports on the radio. Home-study courses such as Gibbons's may have provided a crash-course orientation for a few new voices, but most announcers probably learned the way humans learn to speak, by listening to and imitating others.

By the early 1930s, the first generation of baseball announcers—Hal Totten, Fred Hoey, Quin Ryan, Ty Tyson, Pat Flanagan, France Laux, Tom Manning, and Harry Hartman—were an established part of the baseball world in the Midwest and New England. Their daily calls during the season built a bond with fans, producing an outcry if an announcer such as Hoey was let go. All of the first gang of eight had substantial baseball broadcast careers, but all were gone from the radio booth by the early 1950s. The construction of separate broadcast booths in some cities signaled permanence for radio coverage of the national pastime. In 1933 the influential *Who's Who in Major League Baseball* offered a separate section on Minor League and Major League announcers. The baseball industry overview concluded, "The business of announcing has become a distinct department of the baseball business. Fans swear by their favorites and rely upon their judgment."[88] Baseball writers mocked the foibles of their chattering competition but adapted their own reporting, reluctantly acknowledging that they were no longer the primary source of information about what happened at the ballpark. Despite some acceptance of radio, *Who's Who* also noted the division among baseball owners over the impact of radio on the game. *Who's Who* predicted "that each off-season will see a resumption of the argument as to the benefits or harm in broadcasting."[89] The next chapter examines this continuing baseball "war" with radio.

4   The Baseball-Radio War

Most Major League Baseball owners greeted the emergence of radio in the 1920s with suspicion and apprehension. Owners feared the new medium would reduce attendance and compromise their symbiotic relationship with the newspaper industry. East Coast and American League teams were especially antiradio, while some clubs in the Midwest, especially the Chicago Cubs, were proradio. Initially, teams received limited rights fees, or none at all, for allowing the broadcasting of their games. Thus, there was little economic incentive to let radio in the ballpark gate. However, a few forward-thinking owners saw radio as a positive promotional strategy for selling baseball to new customers, including women working in the home. Radio broadcasts might also charm children, spawning the next generation of fans. Since the games were played during the day, women and children were major groups in the radio audience. As the 1930s dawned, the Great Depression forced owners to consider new options for replacing revenues lost from declining attendance. At the same time, some companies, General Mills in particular, were aggressively promoting the sponsorship of baseball on the radio to sell breakfast cereal such as Wheaties to children. The mounting tensions between some baseball owners and radio erupted during a series of league meetings in the 1930s. These pivotal confrontations between the lords of America's national pastime and the medium that millions used every day to pass the time changed the relationship between baseball and radio, establishing a blueprint that carried over to television.

As wars go, even metaphoric ones, the baseball-radio war of the 1930s was a relatively minor skirmish. Unlike the war on poverty, the war on drugs, or the war on terrorism, the baseball-radio war did not receive much national press attention. A few articles in the *New York Times, Broadcasting*, and the *Sporting News* sufficed to cover the conflict. But behind closed doors, baseball owners debated the future of the national pastime on the radio for more than a decade. Like many regional wars triggered by a broader conflict, the baseball-radio war was never officially declared.

Newspapers versus Radio

The baseball-radio war of the early 1930s was a minor battle in the larger press-radio war. Newspapers owned the news prior to the emergence of radio in the 1920s. Competition among local papers was fierce but limited to members of the daily print club. Radio news developed slowly in the 1920s. As late as 1933, NBC's news bureau consisted of one reporter. Radio news was generally part of a station's "sustaining time," unsponsored programming typically offered to please federal regulators and provided to maintain the station's signal and presence in the market. But newspapers still felt threatened by voices from the ether. Radio could cover news as it happened from the scene and certainly before a print version, even an extra, could appear. Radio speakers could always scoop the printed word. In the 1930s, newspapers all but pulled the plug on their new rival.

In December 1933, the newspaper industry (Associated Press [AP], United Press [UP], International News Service [INS], American Newspaper Publishers Association) and the radio industry (NBC, CBS, National Association of Broadcasters) all but shut down radio news when they signed the Biltmore Agreement at that hotel in Washington DC. The agreement was decidedly one-sided, with major concessions from the radio industry. In the future, radio news would have to be unsponsored (therefore unprofitable), supplied by the newspaper industry's Press-Radio Bureau, and limited to times that ensured that morning and evening newspapers always presented the news first. This outlandish restraint of trade was agreed to by the radio industry because news was not seen as profitable programming and the newspapers controlled the major wire services. The Biltmore Agreement began to fall apart almost immediately; by the end of 1934, independent (nonnetwork) stations, which had not signed the agreement, began to program news extensively and profitably. By the end of 1934, the agreement's restrictions had started to unravel.[1]

Given this context, baseball's radio coverage restrictions were clearly supported by newspapers and were part of the print media's attempts to control its competition. Owners were very aware of the value of newspaper publicity in selling tickets, while, in a classic symbiotic relationship, newspapers sold more papers by extensively covering the national pastime. This comfortable partnership, which had grown into a codependency in the early twentieth century, was threatened by radio's live coverage of the game. Who needed to read about a game they had already heard? At the urging of newspapermen, baseball owners in many markets were generally reluctant to broadcast regular-season games. The owners even denied RCA's request to cover the 1923 World Series but were overruled by Judge Landis.

A Divided Ownership

Although newspaper naysayers could rip radio's reporting, it ultimately fell to the baseball owners to decide if the benefits of radio outweighed its limitations. Large on the benefits side was the promotional value of the broadcasts. Newspapers could only recount the excitement of the recent past, but radio allowed fans to feel the passion of the moment. For fans who had rarely or never come to the ballpark, the dramatic immediacy of the broadcast could help push them through the turnstiles. This was especially true for fans who could listen to the daily broadcast games throughout the long season: women working the home and children, baseball's next generation of fans. Large on the limitations side was a possibility that fans would find the broadcasts too appealing and a convenient substitute for attending the games. Supporting this fear was a dramatic drop in attendance starting in 1931, after a few years of radio broadcasts in many markets. The economic calamity of the Great

Depression was surely driving down attendance, but radio could be a contributing factor. When money is tight, is the appeal of a "free" baseball broadcast not even greater? Owners could not control the economy, but they could control their broadcasts. In addition, broadcasts alienated owners from their longtime supporters in the newspaper industry. On the question of radio, the owners, as they often are, were thoroughly split.

In 1929 the ownership's radio split was described in regional terms: the eastern magnates saw radio "as a dangerous interloper," while their western brethren found "a friend and booster" in the "ether waves."[2] In this era, most of the eastern teams represented larger cities, and most of their attendance came from the immediate metropolitan area. For Jacob Ruppert's Yankees, attendance was always at the top of the league because of the team's preeminent position in the nation's largest market, gigantic stadium, sustained success on the field, and possession of the game's greatest star, Babe Ruth. Given this dominant position, the promotional benefits of radio were easily lost on Ruppert. A new medium might erode Yankee supremacy, while offering opportunities the team did not seem to need.

Unlike the landlocked cities of the East, Midwest teams were surrounded by vast, distant, and lightly populated areas with few big-time entertainment options. The trains, and increasingly automobiles, made these cities accessible to rural populations that were inflating the weekend attendance of many western teams. Many of the western owners believed that baseball on the radio sold the product in the hinterlands and drew substantial numbers of out-of-town guests to the ballpark. Detroit Tigers announcer Ty Tyson recounted, "Folks enclose checks or money orders wanting me to purchase tickets for some game on a day that they expect to be in Detroit. Radio has attracted these people to the ball park, and they admit it." Tyson concluded, "There is little doubt that radio benefits sport."[3]

The Great Owner Debates: Early Rounds

The minutes of National and American League meetings in the 1920s and 1930s are filled with passionate debate over the virtues and vices of radio. The strongest and most consistent proradio voice was Bill Veeck Sr. of the Chicago Cubs, representing the position of his boss, owner William Wrigley Jr. Wrigley had made his fortune selling chewing gum, a product that no one really needs, through the persuasive power of advertising. He and Veeck saw radio as a two-hour daily commercial for their on-field product, which in the 1920s and 1930s was usually a winning one. Their principal ally was Harry Grabiner, representing the Chicago White Sox ownership. The Cleveland Indians management was also a steady radio supporter. Whenever the possibility of banning radio was raised, Veeck rolled out a battery of arguments in favor of the medium.

As early as the February 1927 NL meeting in New York, Bill Veeck defended the Cubs' then-aggressive policy of broadcasting all home games. Veeck proclaimed the broadcasting of games "a good thing." The Cubs had seen their attendance increase since they began broadcasting, especially the attendance of women, who had become interested in baseball through listening to the radio reports. Radio offered "the very best possible advertisement."[4] At the league's December 1929 meeting, when NL president John Heydler said he had a Western Union representative waiting to discuss if "radio broadcasting has been a benefit or harm to the game," Veeck blurted out, "If he is going to say it is a harm, do not have him come."[5]

But the legendary manager John McGraw, representing the New York Giants, wanted nothing to do with the aural medium, noting that during the 1928 presidential campaign, whenever either of the major-party candidates spoke on radio, New York theaters "were nearly empty."[6] McGraw clearly believed the same fate awaited baseball teams should they allow broadcasts. Veeck, now joined by Sam Breadon of the Cardinals, argued that radio brought new customers, especially women, to the ballpark. Not persuaded, some owners were threatening to ban baseball broadcasts. Veeck and his ally's comments were modest compared to a presentation by representatives of the National Association of Broadcasters (NAB).

The NAB Position

On December 10, 1929, William Hedges of WMAQ in Chicago and Henry Bellows of WCCO in Minneapolis told the baseball barons that radio broadcasters gave their teams $15 million worth of free advertising. They made the claim first in the morning at the AL owners meeting and then repeated it in the afternoon at the NL owners gathering. The NAB representatives told the owners, radio's gift "is yours without charge, simply because the broadcasters have the feeling, first of all, that the broadcasting of baseball games is a matter of public service, that it is something that we must carry on to satisfy the great interest that the American people have in baseball." Sponsorship of the broadcasts was only "to defray some of our costs, and in a few instances all of our costs," of those broadcasts.[7] It was the NAB's belief that owners' antipathy toward radio was caused by announcers' errors and unreasonable "panning" of their players. Hedges promised that broadcasters would create a code for sports announcers that would ensure that they promote and fairly report on the teams they cover. Hedges also argued that, just as newspaper publicity had clearly promoted baseball attendance, radio would also help the gate. Radio advertising had helped Pepsodent increase its sales 40 percent in only a few months. It could do the same for baseball. In addition, radio reached out to small communities and made baseball an attraction for Chicago's summer visitors. Announcers received many letters supporting this proposition.

The NAB's arguments worked for the moment. After meeting with its representatives, the senior-circuit owners passed a resolution "that it is the sense of the National League that radio broadcasting is an individual club matter." Seven owners supported the resolution, but Veeck insisted that the Chicago Cubs be listed as not voting because he did not support the league's authority to establish any radio policy affecting his team.[8]

1931: Spoiling for a Fight

Two years later at the joint meeting of the American and National Leagues in Chicago, Veeck developed more fully his argument that radio policy was strictly a club matter. After a couple of years of a hands-off policy, antiradio owners wanted baseball to take a stand on radio. Just before the meeting, the Cubs had preempted the owners' hand for the 1932 season by signing a contract to broadcast its games. Contracts for the 1933 season would be at issue. Before the joint meeting, the American League had passed a resolution that no team should enter into a broadcasting contract for 1933 until baseball could agree on "some definite plan for broadcasting."[9] The same motion was now made and seconded at the joint meeting of the two leagues.

Although Judge Landis was certain of his control over World Series radio rights, he was ambivalent about his role in regular-season radio policy. When asked by Veeck if the commissioner had jurisdiction over radio policy, Landis replied, "I have not given the subject thought to decide whether it comes within the Commissioner's jurisdiction, or comes within the jurisdiction of the two Leagues."[10] Landis never seized control of the radio controversy, and thus it raged in both leagues for several more years.

Over the next several minutes, Veeck outlined his and the Cubs' position regarding radio. First, its seemed strange that anyone would doubt that a team, not the league, should control broadcast policy. "We sell a lot of peanuts at the ball park. People do not say: You can't do this; you have to have the sanction of the two leagues."[11] For Veeck, radio broadcasts of Cubs games were a "form of advertising," and no one had ever questioned a club's right to advertise its product. Second, broadcasts produced goodwill for the Cubs and baseball by offering amusement to all and "playing to men and women who are flat on their backs." He proclaimed that radio is "one of the best good will producers we can possibly get hold of." Third, radio has helped increase "the receipts of the Chicago Club, and of every club that plays at Wrigley Field." Fourth, the broadcasts bring pleasure to many citizens, and to ban them would deprive them of that pleasure. The games have helped make the Cubs an important part of the "civic community." Veeck reported that an NBC telephone survey found that 75 percent of Chicago's afternoon radio audience was listening to game broadcasts. Finally, the Cubs broadcasts did not damage other clubs and were not intended to produce additional revenue. The only "selfish interest that we could have would be in the promotion of baseball."[12]

Countering Veeck's arguments was Sam Breadon of the Cardinals. After dabbling with radio in the late 1920s, Breadon had switched his position and now saw radio, especially from Chicago's high-powered stations, as a threat to his team's attendance. "You say it does not interfere with anybody. When a game keeps people in St. Louis away from St. Louis to listen to a game in Chicago, you are interfering with our business."[13] Veeck conceded that very long distance broadcast of more than one hundred miles might be a problem for other clubs, but he needed more than a fifty-mile limit because, he said, "we draw a great many people from a distance greater than fifty miles, and we are entitled to that, if by our progressiveness [in radio policy] . . . we can interest them in our game."[14]

Finally, because it never hurts to praise the boss, Veeck appealed to the ethos of William Wrigley Jr. who was "as great a salesman as ever trod the earth": "[The Cubs] had benefit of his counsels, and he is absolutely convinced that radio, next to a winning ball club, is the greatest producer of admissions that we have. When I talk to you about a man of that sort, you cannot laugh it off, because he has had experience in advertising. He has had experience in merchandising. He has had experience in mob psychology, and that is his reaction."[15]

As the meeting continued, Veeck received some support from Bill Evans of the Cleveland Indians, one of the few teams receiving rights fees for their games. When Judge Landis finally called the question, the motion to delay signing contracts for the 1933 season was passed. The motion carried, but as in 1929, Veeck had the Cubs recorded as "not voting on this question."[16] The owners agreed that no contracts would be signed for the 1933 season until after the radio issue was reviewed at the 1932 meetings.

1932: A Slippery Slope to the Status Quo

The following year's joint meeting produced another skirmish in the baseball-radio war. Veeck came to the meeting with a league motion that reflected his position. Prior to the meeting, the NL passed, by a 5–3 vote, a motion stating, "For the purposes of the joint meeting, it is the sense of the National League that each club has and shall have the right to regulate its own affairs with reference to radio, provided that it does not materially interfere with any other Major League Club."[17] The motion reflected Veeck's "hands-off" position with a concession to the Cardinals' concern that one team's radio broadcasts should not "materially interfere" with another club's rights. However, Breadon found the motion's language too vague and did not support it. Although Veeck's arguments convinced some wavering owners, the NL owners were still clearly divided on the radio issue.

As the 1932 joint meeting continued, Breadon introduced a new concern about radio. The medium might harm baseball's old-media newspapers, which, he claimed, had "built up our business" for the past fifty years.[18] Breadon then read a long letter from the chairman of the Radio Commission of the Newspaper Publishers Association, which documented the competition that radio posed to newspapers. Clearly, radio could always disseminate information faster than newspapers.

Ignoring the NL's earlier "hands-off" motion, Breadon launched a frontal assault on radio. He introduced a motion at the joint meeting "that all broadcasting be eliminated from the Major Leagues; that is to say, that all Major League clubs be prohibited from broadcasting Major League ball games."[19] The motion produced an immediate response from Veeck: "Mr. Chairman, the position of the Chicago Club is this: It believes that it has certain inherent rights and that it acquired those rights when it purchased the franchise in the National League. It holds that one of its rights is the advertising of the only product that enables it to exist. That product is baseball. We hold that so long as we advertise our product in a business-like, decent, honest and honorable method, there is no man in this room who has the right to say that we shall discontinue that right." Veeck was declaring an "inalienable right" for owners to advertise, and "the Chicago Club will adhere strictly to whatever rights it thinks it possesses." Later, he added, "I would be a traitor to my organization if I held views of that sort and did not defend them upon every occasion."[20] Veeck then revisited many of his earlier arguments: radio advertises the product, it brings women and other new fans to the ballpark, and it helped Wrigley build the Cubs into a successful franchise. The representatives of the two Boston teams (Red Sox and Braves) joined with Veeck in praising the positive power of radio, particularly if you have a solid team and a talented announcer. Harry Grabiner, representing the crosstown White Sox, also offered support for Veeck's proradio vision.

But the argument that won the day was a classic "slippery slope" gambit. Ironically, it was articulated by Leo Bondy, who represented the antiradio New York Giants. If the leagues regulate radio today, what will they regulate tomorrow? Or as Bondy put it, "If we start to regulate the other man's business with radio no one knows where that will finish."[21] While many owners feared radio, they feared league interference in their business even more. Bondy's appeal was so powerful that it convinced Breadon to withdraw the "no radio" motion, as he finally conceded, "No one is more jealous of his rights than I am. . . . I think it would be a dangerous precedent to allow a meeting of this kind to tell us how we are going to run our clubs."[22] For the 1932 joint meeting, the issue was resolved. At the 1933 owners meeting, the clubs agreed once again to stick with the status quo and let teams decide on their own policy.

1934: The Last Round

In 1934 the antiradio forces pushed to reduce radio's influence over baseball. The St. Louis teams moved to remove radio from Sportsman's Park, while the Yankees convinced their New York rivals to agree to a five-year ban on Gotham broadcasts, including re-creations. But at the same time, sponsors were increasingly stepping up to pay for baseball broadcasts. In Chicago, Walgreen's paid WGN $45,000 for baseball ads for the 1934 season,[23] while Prima beer gave WBBM $40,000 for advertising on ball games.[24] Nationally, other sponsors, especially General Mills, were signing contracts to sponsor broadcasts of Major and Minor League games.

The final stand for the antiradio forces came at the December 1934 American League meeting. AL president Will Harridge introduced a rule proposed at the earlier joint meeting "that in the 1936 season and thereafter radio broadcasting of the official league championship games [regular-season games] shall not be permitted." Yankees owner Jacob Ruppert moved for adoption, and the motion was seconded.[25] The owners then discussed the issue once again. Harry Grabiner of the White Sox argued that broadcasting did not harm a team's attendance, if "your club is up." Ed Barrow of the Yankees countered, "Broadcasting does not help us at all."[26] Of course, the Yankees were not broadcasting their games, so radio could not help. The discussion continued off the record. Finally, the question was called. The Yankees, Browns, A's, and Senators supported the motion to end broadcasts starting in 1936. The White Sox, Indians, Tigers, and Red Sox opposed it. The tie vote killed the motion. With the outright broadcast ban lost, Browns president L. C. McEvoy proposed a one-thousand-watt power limit on any station carrying baseball broadcasts. There was no second to the motion. Then Grabiner moved "that broadcasting of games in the American League be left to the local clubs to handle as they see fit, as they have in the past."[27] Predictably, Grabiner's "local autonomy" motion failed with the same 4–4 split in the vote. But the defeat did not matter, since the absence of any radio policy meant that the decision to broadcast was "left to the local clubs to handle as they see fit" anyway.

The AL vote reflected how the league's position on radio was shifting. In the late 1920s and early 1930s, the antiradio faction was the majority, but strong arguments by Veeck and others held them at bay. By 1934 the owners were evenly split, and antiradio forces, having failed to force a radio ban on at least three occasions, were losing ground. While most owners were still very concerned about radio's negative effect on attendance, they were not willing to "to regulate the other man's business."

Later that year, the cereal makers General Mills and Kellogg convinced the St. Louis teams to reenter the radio arena for the 1935 season.[28]

Although several teams shifted their positions, the owner split over radio continued throughout the decade of the 1930s. While the Yankees and their weaker New York–area rivals maintained a radio ban until 1939, three forces made radio increasingly attractive to owners: the Great Depression, the radio advertising boom, and the surprisingly gradual move toward night baseball.

Winds of Change

The economic calamity that was the Great Depression triggered a rapid decline in Major League attendance. Between 1924 and 1929, MLB attendance ranged between just over nine and just under ten million and then peaked at 10,132,262 in 1930, a figure it did not reach again until 1944.[29] In 1931 attendance declined to 8,467,107, in 1932 to 6,974,566, and in 1933 to 6,089,031, a 40 percent decline from its 1930 peak. The owners quickly reacted to the 1931 dip in attendance by cutting costs. At their 1931 December meeting in Chicago, the magnates passed a joint resolution to reduce players' salaries. Later they reduced rosters from twenty-five to twenty-three, laying-off thirty-two players. Even umpires were cut from twelve to ten in each league.[30] But cost cutting did not fully compensate for vanishing fans. By the end of the 1932 season, teams "had collectively lost $1,201,000, for a loss margin of 15 percent."[31]

Given the owners' declining fortunes, some of their actions seamed irrational. MLB had reached its record attendance in 1930, the year of the live baseball. Fans seemed to like more offense, but owners moved to change the ball, giving pitchers a better grip, and the National League voted to deaden the ball, and perhaps some fan interest, for the 1931 season. Fans polled by *Baseball Magazine* had voted 957 to 451 to leave the 1930 "jackrabbit" ball unchanged.[32] But still stranger was the entrenched resistance to night baseball. Day baseball games during the workweek reduced the number of potential days that most workers could come to games from seven to two, making many weekday games baseball's own version of radio's sustaining time. An obvious way to boost attendance would be to make the product available to as many interested customers as possible. Sunday baseball had helped grow attendance, and so could weeknight games. The Minor Leagues were proving that baseball could be played successfully under the lights and bring new customers through the gates.[33] Night baseball would also make the sport much more attractive to radio sponsors, who knew that the largest radio audiences were reserved for evening hours. But throughout MLB's own great depression of the early 1930s, it stuck to daylight ball, waiting until 1935 for its first major night game, hosted by the Cincinnati Reds, under the leadership of GM Larry MacPhail. Despite an average night-game attendance for Reds games that was three and a half times greater than the average daytime figures in 1935, it was three more years before a second MLB team, the Brooklyn Dodgers, now led by MacPhail, played some games under the lights.[34]

Another force for change in baseball's radio policy came from the real power in radio: advertisers. While the radio industry tepidly accepted advertisers' support starting in the early 1920s, by 1930 advertisers were calling the shots. Major network programs were produced by advertising agencies, with commercial content woven into the entertainment. The Great Depression did not affect radio ad growth as much as it did other advertising forms. Radio prospered during the 1930s, driven by its growing penetration in American homes. With major networks limited to four (NBC Red, NBC Blue, CBS, and Mutual) and the number of stations stagnant, advertisers needed to expand the commercial part of the radio schedule into daytime hours. Baseball represented cheap and appealing programming to help fill the daytime hours. No actors needed to be hired, and no studio needed to be booked. A single announcer, some equipment, and a ball game would suffice. One sponsor, General Mills, had a passion for the game, seeing it as an exquisite vehicle for peddling high-profit breakfast cereals to young people. Wheaties, "the breakfast of champions," needed daytime programming to sell the product to the American boy. In the 1930s, General Mills became a leading radio sponsor of both Major and Minor League baseball games (see chapter 6).[35]

As attendance declined, many owners continued to press for a broadcast ban, but opinions outside the baseball cartel were changing. Whenever consulted, the public had always supported broadcasts of games. For example, a 1936 survey of Kansas City radio listeners found that 81 percent listened to play-by-play broadcasts of baseball games, 87 percent believed that the broadcasts increased attendance, and 39 percent indicated that baseball was the broadcast they listened to most frequently.[36] The *Sporting News*, clearly antiradio in the 1920s, now believed that broadcast policy should be locally determined, arguing that "there can be no doubt that the advantages of the radio as a promotional medium should not be overlooked, and these benefits should be stressed, so that magnate, official and player alike will understand that it is part of their job to make use of radio opportunities."[37]

As attendance began a steady ascent in 1934, radio was increasingly seen as a promotional friend for baseball. It also contributed directly to a team's bottom line, as rights fees increased in direct proportion to advertisers' interest. By 1935 nine of sixteen MLB teams were broadcasting home games, while even some radio-resistant clubs allowed broadcasts or re-creations of a few games. When the five-year New York–area ban expired after the 1938 season, every Major League club entered the radio era. Waged in the context of the larger press-radio war, radio had finally won its battle with baseball. However, the terms of the new peace were yet to be written.

5 The World Series Triggers
a National Obsession

While the financial health of Major League Baseball has never been better, one sore spot for the national pastime today has been the declining television ratings for the World Series. At its peak in 1972, the World Series had a 58 share, nearly 60 percent of the television viewing audience.[1] The 2012 Series between the Giants and the Cardinals produced a 12 share, less than 21 percent of its peak audience.[2] This striking drop is often considered an index of the declining interest in baseball. In public-opinion polls, football long ago surpassed baseball as the nation's most popular sport. The game is too slow, the argument goes, and not violent enough for modern fans, especially younger ones; consequently baseball is destined to become a secondary sport in the United States. While that future may await baseball, the declining World Series ratings do not necessarily reflect a declining interest in Major League Baseball.

The erosion of World Series shares has more to do with the changes in video distribution than shifts in fan interest. The monster ratings of the late 1970s were a product of a restrictive television environment dominated by three major commercial networks. Those three networks captured 90 percent of the viewing audience in prime time. The same three networks, plus Fox, now garner 35 percent of the nation's prime-time viewers.[3] Baseball now competes in a crowded sports world packed with NCAA, NFL, NBA, and NHL contests, as well as those from many less popular sports. The drama of the World Series may be as compelling as ever, but its television stage has shrunk significantly.

The World Series became a national obsession in the 1930s because it commanded the nation's largest radio stage. At its height in 1938, four national radio networks (CBS, NBC Red, NBC Blue, MBS) and over half of all stations, including the nation's most powerful, carried baseball's Fall Classic. Fifteen announcers covered some part of the World Series for those four networks.[4] The World Series was so important that Niles Trammell of NBC, the nation's largest *commercial* network, told Judge Landis the World Series "was too big to be commercialized." He continued, "base ball is such a part of American life it should be carried on a non-commercial basis and should be made available to all radio stations regardless of whether they were network stations or not."[5] In the 1930s, the World Series was the only game in town, in everybody's town.

World Series: Judge and Jury

By 1938 Judge Landis had exercised absolute authority over radio coverage of the World Series for fifteen years. In 1923 he overruled the NL owners' resolution, refusing WEAF's request to broadcast the World Series. The commissioner of baseball controlled the Series, and that authority extended to any radio broadcasts. In the matter of the World Series, Landis was a hands-on administrator. Radio networks and their announcers knew who was in charge, as one celebrated voice of the game was to discover. Starting in 1923, Graham McNamee developed a national following for his Series calls. But past success did not ensure future selection. In September 17, 1931, McNamee, the voice synonymous with the World Series, wrote the commissioner asking his "permission to broadcast the World Series over the networks of the National Broadcasting Company." McNamee noted that this would be his ninth Series, making him "very anxious to stretch it to ten before stepping aside for someone else."[6] Landis granted McNamee's World Series wish but only if he served as "color" announcer. Hal Totten and Tom Manning would handle NBC's play-by-play call.

Until Landis's death in 1944, the networks trod lightly in their negotiations with the temperamental commissioner of baseball. World Series arrangements were made only shortly before the Series commenced. McNamee's 1931 letter, indicating that announcer selections were not set, was sent less than two weeks before the start of the 1931 World Series between the Cardinals and Athletics. In 1932 Landis held a meeting with NBC and CBS representatives just eleven days before the Cubs invaded Yankee Stadium for the start of the Fall Classic. By late August 1938, one month before its start, Landis had not even decided if the Series would be sponsored.[7]

The commissioner carefully guarded his prize property. In early 1938, NBC released to its stations a list of "NBC Outstanding Sports Broadcasts" that it anticipated reporting on but not necessarily covering live. The NBC list included the "All Star Baseball Game, July 6, Cincinnati, Ohio," and "World's Series opens, October 7." Landis interpreted this to mean that NBC was promoting play-by-play coverage of both events, months before he made his decision. He wrote the network demanding, "Will you be good enough to tell me who authorized the National Broadcasting Company to put out these publications?"[8] The network quickly responded, "[The release was] merely notification to the stations of what service we will probably give, and at no time do we specify that it will be from the scene of action."[9] Although NBC vice president Niles Trammell thought the network provided "a very good explanation," he instructed his staff that before such future proclamations, NBC should "get the Judge's permission": "This is a rather delicate situation and he is unusually temperamental. . . . Let's tell him in advance and he will usually let us do it."[10] Translation: "do not provoke the Judge."

In general, the networks accepted Landis's conditions, although they grumbled about them in their internal correspondence. After the 1933 Series, NBC and CBS agreed that they must fight back if Landis got too unreasonable. NBC executive P. G. Parker wrote John Royal, NBC's programming manager, that Landis subjected the networks to "further intimation" by suggesting announcers in future years "must be those who were experienced in handling the play-by-play thru the season."[11] Royal responded that the networks would only be pushed so far: "I have already talked to Columbia, and if the Judge gets too dictatorial we both will agree not to take the World's Series."[12] But shunning the World Series would be a public-relations nightmare for the networks. They had more to lose than Major League Baseball. Despite occasional network bluster, the judge held all of the cards.

While the networks backed off from direct threats to Landis, they did try to manipulate the commissioner. NBC's Phillips Carlin, long associated with the Series, wanted to promote the network's upcoming coverage of the 1932 World Series with a half-hour special after the regular season concluded. He wanted the managers and captains from the NL and AL teams, as well as Babe Ruth and Landis, to appear. He told Parker, "Please approach Judge Landis, making him feel that [the program] is his own idea." NBC's World Series special "may tickle him, particularly if he thinks he is arranging the program."[13]

Landis met each year with network representatives and announcers to review the "Landis rules" of World Series coverage. In the earlier years, the commissioner saw broadcasts of the World Series as a public service; they were to be unsponsored. Radio was to report the games; interviewers were not to pester players or managers. Though carried by the national networks, the games also would be available to all stations. The commissioner chose the announcers. A 1932 NBC memo reviews the judge's conditions. In addition to specifying the play-by-play announcers and analysts, Landis gave NBC and CBS five mandates:

"1 - There will be no commercial sponsorship of the Series or any individual game.

2 - Any broadcasting station not regularly connected or associated with either National or Columbia may secure the broadcast if they so desire and are willing to pay the necessary line costs to connect their station to either one of the two networks at the nearest point.

3 - Local stations who have regularly broadcast baseball games during the season, that is, in New York and Chicago, will be permitted in the case of Chicago stations to do the local games and in the case of the New York stations to do the games played in New York.

4 - Special pickup of players of either team from the clubhouse or field may only be made following the conclusion of the Series and the final game.

5 - No player, manager, ex-player or ex-manager of either league will be permitted to serve as an announcer during the Series."[14]

While the judge changed his mind about sponsorship, and later exclusivity, he maintained control over the announcers and their coverage throughout his tenure. The networks would submit names, but the judge confirmed or denied the request.

The announcer Red Barber was clearly impressed by the judge's instructions in preparation for his first World Series broadcasts in 1935. After congratulating the assembled announcers for being "the best in your business," Landis proceeded to remind them that the players, managers, and especially, umpires were also "the best in their business." He also noted, "One announcer, you gentlemen know him, . . . isn't here, . . . and I don't have to go into that." Barber knew the reference was to Ted Husing, who, despite support from CBS, was off the Series because he second-guessed umpire decisions during the 1934 contests. Then Landis told the announcers that it was their job to report what happens on the field, not comment on why it happens. "Gentlemen, you report. Report everything you can see. Report what the ballplayers do, but don't feel sorry for them or rejoice for them. Report what they do. That's all the listeners [especially listener Landis] want to hear." Then Landis offered a dramatic personal example of what he meant by "report." "Suppose a ballplayer . . . walks over to where I'm sitting in a rail box, he leans in to me, and he spits right in my face. Report each step the player makes. . . . Report but don't feel disturbed about the Commissioner. That will be my affair after I have been spit upon. Your job is to simply to report the event."[15] Barber took the judge's command to "simply report the event" as his personal announcer's mantra. In the coming decades, he became the dean of the "journalism-first" school of baseball announcing.

The Ty Tyson Affair: Landis Offers a Compromise

Networks clearly catered to the commissioner. In June 1938, NBC even secured Mrs. Landis tickets to the network's *Rudy Vallée Show*. Niles Trammell telegraphed John Royal, "Landis is a very important factor in our lives so far as World Series broadcasts are concerned and I think it is very necessary that Mrs. Landis come away from the studios with very favorable impression."[16]

While the networks might be contrite, Landis could be influenced by public outcry. Major League Baseball appointed Landis its first commissioner to restore its integrity after the Black Sox World Series scandal. Thus, he took every aspect of the game's integrity very seriously, including its World Series radio coverage. He insisted on objective, unbiased reports of the games. As noted earlier, at first Landis would not allow ex-players or managers to call the games because they might favor their old teammates or league. In 1935 he finally allowed a former player, Indians announcer Jack Graney, to call the Series for CBS because enough time had passed since his playing days. Landis told Graney, "By now you've forgotten you ever played baseball."[17] The judge always believed his announcer choices were in the best interests of the game and protected the integrity of the Series broadcasts.

For the first years of the Series broadcasts, the networks used their own staff announcers for the Series: primarily Graham McNamee at NBC and Ted Husing at CBS. But as regular-season announcers became hometown celebrities in the late 1920s and early 1930s, the fans of pennant-winning teams wanted to hear those familiar voices describe their teams' fortunes in baseball's biggest games. In Detroit, the hometown celebrity announcer was Ty Tyson. On August 28, 1934, D. U. Bathrick of J. Stirling Getchel, the ad agency that represented Tyson's sponsor on WWJ, wrote Royal, "We cannot ignore the wishes of over 100,000 radio listeners, who have been hearing Ty broadcast all summer" and who had signed a petition supporting his inclusion on the NBC crew.[18] Three days later,

NBC president Merle H. Aylesworth was told the petition now had two hundred thousand signatures from nine states and parts of Canada. The final tally was expected to reach three hundred to five hundred thousand.[19] But the petition backers were preaching to the saved. Royal wrote Parker, head of NBC's Chicago office, that he wanted "to use Ty Tyson to please all the Detroit listeners." But he cautioned not to "take up this matter with the Judge as yet."[20] However, Landis had already made up his mind about Tyson.

The commissioner was peeved that Tyson told Detroit newspapers that he expected the Tigers to win the upcoming Series over the St. Louis Cardinals. From this, Landis concluded that "Tyson was biased or prejudiced in favor of Detroit," and "there was doubt as to his ability to give an impartial description of the Series."[21] The judge also believed the *Detroit News* was behind the pro-Tyson petition because the paper had covered the story in its pages. Tyson was also a valuable employee.

When the commissioner rejected NBC's request to put Tyson on the series, the *Detroit News*, WWJ's owner and Tyson's employer, was shocked at the decision. Director of Sales Jefferson Webb wrote Royal, "The newspaper and the station kept entirely out of it [the petition]." Further, Tyson's attachment to an AL team did not mean he would be biased. Judge Landis "might as well not have American League umpires if he feels this to be any reason to object."[22] Ordinary Detroit workers also wrote Royal in support of Tyson. "We have followed baseball for many years—we know a bunt from a goal-post and wish our announcer to know at least as much as we do. . . . We solemnly maintain that if Ty doesn't do the play-by-play descriptions that we will listen to Ted Husing over CBS."[23]

Ultimately, the pressure from the public and NBC pushed Landis to reconsider and allow Tyson to serve his fans. Landis would not let Tyson call the Series on NBC, but he could call the game for WWJ. There would be no chance for any Tyson prejudice to reach a national audience. Although Tyson's call would be strictly local, his loyal listeners would be placated. Tom Manning and Ford Bond would do play-by-play on NBC, with Graham McNamee handling the pregame. On CBS, France Laux and Pat Flanagan would call the games and Ted Husing the preliminaries.[24] While the inclusion of Tyson, the Tigers announcer, triggered a tempest of public outcry, the addition of Laux, who called Cardinal games for KMOX, to the CBS crew produced no concerns about impartiality from Landis. Tyson made the mistake of offering his opinion about the Series outcome in the press. Laux had not, or if he had, the commissioner had not seen it.

Commercializing the World Series

The Tyson affair was a minor concern compared to Landis's biggest 1934 Series decision. For the first time, World Series coverage would be sponsored. In this as in most radio matters, Judge Landis worked independently without network input. As late as May 1934, the commissioner in discussions with Parker about possible sponsorship of the All-Star Game and World Series told Parker that if advertisers approach about sponsorship, "he was not favorable and would so inform anyone making inquiry of him," but "these interests might approach individual club owners who for purely selfish reasons might feel differently"; when the matter came before him, however, he would be opposed to it.[25] In July, NBC's Royal was told that Landis was planning on having recordings of the All-Star Game to document any commercial references.[26] Landis appeared committed to maintaining a commercial-free All-Star Game and World Series.

Landis's response reassured NBC. Most of the network's leadership had long maintained that the World Series and other sports events of national significance should not be sponsored but presented as sustaining programs. The NBC files of the early 1930s show repeated documentation of the network's position. As late as September 1934, Royal was insisting that commercial sponsorship of the World Series "is something we should never do."[27] Edgar Kobak, NBC's eastern division manager, clearly articulated the network's position on World Series commercialization to his sales department:

It has been our policy not to broadcast commercially any World Series Games. We have been anxious to broadcast the World Series on a sustaining basis as we believe that major events of this nature should be broadcast as a service to our listening audience and should be secured by us as part of the program service that we render to different stations. Major events in the field of sports as well as any other fields represent one important phase of our own duty and responsibility to our listening audiences. The minute we begin to commercialize this type of service we will soon have difficulties on our hands from various groups that are not friendly to broadcasting.[28]

Commercialization of major sports and news events would violate the network's public-service standards and provoke the critics of commercial radio at time when the advertising-supported model of broadcasting was taking firm root in American culture. In addition, it was sponsors and Major League Baseball, not NBC, that had the most to gain from a commercialized Series. The rights would give baseball a big payday. The vast audience would give the Series' sponsor tremendous exposure. NBC would receive only its time charges.

As the 1934 season wore on, rumors of change in World Series policy stirred advertisers' interest. In May, a representative of Benton & Bowles advertising agency, on behalf of an unnamed client, wanted to be contacted if the Series became available.[29] D. U. Bathrick of J. Sterling Getchell, Socony-Vacuum Oil's agency, wrote Royal that if the commissioner changed his mind, Bathrick wanted the first option for his ad agency.[30] Lord & Thomas agency also inquired on behalf of its client Lucky Strike. The agency hinted that the cigarette maker might pay $100,000 for rights to the games.[31] All together, NBC was approached by "five very prominent manufacturers" willing to sponsor the Series, if NBC could obtain rights.[32] Increasingly, the network was concerned that advertisers might "lose faith in any explanations [it] might give them" if Landis switched directions.[33]

Landis was indeed switching directions. After four years of economic depression, the potential for a big payday was difficult to resist. By mid-September 1934, the networks were aware that Landis had cut a $100,000 deal with the Ford Motor Company for the rights to sponsor the World Series. The players received $42,000 and the clubs the rest. CBS quickly agreed to carry the Series as sponsored programming. NBC asked to carry it as sustaining but were refused. Kobak articulated the network's awkward situation. NBC was "placed in a peculiar spot": "If we refused to take the Series commercially we could not have it on a sustaining basis. It was felt by the executives of the company . . . that while our principle of sustaining service was right, we could not afford to take a chance and refuse to take it commercially and thereby deprive our stations and listeners of this series."[34]

NBC was disappointed that Landis had not opened the bidding for the rights to the Series, allowing the networks and potential sponsors to participate. Royal wrote, "I still believe that the Judge should have told us that the pressure on him was too great, and they had finally decided to broadcast it with a sponsor."[35] Although Landis probably got less for the rights than he could have from competitive offers, he cut his own deal with Ford.

Judge Landis's decision in September 1934 to commercialize the World Series is a milestone in the history of sports media in the United States. Prior to the judge's decision, the World Series had been too important to the nation to commercialize. Even the commercial radio networks saw the World Series as an event of national prominence that should not be stained by commerce. But at a time when teams typically received a few thousand dollars or nothing at all for the broadcast rights to their home games, the judge hauled in $100,000 for the rights to four to seven October contests. His contract with Ford made the World Series too important to be unsponsored. There would be no turning back. The era of sports as public-service programming faded to silence.

Landis's decision to commercialize the World Series forced the networks to reconsider their policy of offering major national sports events as sustaining programming. If commercialism was forced on them, how could they best manage the new reality? Should the networks simply allow sponsors to buy the radio rights from owners and pay the webs for their time charges? Or should the networks buy the rights and negotiate the best deal with the sponsors, as John Shepherd III of the Yankee Network had done with Red Sox and Braves radio rights?

NBC's initial position was to secure rights to major sports events. CBS had decided to accept sports on a commercial basis. For NBC to protect its standing with affiliates and advertisers, it had to alter its position and begin to secure rights. The network identified four major events to pursue: heavyweight championship fights, the Kentucky Derby, the Rose Bowl, and first and foremost, the World Series. The first foray was for the network to try and obtain exclusive rights to the 1935 Series from Commissioner Landis for the same $100,000 rights fee paid by Ford. NBC executives worried about the high costs of these marquee events but maintained, "It is virtually essential that we have them," or "we would find the Columbia Broadcasting System broadcasting certain of these sporting events on an exclusive basis."[36] The next April, they made inquiries with Ford's ad agency, N. W. Ayer & Son, to see if Ford planned to pick up its option on the 1936 Series.[37] NBC also sought to control the situation by working with, rather than against, CBS.

CBS president William Paley and NBC president Merle H. Aylesworth agreed to force any sponsor buying World Series rights to buy all three national networks: CBS, NBC Red, and NBC Blue. Paley thought neither company could afford to buy exclusive rights to the Series. He also believed Commissioner Landis wanted the games carried on all networks. The "gentleman's agreement" forbid either company from buying exclusive rights to the Series.[38] The agreement also demonstrates collusion between the networks. By colluding, CBS and NBC forced a sponsor to pay the network charges of both companies, if the advertiser wanted national exposure for the World Series. If no sponsor were willing to buy all three networks, NBC and CBS would still broadcast the series as sustaining programming. But neither network would "pay one cent for the World Series on a sustaining basis."[39]

Royal was troubled by the agreement. "I don't think the agreement is worth the paper it's written on, if it ever was written. In the first place, I think it illegal and if either NBC or Columbia tried to enforce it, it would be very embarrassing."[40] By October 1935, NBC and CBS had mutually agreed to allow each other to purchase rights to sporting events "for sustaining purposes." CBS was already competing with NBC for rights to sponsored heavyweight title fights. CBS's charge into sports fired up Royal. "They have thrown down the gauntlet and I think we should give them a darned good licking. My suggestion is that we go out and buy all the important events now. Most of them we can sell. We might have to take a loss on one or two, but in the long run we will keep NBC out in front where it belongs."[41] Clearly, networks' efforts to collaborate on the negotiation of sports broadcast rights were doomed. The gentlemen had agreed to disagree.

In retrospect, networks' attempts to avoid competition for exclusive rights to the World Series were consistent with their views at the time of how the radio industry should work. Sponsors through their advertising agencies created programming that the networks aired for a fee. Networks would produce news and special events as part of their public-service commitment, but sponsors packaged entertainment programs. Networks might refuse to sell a particular time period or refuse a particular program, but in general, they were pleased to sell time at their regular rates to any legitimate advertiser. Only after congressional hearings, provoked by the rigging of advertiser-produced television quiz shows in the mid-1950s, did networks become the major procurers of their own entertainment programming.

Redundant Coverage

Ford sponsored the World Series for a second time in 1935, although the contract was not finalized until mid-September. The rights fee was once again $100,000. Both CBS (ninety-six stations) and NBC Red (seventy-nine stations) broadcast the games commercially.[42] Ford also agreed to use the recently formed Mutual Broadcasting System, including major stations in Detroit (WXYZ), New York (WOR), Chicago (WGN), and Cincinnati (WLW). However, the fees for so many networks were becoming too much for the company to stomach. In 1934 Ford's ad agency, N. W. Ayers & Son, at first refused to pay NBC for announcer costs. Later, the parties settled the dispute by each paying half the costs.[43] In 1935 Ford refused to buy NBC Blue, as it had the previous year, forcing NBC to carry the Series as sustaining on its junior network. Out of pocket, NBC paid the Blue stations their regular commercial rate. The network felt betrayed by CBS, which they thought had agreed to force any sponsor to buy all CBS and NBC networks for the World Series. According to NBC, CBS "conveniently interpreted [the] agreement only to include the Red network."[44] The four national chains gave the World Series its greatest national exposure, and the arrangement remained the same in 1936.

The $100,000 rights fee was only the start of Ford's costs. Each commercial network required additional time charges. In 1937 Ford picked up its Series option with Commissioner Landis, paying baseball another $100,000. But facing an additional $175,000 in network time and line charges, the automaker decided to punt. The Series, an all-Gotham rematch between the Yankees and the Giants, did produce the smallest audience of any previous Series. Landis gave Ford permission to resell the rights, but no takers were forthcoming.[45] The networks (CBS, NBC Red, NBC Blue, MBS) decided to carry the Series sustaining.[46]

Ford's exit left the commissioner scrambling for new buyer. The commissioner approached Coca-Cola, but the company declined. Although its advertising manager supported sponsorship, the company was committed to spreading its advertising dollars broadly, rather than on an event with a four- to seven-day focus. In late August 1938, Landis offered the rights on an exclusive basis to NBC's Trammell. While NBC had pursued other sports exclusives, the World Series was different. Trammell, making it clear to Landis that he was offering "his personal and unofficial opinion," told the judge that denying the Series to other networks would be a mistake. If NBC took exclusive rights, over two hundred stations affiliated with CBS and Mutual would be "deprived of carrying the largest feature broadcasting has to offer." Since newspapers owned many of the jilted stations, Trammell told Landis, "the trouble an exclusive arrangement would develop was something I would not care to face." Landis worried that players would lose about $800 each if no sponsorship was forthcoming, and "he would not be able to explain to them his reasons for not selling it."[47] Landis then asked if NBC might take the games exclusively, if he found a sponsor willing to pay $100,000 for the rights and another $150,000 to NBC for facilities. Eschewing the other networks would save the sponsor about $150,000 in World Series costs. Trammell suggested that Landis might approach the three network owners—CBS, NBC, Mutual—with a plan to purchase the long-term rights to the World Series, so that it could be broadcast by all three on a sustaining basis. But the fee would have to be substantially under the $100,000 the commissioner was accustomed to receiving from Ford. Ultimately, the commissioner could find no new sponsor at his $100,000 price, and the 1938 World Series was broadcast sustaining.

A Mutually Exclusive World Series

The loss of $100,000 for World Series rights in 1938 pushed Commissioner Landis to seek a new exclusive arrangement. With two networks and the largest number of affiliates, NBC was clearly the best choice among the commercial networks to maximize exposure. But NBC was also committed to broadcasting the World Series sustaining and had turned down the judge in 1938. As is often the case in an oligopolistic industry such as network radio in the late 1930s, the newest and weakest member is the one most willing to innovate. Industry leaders can stand on their principles and profits, but newcomers must seize and exploit fresh financial opportunities. Network radio's novitiate in 1939 was the Mutual Broadcasting System (MBS). Now, MBS had a new partner in baseball and the World Series a new sponsor, the Gillette Safety Razor Company.

On August 17, 1939, Gillette president J. P. Spang Jr. and MBS general manager Fred Weber signed an agreement paying baseball $100,000 for rights to the 1939 Series broadcasts and giving MBS and Gillette an option for the 1940 contests. *Broadcasting* estimated that Gillette would pay $225,000 in rights and network charges. The new deal allowed baseball to recapture its $100,000 rights fee while lowering the sponsor's costs by requiring payment to only one network. For the sponsor, redundant exposure on several networks was simply not worth the additional network fees. While Landis approved the deal, it was orchestrated by Frank Schreiber, the director of public relations for WGN in Chicago.[48]

The contract was the most significant in Mutual's brief history, and MBS broadcast the signing coast-to-coast. The baseball announcer Bob Elson hosted the broadcast, which featured Landis, although he did not speak; Leslie O'Connor, Major League Baseball's executive secretary; the American and National League presidents, Will Harridge and Ford Frick; and Gillette's president, J. P. Spang.

Fortunately, WOR in New York made a transcription recording of the historic signing because it could not air the MBS broadcast live. The recording documents why Gillette was willing to pay so much for the World Series. When Elson asked Spang why Gillette wanted the Series, he asserted its primacy in the hierarchy of sporting events: "We are sponsoring the World Series because it is the nation's greatest sports attraction. There is no event in all sportsdom that equals the kick of the World Series and no other sport commands the sustained interest that baseball holds." The sponsor also promised to "not burden the broadcasts with commercials. Listeners will not miss a single thrill of any game. The play-by-play reporting of the Series will be the big show."[49] Spang's praise for the Series was more than puffery. Gillette sponsored the World Series exclusively for nearly three decades. For a generation, Gillette was linked in the public mind with baseball's Fall Classic.

MBS's exclusive deal angered CBS and NBC, which had carried the World Series every year since 1927. The two networks still wanted the Series. On behalf of both networks, NBC's Trammell contacted Spang to see if Gillette would allow the two networks to cover the Series free of charge if they also provided "free courtesy announcements" for the company during the Series. Spang refused, citing the exclusive contract with MBS. Trammell also contacted Landis to see if the networks could continue their annual tradition, but Landis also refused. Echoing the commissioner's earlier position, Trammell argued that the World Series was "an outstanding sporting event with a national following" that should receive the widest possible exposure. But networks had already established precedents for exclusive coverage of major sports events. Landis reportedly believed that the Series was "of no greater interest than the Kentucky Derby, Rose Bowl game, and numerous boxing events that have been carried exclusively."[50] Clearly, the World Series was important but not so important that it had to be shared with all interested networks.

Rebuffed by the commissioner and Gillette, the networks made it clear to their affiliates that they did not want them to preempt network programs to carry MBS's coverage of the World Series. On August 22, 1939, NBC executive William Hedges telegrammed the company's affiliates:

> IT APPEARS NBC'S PRESENT PLAN WILL NOT PERMIT BROAD-
> CASTING OF THE WORLD SERIES GAMES THIS SEASON. OUR
> COMMERCIAL PROGRAMS WILL BE BROADCAST AT THE SAME
> TIME AS THE GAMES AND THOSE COMMERCIAL PROGRAMS
> ARE OF GREAT IMPORTANCE TO BOTH YOU AND US. I AM
> SURE OUR SPONSORS EXPECT ONE HUNDRED PERCENT CO-
> OPERATION FROM ALL OF US IN CARRYING THEIR PROGRAMS
> WITHOUT INTERRUPTION. I AM CONVINCED WE CAN ASSURE
> OUR SPONSORS THAT ALL OF OUR AFFILIATED STATIONS
> WILL LIVE UP TO THEIR COMMITMENTS AND ABIDE BY
> THEIR CONTRACTS WITH US. WE ASSUME YOU ARE IN COM-
> PLETE ACCORD WITH THESE VIEWS.[51]

On October 4, NBC sent a follow-up message from Hedges, reiterating, "OUR COMMERCIAL CLIENTS EXPECT THEIR PROGRAMS TO BE BROADCAST AS USUAL.[52] MBS reported to the Federal Communications Commission (FCC) that the other networks were pressuring affiliates to refuse its World Series coverage. Despite the network pressure, Mutual told *Broadcasting* that thirty-eight NBC Red or Blue affiliates and eight CBS affiliates were planning to air the World Series as of late September 1939. Ultimately, 238 stations carried coverage of the Yankees' four-game sweep of the Reds.[53]

NBC and CBS were pressuring affiliates at a very bad time. The FCC had been investigating network control over affiliate programing for six months. Although the FCC hearings on the matter had closed, MBS had charged that NBC's and CBS's long-term affiliate contracts "had stifled its development."[54] MBS's FCC inquiry about network interference with its offering World Series to all stations produced a response in early November. The FCC's Network-Monopoly Committee surveyed all U.S. stations regarding their participation in the Series. Among the information the FCC wanted to know was if the station broadcast the games, if the games were offered but the station refused, if the station had agreements that would not let it broadcast the Series, and "whether any attempt was made by any person or organization to influence or persuade [the station] against broadcasting the programs."[55] Responding to the FCC's inquiry, NBC provided transcripts of the telegrams sent to affiliates on August 22 and October 4, 1939, reminding them of their obligation to carry the network's sponsored programs during the Series.

The data collected by the FCC added to its collection of evidence showing that NBC and CBS exerted considerable control over affiliate programing and advertising rates. Although the Communications Act of 1934 clearly placed the responsibility and accountability for programming in the hands of licensed broadcast stations, networks, which were not licensed by the FCC, were actually controlling their stations' air time through long-term, exclusive network-affiliate contracts.

The FCC's 1941 Chain Broadcasting Rules (upheld by the Supreme Court in 1943) dramatically altered the conditions of network-affiliated conduct. Network contracts could no longer require exclusivity; affiliates could take programs, such as the World Series, produced by other networks. Stations were required to maintain control of their programming and were granted the right to preempt a network program anytime the station believed it did not serve the public interest, convenience, or necessity. Networks could not interfere with stations' advertising rates, except for network programs. Perhaps most significantly, the FCC forbid stations from affiliating with any company owning more than one broadcast network, effectively forcing NBC to sell one of its networks. In 1945 NBC Blue became ABC. While the flack over baseball's first network-exclusive World Series in 1939 was not the only rationale for the Chain

Broadcasting Rules, it certainly gave the FCC a high-profile example of how network dominance over affiliates could sabotage the public interest.

World Series Radio in the Television Age

The pattern established by Landis, a commissioner-negotiated deal with an individual sponsor for the World Series, became the norm for the radio and eventually the television age. From 1934 through 1966, the World Series, when sponsored, featured one advertiser, Ford from 1934 to 1936 and Gillette from 1939 to 1966. Three different commissioners— Landis, Albert B. "Happy" Chandler, and Ford Frick—negotiated a series of World Series (and All-Star Game) contracts, often without competitive bidding. In 1966 MLB negotiated the first World Series contract for television and radio directly with a network, NBC. For the 1967 and 1968 World Series and All-Star Game, the network owned the rights and sold time to multiple advertisers, effectively canceling the single-sponsor model.

The stable relationship that evolved among MLB, Gillette, and Mutual was reflected in the rights fees for the World Series. From 1939 to 1945, Gillette paid the same $100,000 for radio rights for the Series that Ford had paid in 1934. The low-inflation, even deflationary, economy of the Great Depression likely is one reason for the stagnant fees. The commissioner's failure to find any taker in 1938 probably made him shy about demanding more for World Series rights. When Happy Chandler negotiated his first rights contract for the 1946 World Series, the fees finally jumped to $150,000, a 50 percent increase.[56] But Chandler's fee structure also stagnated.

Throughout the early 1950s, World Series radio-rights fees remained relatively stable. From 1951 to 1956, Gillette paid the following: 1951, $150,000; 1952, $200,000; 1953, $175,000; 1954, $150,000; 1955, $150,000; and 1956, $125,000. But now the radio fees stagnated because of the emergence of a new medium, television. Even in the early 1950s, TV was bringing in $925,000 in World Series rights each year. Radio rights had become an afterthought and not subject to much change.[57] For the next two decades, Series radio rights were sold along with the TV rights and became an even smaller piece of the World Series rights pie. Only when CBS Radio purchased separate radio rights in 1976 did the radio version of the World Series start to become financially relevant again (see chapter 10).

The 1930s and 1940s were the golden age of the World Series on the radio. Exposure on multiple networks throughout the 1930s gave the Fall Classic its greatest national exposure and helped it maintain its position as the nation's most important sports event. Even with the granting of exclusive network coverage to MBS in 1939, the World Series continued to be preeminent. Mutual's policy of allowing nonaffiliated stations to carry the Series gave it wide, national exposure. In the broadcast-television era, with commercial television competition restricted to three networks, the World Series still commanded a vast national stage. But as the NFL became the most successful sport of the television era, the World Series took a second seat to the Super Bowl in annual lists of the top-rated sports telecasts. However, the World Series was still the highest rated championship *series* among all sports. This picture changed rapidly as cable and satellite distribution of a plethora of new channels fragmented the television audience. The era when nearly 60 percent of the television audience watched the World Series faded into history, as had radio's dominance of World Series coverage four decades earlier.

6   Advertisers Expand Baseball Coverage

Three organizational players created baseball on the radio: the team owners, the radio industry, and advertisers. That trio has remained in place throughout the history of the broadcast game but has not always demonstrated a "balance of powers." Beginning in the late 1920s and throughout the next decade, the power of advertisers to dictate conditions of radio's coverage of baseball grew precipitously. Pressure from advertisers helped to convince reluctant clubs, even the powerful New York teams, that the live game should be shared with the public beyond the ballpark walls. Advertisers also pushed major network stations out of regular-season baseball coverage, as they demanded station clearance for their sponsored daytime network programs. The influence of major radio advertisers, particularly General Mills and Socony-Vacuum Oil Company (now Mobil), made baseball a staple for independent (non-network) stations in both Major and Minor League cities. As baseball moved from a daytime game in the 1920s and 1930s to a nighttime entertainment option in the 1940s and 1950s, the advertisers changed but not their influence. Cereal makers selling to children and housewives made way for beer and cigarettes makers selling directly to men with children, the next generation of smokers and drinkers, in the on-deck circle.

At the dawn of radio in the United States, advertising was only one of the options for bankrolling the new medium. Many radio stations were founded as a public service by department stores or newspapers.

Stations offered the side benefit of promoting their owners' interests. Universities and philanthropists launched other stations as educational outlets. Radio-equipment manufacturers, including Westinghouse, RCA, and General Electronic, supported stations to create a market for their radio receivers and tubes when the military's demand for radio equipment dropped after the First World War. It was a telephone company that first sold radio time.

AT&T developed the New York–based station WEAF to offer "toll broadcasting," a toll (additional charge) call directed to the general public rather than to a particular individual phone. According to AT&T's February 11, 1922, announcement, the station would offer "no program of its own, but provide the channels through which anyone with whom it makes a contract can send out their own programs."[1] Businesses could "call" anyone listening on a wireless receiver within the range of WEAF. On August 28, 1922, for a fee of fifty dollars, the Queensboro Corporation presented a ten-minute message selling apartments in its complex in Jackson Heights, Long Island.[2] The radio commercial was born.

The initial reactions to AT&T's first attempt to bind radio to advertising were harshly critical. The trade publication *Radio Dealer* attacked AT&T's plan for WEAF, accusing it of pursuing "mercenary advertising purposes." Even the probusiness, and future Republican president, Herbert Hoover thought that it was "inconceivable that we should allow so great a possibility for service . . . to be drowned in advertising chatter."[3] AT&T, for its part, was more interested in linking stations and producing equipment than entering the new business of selling advertising. Also, after discovering that few people would listen exclusively to commercial messages, AT&T was forced to provide information and entertainment to attract listeners to its station. Indeed, the yoking of radio and advertising was a gradual process. As the historian Susan Smulyan carefully documents in her book *Selling Radio*, "nothing about the process [of commercializing radio] was inevitable, and every step involved conflict."[4]

At first, most radio programming was unsponsored. This unsponsored programming, also called sustaining time, gradually disappeared from broadcast media. In the 1920s and 1930s, networks saw major national sporting events, and especially the World Series, as public-service programming that should not be commercialized but broadcast on a sustaining basis. Major increases in commercialization of radio occurred during World War II. Paper shortages limited print advertising, but radio could expand its commercial time. In addition, the taxing of excess profits made the expense of radio advertising more palatable. Previously unsponsored time became sponsored. Commercial sponsorship of virtually all radio and, later, television programming become a cultural norm. In the 1980s, a similar transformation occurred in television, when consumers gradually began to accept paying a monthly fee for cable or satellite television embedded with commercial programming as the new natural order for a previously "free" (advertiser-subsidized) medium.

For baseball, Word Series broadcasts were the most forcefully protected from the stain of overcommercialization. The combination of a monolithic commissioner, radio-wary owners, a Major League–level monopoly, and an American culture increasingly suspicious of advertising kept the crown jewel of all sports broadcasts unsponsored until 1934. The World Series was simply too important an event to be presented as anything other than an unsponsored public service by NBC and CBS. Indeed, for years the radio networks were adamant in this view. For reasons examined in the previous chapter, NBC believed firmly that the World Series was a public trust and that its broadcast should be unsponsored. When sponsorship finally came to the Series, it was the Ford Motor Company and its ad agency, N. W. Ayer & Son, that made a deal directly with Commissioner Landis. The financial problems faced by baseball in 1934, reflected in a decline in attendance from slightly over ten million in 1930 to just over six million in 1933, certainly forced the commissioner to consider commercialization. But it is also clear from Smulyan's overview of the commercialization of radio that by the mid-1930s networks, stations, and advertisers had overcome the backlash to commercialization and had managed to suppress most noncommercial alternatives. The Communications Act of 1934 legislatively normalized commercial support for the industry.[5]

The development of national and regional radio networks established advertising as the basis of financial support for radio. Newspapers, universities, or a committed hobbyist or philanthropist could support individual stations as a public service or a promotional tool, but networks required significantly more resources. They needed resources to pay for top-quality programming and to pay AT&T's substantial connection charges. In the era before satellites or microwave relays, the most reliable connections came from AT&T's landlines; these were costly wires that had to be strung pole to pole, station to station, across a continent. While attempts were made to use shortwave radio relays and high-powered "superstations" to support a national radio presence without landlines, neither option was as technologically viable. In the 1920s and 1930s, AT&T's landlines were the best, and most expensive, means of creating networks.

Programming was also becoming more expensive. After the initial novelty of radio wore off, stations needed better programming to attract an audience and to distinguish themselves from the cacophony of competitors. Bedtime stories, piano music, and unpaid local talent might fill a local station's time, but networks needed star attractions. To cover these costs, stations needed steady revenue and advertising. Increasingly, baseball, a sport that had long been a staple for U.S. print media, accommodated the needs of radio as well.

The Network Baseball Problem

Although substantial regional networks operated from the early days of radio, the creation of NBC (National Broadcasting Company) in November 1926 signaled the beginning of national network radio, or what the historian Erik Barnouw labeled the "Golden Web."[6] NBC's first nationally broadcast sports event was the 1927 Rose Bowl, but the network, along with the emerging CBS (Columbia Broadcasting System), broadcast that season's World Series from coast to coast. Since the World Series was limited to a maximum of seven afternoons a year, it created minimal conflict between the networks and their affiliates. However, regular-season games were a very different situation.

When the owners allowed Major League games to be broadcast locally, the games were very popular. Local stations could make a substantial profit on radio broadcasts, even after owners began demanding rights fees for their games and even with competing stations carrying the same game. But the broadcasting of local baseball games by a network affiliate meant that any network programs offered during game time for the six-month season were preempted by the network affiliate. One of the greatest assets of a network is the ability to deliver a national audience to national advertisers, but each affiliate that carries baseball diminishes that potential national audience. Even though baseball was popular, networks began to demand that affiliates and their owned and operated stations drop the seasonal sport, so that they could clear stations for the much more lucrative year-round nationally sponsored programs.

The NBC network's correspondence of the early 1930s includes several rounds of confrontation over baseball broadcasts by affiliates. By 1933 W MAQ, the NBC-owned Red network station in Chicago, had been broadcasting regular-season games for eight years. However, NBC's national sales manager, Roy C. Witmer, complained about the impact of baseball on other sponsored programming, protesting "strongly against the sale of WMAQ Chicago to General Foods for the sponsorship of Chicago Baseball Games on the grounds that WMAQ was thereby lost to certain network commercials who, in consequence, had to take other stations in Chicago,—that procedure of course being diametrically opposed to the underlying reason for acquiring control of any station."[7] However, the broadcasts, which produced $30,000 in revenue, had become an institution in Chicago. Initially, the baseball broadcasts forced only a few changes in the advertising schedule that could be accommodated by moving sponsored programming to a sister NBC station in Chicago. However, the unpredictability of baseball soon exacerbated the conflict.

On April 30, 1930, because of rain delays, a double-header finished just before 8 p.m. central time, causing the cancellation of the *Chase and Sanborn* program on WMAQ. The Standard Brands–sponsored program had been bumped by baseball, sponsored by Standard's chief competitor, General Foods. As Witmer put it, "General Foods put their competitor—Standard Brands—off the air. That was fun!"[8] While the station could have solved the problem by suspending game coverage and switching to the network, listeners would have been outraged. Witmer said, "Troubles coming out of a deal of this kind are endless."[9] But in an earlier letter, NBC president Niles Trammell vigorously defended baseball on WMAQ, implying that, if no sponsor were available, the games would have to be carried as a public service: "To discontinue the broadcasting of baseball by Station WMAQ would mean that we are taking a definitive step in obliterating what is left of this station's local identity and association with local events in Chicago. We have always sold the baseball games on WMAQ, and as long as I have anything to do with it, we are going to continue to sell them. It means $30,000.00 to the Company for a broadcast we would be forced to do if we didn't have a sponsor."[10]

Trammell's March 1933 letter illustrates the difficult position of network stations in markets with established baseball broadcasts. On the upside, baseball created local identity. Advertisers wanted the broadcasts, listeners wanted the broadcasts, some teams—especially the Chicago Cubs—wanted the broadcasts, and many network executives wanted to continue them as a public service. On the downside, the network sales staff, on the frontlines with national advertisers and their agencies, faced the development of further "troubles" that seemed "endless." While $30,000 in station revenue from baseball was impressive, baseball broadcasts risked angering national advertisers, including Standard Brands, that were the financial pillars of network radio.

Within months, Witmer raised the local baseball broadcast conflict again. This time it was in Cleveland, a market that presented an even bigger problem, since the network had no second station in the market to which it could send baseball-bumped shows. According to Witmer, "The moment we sell a program of this kind, which must be broadcast whenever the ball games are scheduled by the American League, it means that network commercials must stand aside which is exactly the reverse of NBC policy. Either that or the time for approximately two hours each afternoon is blocked on the network. . . . I am opposed to this proposal just about 100%."[11] Witmer's position won the day in Cleveland. Indians games shifted to WHK, a CBS station.

In Chicago, the NBC affiliate continued to carry games through the 1934 season but with some changes to accommodate the network sales department. Sunday games were dropped because there were too many conflicts with the network's schedule. In addition, if game coverage spilled into times when Red network commercials were scheduled, the commercials would be aired and then the station would return to the baseball game.[12]

A second issue was the $30,000 fee for baseball coverage, which was substantially less than the $52,560 WMAQ would earn if it charged the standard rate-card fees for sponsored programs (two hours per day, six days a week, for twenty-six weeks).[13] WMAQ's management noted that the $30,000 charge was consistent with the amount charged for the two previous seasons and that it was a bargain, considering the elimination of Sunday games. In addition, WMAQ's Lloyd C. Thomas argued, "There are certain classes of local broadcasting that should be put on the air for the benefit of the station and the audience, no matter whether they are sponsored commercially or not. These include time signals, weather and temperature reports, financial and live stock market reports, and in the case of Chicago particularly, play-by-play baseball reports."[14]

Witmer did not buy into Thomas's public-service argument for baseball: "Frankly, I do not see that the broadcasting of a baseball game could be construed as different from any other program as far as the price of the station is concerned. I have heard much said about it being a public service and the great interest shown by the people of Chicago in listening to these games, but in what respect is that different from any other program?"[15]

NBC executive P. G Parker quickly responded that NBC makes other exceptions to the standard rate card, such as American Tobacco Company's sponsorship of the Metropolitan Opera broadcasts.[16] Ultimately, the elimination of Sunday games was a deal breaker for General Foods, and it decided not to sponsor games on WMAQ in 1934.[17] In 1935 NBC used its two-network advantage. WMAQ's Cubs and Sox broadcasts, called by Hal Totten, shifted to WCFL (the Voice of Labor), a part of the NBC Blue Network that carried much more sustaining (unsponsored) programming.[18]

When the baseball broadcast conflict involved stations owned by the network, such as WMAQ, NBC could force the desired outcome, but affiliated stations were another situation. In late 1935, NBC met with representatives from the *Detroit News* station WWJ, now part of the Red network. WWJ wanted to continue its long-standing Tigers broadcasts. NBC wanted clearance for sponsored afternoon network programs in the nation's sixth-largest market. When NBC tried to enforce its affiliate contract and compel WWJ to quit the Tigers broadcasts, the station threatened to cancel its contract with NBC. NBC executives met and formulated a plan to have the station delay broadcast of NBC-sponsored programs that were bumped by baseball, using electrical transcriptions (recordings).[19] But NBC executive Edgar Kobak was concerned that Proctor & Gamble, the sponsor most affected, would balk at the change. "Detroit is a big market and we do not like to try to sell daytime without being able to deliver Detroit. I do not think it is good programming to put these daytime shows on in the evening."[20]

To break the impasse, Herbert Ponting, general manager of the *Detroit News* and WWJ, and an associate came to New York to meet with the network brass. The group reached an agreement for WWJ to buy back from NBC the 3–6 p.m. time slots for the baseball season, with a potential profit of over $14,000 to the station, even after paying NBC for the time.[21]

A period of frustrating negotiations between WWJ and NBC ensued. In 1936 WWJ paid NBC for the baseball time, but the profit projections for WWJ were overly optimistic and the station lost money on baseball. The 1937 season brought a new round of negotiation. NBC was willing to continue the 1936 arrangement, but WWJ wanted more. Facing the cost of a new million-dollar radio facility, the station needed profits from baseball, not losses. A number of options were considered, including delayed broadcasts and partial cancellations of Proctor & Gamble programs. WWJ even considered offering the Tigers games as sustaining programming, while the sponsored broadcasts were presented on another

Detroit station. Using this strategy, WWJ could claim baseball as public-interest programming, exempting itself from NBC's sponsored-program clearance policy. But the station still wanted to make a profit from baseball and produce profits for other stations. As of March 4, 1937, the network and its key Detroit station had "reached an impasse."[22] Despite the crisis, WWJ continued to carry Tigers games, with Ty Tyson calling the action, through the 1942 season.

Baseball remained a thorn in the network's side. Problems cropped up even in Minor League markets. In May 1938, Witmer was informed that the Blue Network station WMFF in Plattsburg, New York, would be carrying Northern New York–Vermont League games starting in June and dropping network programming. By July, two additional stations were tagged for conflicting baseball broadcasts.[23] Witmer responded that "advertisers are becoming conscious of the fact that if they buy a late afternoon period, it will be interfered with by baseball. Hence, one of the most valuable and lucrative periods of the day is beginning to be frowned upon."[24] An increasingly frustrated Witmer summarized, once again, the network's baseball problem in an August 1938 letter to Albert H. Morton:

> I am heartily in favor of local baseball programs but I am even more in favor of Network commercial programs. We cannot have both. Basically network commercial programs must come first. Obviously, then, the only way that local baseball can be handled is like any other local account—this is, on a removal basis. That, however, also has its bad aspects—worse than the average local commercial. For instance, now that KDKA has been broadcasting baseball games and Pittsburgh listeners have formed the habit, it would be very bad in my opinion to drop the games in favor of network commercial programs, much worse than the average local commercial which can be moved and still heard. You cannot move baseball. Either you have it or drop it entirely.[25]

Regular-season baseball was an intensely local product that created a loyal, vocal audience that wanted all the games to be broadcast live and complete. Transcribing for later broadcast or, worse yet, leaving the action before the game ended was not acceptable. Baseball was a great local-station product, promoting the localism that the FCC favored in the broadcast regulation of the era. But it compromised the network's most important product, its national audience.

A month later, Trammell tried to bring closure to the baseball problem by codifying the Blue Network solution. Trammell argued that Blue Network stations should be allowed to carry baseball with the understanding they would record network commercial shows and broadcast them at a later time period approved by the sponsor. Trammell believed the commercial conflicts would be limited: "During the past two or three years, we have not sold any time on the Blue Network in the afternoon before 6:00 o'clock." Baseball would also give stations an opportunity "to increase their billing materially," and it "is a tremendous audience-builder."[26]

NBC was amassing evidence of just how big an audience-builder baseball was. Pittsburgh station KDKA and San Francisco station KGO found that baseball had "done more to build up the afternoon audience of those two Blue stations and to change the listening habits of their communities towards them than anything the stations ha[d] done in the last five years of their operation." Surveys from Cleveland found that WCLE's afternoon ratings jumped from 9.2 percent to 46.5 percent after baseball was added. In Boston, WAAB had a 9.0 percent morning audience share that leaped to 40.1 percent for the afternoons with baseball broadcasts. According to the Crossley survey for July 1938, baseball had a higher rating than the Rudy Vallée program, a prime-time hit.[27] NBC Washington vice president Frank Russell also wanted baseball in DC, citing evidence from the Yankee Network's John Shepard that baseball had helped push WAAB's entire 2–7 p.m. time period into second place in Boston, even though WAAB was not the network's primary outlet in the market. "I know of no better argument to schedule baseball broadcasts than the one of improving our afternoon audience and certainly it is sufficient to overcome considerable objections to the idea."[28]

Baseball: The Breakfast of Champions

NBC also was facing a big baseball push from General Mills, which wanted network stations in New York, Chicago, Cleveland, Pittsburgh, Boston, and Washington DC to accept baseball for the 1939 season. The New York market had finally come into play after a five-year ban on radio agreed to by the three Gotham franchises. CBS had already created a special two-hour rate for baseball by sewing up CBS stations in Philadelphia and St. Louis for the 1939 season. From an advertising perspective, the baseball battle was between sponsors targeting primarily women with fifteen-minute soap operas and General Mills, targeting youngsters with ads for Wheaties, "the breakfast of champions."

General Mills regarded baseball as a major sponsorship opportunity throughout the 1930s. As a national advertiser, General Mills needed to make the baseball connection beyond the eastern-midwestern range of Major League Baseball, and it found many ways to do so. It sponsored Minor League Baseball as aggressively as big league ball. Just as the Minor Leagues exploited night baseball first, many of them also welcomed sponsored broadcasts of their games and a new revenue flow before their Major League superiors capitalized on the opportunity. General Mills also brought Major League action to Minor League cities, using re-creations of Major League games. For example, in 1933 Iowa stations WOC and WHO began offering General Mills–sponsored re-creations of Cubs and White Sox home games with "Dutch" Reagan—the future president Ronald Reagan—calling the games. The makers of Wheaties claimed more than sixty-five thousand letters of support for the broadcasts.

To alleviate the tension with the local Minor League club over territorial invasion, General Mills worked directly with the local Minor League club, sponsoring "kiddies parties" at the local park, most-popular-player contests, and interviews with Minor League players and managers during Cubs and Sox re-creations.[29] When home games were already under contract by another sponsor, General Mills would sponsor re-creations of road contests. In Cleveland, for the 1935 season, General

Mills sponsored re-creations of the Indians' away games for the first time at the cost of $10,000.[30] Of course, when live broadcasts of Major League home games were available, General Mills bid aggressively for the rights. In 1935 it locked up one of the competing Cubs and Sox broadcasts on WBBM.

By the dawn of the 1936 baseball season, *Broadcasting* acknowledged General Mills as the "biggest buyer of athletic broadcasts, . . . sponsoring baseball in all parts of the nation." In addition to the Chicago teams, the *Broadcasting* summary notes General Mills sponsorship of Boston Red Sox and Braves games on the Yankee Network; Red Sox games on a Charlotte, North Carolina, station that had adopted the team for the season; road-game re-creations of the Birmingham AL Southern League games; contests of the Seattle franchise of the Pacific Coast League; and the aforementioned Indians road-game re-creations on WGAR. Because of NBC network commitments, WGAR would not broadcast Tribe home games but instead made a series of "sidewalk broadcasts outside the ball park."[31]

In 1936 David D. Davis, the president of General Mills, approached both the American and National Leagues with a plan to buy the broadcast rights to as many league clubs as possible for a flat sum of $200,000, to be divided evenly among the clubs. NL president Ford Frick and the league owners were concerned that the American League might take the deal, partly because the same lawyer was representing General Mills, broadcast stations, and the American League in what appeared to be a conflict of interest. Frick was solidly against the idea, telling the owners, "I don't want our league to become a breakfast food league by having 'Wheaties' take over all our broadcasting and having every National league ball game played for General Mills."[32]

But the American League or "junior circuit" was not at all happy with General Mills. While the National League was discussing whether it should work jointly with General Mills, the American League was accusing the company of sponsoring bootlegged broadcasts of Boston and Philadelphia games on WMCA in New York. American League attorney Joseph C. Hostetler arranged for stenographers to transcribe the WMCA broadcasts to show that WMCA was reconstructing the games from General Mills–sponsored broadcasts rather than telegraphic information. His evidence supported the use of the broadcasts because errors in the telegraph dispatches were not reported by WMCA, while the correct calls made by announcers observing the action on the field were. When word leaked to WMCA that the AL was monitoring its broadcasts, it began "deliberately misdescribing [sic] the plays." Hostetler flatly told the American League owners, "General Mills are sponsoring the theft of the game by the New York station" (WMCA).[33] General Mills was using its own sponsored Boston and Philadelphia broadcasts to light up the blacked-out New York market, denied radio access to its home teams' games by the 1934 broadcast band. Ed Barrow of the radio-adverse Yankees saw General Mills as the main problem. "If you can scare off this Wheaties crowd you have probably got everybody else licked."[34] General Mills' aggressive baseball broadcasts pushed forced the owners in both leagues to develop radio policies that would provide a legal basis to defend their ownership of radio rights in court, making "it clear who is the owner of this thing [broadcast rights] we are trying to protect."[35]

With General Mills clearly aware that it must overcome owners' resistance to radio and quell fears about radio's effect on attendance, the company worked to promote attendance at the ballpark. In addition to children's parties at the park and most-popular-player contests, the company created a contest for announcers, aimed at promoting attendance. The station whose team showed the greatest increase in attendance during the 1936 season would win a fifty-six-inch silver cup, and the team's announcer would receive his own smaller trophy. Radio announcers whose teams reached a targeted percentage attendance increase would be awarded Elgin wristwatches. David Davis told *Broadcasting* that the company's sponsored broadcasts were "designed to be of direct benefit to baseball clubs, stations and the company." General Mills also invited suggestions from owners regarding how they could work cooperatively to increase attendance.[36]

Securing Substantiated Facts

Perhaps General Mills' most aggressive move was an attempt to "prove conclusively that baseball broadcasting, properly handled, definitely increases attendance at the parks."[37] The company commissioned the Market Research Corporation to conduct a survey of 12,490 people in the Philadelphia area in June 1936. The survey focused on the impact of the broadcasts initiated that year on Phillies and Athletics attendance. General Mills claimed that Judge Landis requested that it separate *facts* from *opinions* about broadcasting effects on attendance and that "as by far the largest sponsor of baseball broadcasts," the company "undertook through a survey to secure substantiated facts to serve as a basis for determining the value of broadcasting in stimulating increased attendance at baseball games."[38]

Philadelphia was selected because the city had finally started receiving games, its teams' performance were consistent compared to the previous year, its teams had increased attendance during the first ten weeks of 1936, and its broadcasts originated from a "powerful broadcasting station with a thoroughly competent announcer."[39] Respondents were surveyed at gas stations, parking lots, ferries, and street intersections. The results as reported by General Mills seemed to support its contention that broadcasting helped attendance more than it harmed it. Of the respondents who went to more games, over 90 percent were baseball listeners, compared to about 80 percent of those who went to fewer games. Of those attending more frequently, 18.6 percent claimed they were "doing so because of the interest aroused by the broadcasts." Of those attending less, only 4.1 percent "stayed away because they prefer listening to the broadcasts." Market Research Corporation also claimed that its data showed that game broadcasts produced "a net gain of 49 per cent in attendance."[40] Surveys also allegedly indicated that attitudes toward the sport and personal factors were more likely to keep people away from games, while the interest stimulated by radio broadcasts was a significant motivation for attending games.

While the results seemed to support General Mills' contention that "broadcasting increases baseball attendance," the sample was not randomly drawn and, thus, not necessarily representative of Philadelphia baseball fans. Given the topic, it is entirely possible that fans excited about the newly authorized broadcasts coming to Philadelphia, long after most other Major League cities, were more likely to participate in the survey than fans less interested in broadcasts. Broadcast fans might have feared that Philadelphia owners would take the gamecasts away if they suspected that they hurt the gate. Also, the survey was only a snapshot taken just after radio came into the market; any long-term impact of radio is unknown. Given the relatively low percentage of respondents who indicated that radio actually was a factor in their attendance, either positive or negative, at a time when baseball broadcasts were still a novelty, it might be reasonable to conclude that the broadcasts had only a modest effect, positive or negative.

While General Mills found that the results supported its own interest in increasing baseball broadcasts, baseball owners were far more skeptical. Mark Twain once wrote that there are three types of lies: "lies, damned lies, and statistics." Some owners clearly thought that General Mills' survey results constituted the third category of deceit. At a July 1936 American League meeting, Phillies owner John Shibe exploded at the suggestion that Wheaties' (General Mills') broadcasts "saved you in Philadelphia": "They are God damned liars. And I will tell them say so. They are nothing but a lot of God damn lying bastards. Saved us! Christ, they didn't save us. They kept them away from the park. . . . They are God damned liars. I told you that before, right in this room, but it didn't seem to register."[41]

At the time of the General Mills survey, Shibe had only recently become A's president, following his brother Tom's death. The brothers inherited the team from Ben Shibe, the founding owner, in 1922. They were longtime members of the AL's antiradio club, and John Shibe clearly regretted the decision to allow broadcasts for the first time in 1936. His presidency was brief; his death in July 1937 reduced the antiradio faction by one. While the new majority owner, Connie Mack, was seventy-five, hardly a youthful figure, he was nonetheless more accepting of the new radio reality.

Company Men: Training Announcers

The commercialization of baseball broadcasts had professionalized the art of baseball announcing, raising the bar for the voices of the game by generating standards and expectations for their jobs. The 1937 season saw General Mills increase its sponsorship of baseball to eighty stations, "the most extensive baseball sponsorship in the history of radio." The company planned to spend over $1 million on baseball. General Mills' ad agency, Knox-Reeves Advertising, developed a promotional campaign aimed at professionalizing baseball announcing. It started with a conference in Chicago attended by sixty-two baseball announcers. According to *Broadcasting*, the objective was not to standardize broadcasts but "to discuss fully the whole conception of modern baseball broadcasting, exchange ideas and discuss mutual problems so that better broadcasts of the games would result." However, the conference included direct instruction using transcriptions (recordings) to illustrate "both desirable and undesirable ways of announcing games" and newsreels to demonstrate "the incorrect way of broadcasting a ball game." Announcers were also told that the majority of the baseball audience is "a flexible, floating audience that changes from minute to minute and day to day. The habitual day in and day out listeners represent only a small portion of the total audience." To reach this changing audience, "General Mills sells Wheaties constantly at every hour of the game on every broadcast," changing ad copy frequently to save habitual listeners "from monotonous repetition." After the baseball announcers' conference in Chicago, Knox-Reeves followed up by providing three field operatives, assigned to the East, Central, and West/Southwest regions, helping announcers "in every way to make their broadcasts more effective to the baseball club, the station, and the sponsor."[42]

General Mills' leadership in professionalizing baseball announcing filled a void left by the radio-divided baseball owners. While the number of owners openly resisting radio was decreasing, few owners saw the professional training of baseball announcers, now entering their second decade of work, as their responsibility. In 1937 the American League did appoint L. C. McEvoy as its first radio director but did so to remind announcers that their job was to offer play-by-play accounts of game action, not to "criticize umpires, players, managers, or anybody else, or to visit the dugouts or mingle with players on the field."[43]

The professionalization of announcers also standardized their presentation of commercial copy and codified its routine insertion into the play-by-play. Predictably, this new intrusion did not go unnoticed. The increasing commercialization was especially noted in Detroit, where sponsors had for many years limited ads to announcements at the start and end of each game. H. G. Salsinger, the veteran sports editor from the *Detroit News*, ridiculed the increasing "advertising tripe" in the Tigers broadcasts on WWJ, a station owned by the *News*. "The plugs they [General Mills] demand are more frequent, prolonged and bizarre than the plugs of a wagon show barker extolling the virtues of rattlesnake oil." Salsinger wrote a mock "broadcast" of a Tigers game in which the mythical product "Grippo" became the announcer's primary focus, with game action falling by the wayside. The headline to one of Salsinger's journalistic jabs read,

Who Won the Game?
Grippo Always Wins
Tigers Lead—Hurray for Grippo!
Browns Come from Behind—
Hurray for Grippo!

Salsinger reported that sponsors criticized both Ty Tyson of WWJ and Harry Heilmann of WXYZ for not inserting enough commercials during the game. "The Messrs. Tyson and Heilmann believed they were giving the radio audience a pain in the neck as it was and were heartily ashamed of themselves, but not so the sponsors." For Salsinger, the new AL radio director's main job should be "to censor the commercials of the sponsors of baseball broadcasts and see that they are kept within dignified limits, but strangely enough the baseball broadcasts this year have passed all limits. They were never before as bizarre and blatant, and as stupid, as they have been this season."[44]

Salsinger's conception of the director's function was mistaken. The radio director could complain but not censor baseball broadcasts. And with over $1 million invested in baseball broadcasts, General Mills' demands would carry more weight with announcers and their stations than would the American League's radio director. Indeed some announcers worked not for stations but for General Mills. When the legendary Dodgers announcer Red Barber came to Brooklyn in 1939, he was in the employ of the makers of "the breakfast of champions," not the owners of "dem bums."

Oil and More Cereal

While General Mills was the leading promoter of baseball broadcasts, oil companies and General Mills' main cereal rival, Kellogg, were also finding baseball good for business. In 1937 General Mills teamed with Socony-Vacuum Oil Company to cosponsor American League and National League team broadcasts in eight markets: Boston, Philadelphia, Chicago, St. Louis, Detroit, Cleveland, Cincinnati, and Pittsburgh. General Mills also shared sponsorship of all eight American Association teams with Socony-Vacuum.[45] The two companies cosponsored a "Round Robin" in which Major League announcers Ty Tyson and Harry Heilmann of the Tigers, Jack Graney of the Indians, and Harry Hartman of the Reds served as guest announcers on one another's stations.[46]

Atlantic Refining Company sponsored four hundred games, including away- and home-game re-creations of Pittsburgh Pirates contests and the games of four New York–Pennsylvania League teams. Atlantic promised to limit commercials to five minutes per game following the third, fifth, and seven innings and at the end of the contest. Announcers urged fans to "come out and see the home town team." Unlike General Mills' announcers, Atlantic's were "forbidden to tie in the product with spectacular plays on threat of instant dismissal."[47] Another oil company, Sinclair Refining, offered listeners Babe Ruth, baseball's most famous retired player, on a twice-a-week CBS coast-to-coast program.[48]

General Mills' chief cereal rival, Kellogg, was also active in baseball broadcasts. In Chicago, Kellogg spent $130,000 on Cubs and White Sox regular-season game broadcasts on WJJD. The cereal maker also expanded coverage into the preseason, spending $10,000 on lines to bring Chicagoans games from Yuma, Phoenix, Tucson, Bisbee, and El Paso.[49] Kellogg promoted its new WJJD broadcasts in five Chicago newspapers and on billboards. The company also arranged for visits by baseball players to Chicago playgrounds. The best "baseball boys" from the playgrounds were brought to Wrigley Field for instruction and the opportunity to play games against one another in the Major League park. The best team won a "scholarship" to further its baseball education. Joining announcer John Harrington were celebrity guest color men, including the comedian Joe E. Brown and the retired baseball stars Mordecai "Three-Finger" Brown, Walter Johnson, Johnny Evers, Joe Tinker, and Tris Speaker. In addition to Chicago, Kellogg was the sole sponsor on KMOX in St. Louis and in five larger Minor League markets.[50]

For the 1938 season, General Mills planned to spend more than a $1 million on baseball once again. It sponsored a second baseball announcers' conference in Chicago attended by the presidents of both leagues. A second, smaller conference for West Coast announcers was held in Los Angeles. General Mills sponsored baseball on over seventy-five stations, sharing sponsorship with Socony-Vacuum on twenty-six stations. The home of Wheaties signed several Major League players to offer testimonials for "the breakfast of champions." B. F. Goodrich increased its cosponsorship with General Mills from five to twenty stations, including six of eight Pacific Coast League teams. Working with grocers, Wheaties was featured in several special "Welcome Home Sales" tied to a team's return from a road trip.[51]

To keep up with General Mills, Kellogg dramatically increased its baseball exposure, sponsoring broadcasts on sixty stations from New England to the Far West, including eight Major League clubs. To expand big league ball west of the Mississippi, Kellogg allowed fans in the Rocky Mountain region to vote for the American League games they wanted re-created on three stations.[52]

The predominance of cereal makers and oil companies as baseball sponsors illuminates the clear audience bifurcation in the era of daytime baseball. The weekday audience included large numbers of women and youngsters. The weekend audience skewed more toward adult males. Cereal makers sold to kids and their mothers, who wrote the grocery list; oil and tire companies sold to the males who bought automobile products for the family car or who traveled during the workday and listened on their vehicle's radio. However, now that General Mills had forced the owners to embrace radio fully, other product categories were joining the advertiser mix. Even the owners understood why baseball appealed to so many sponsors. As the attorney Joseph Hostetler told the American League owners, "You can't think of a program that has anything like the universal listen-in appeal. . . . We not only give it to the listeners with that listen-in-appeal, but we give it to them [advertisers] for a 2-hour period during which practically nobody turns off unless he has got to go somewhere . . . because he wants to hear the next half-inning. So you have got a two-hour program, 156 days, with 18 breaks in every program of about a minute or longer, and there is nothing just like it on the air."[53]

In 1938 P. Lorillard Company, manufactures of Old Gold cigarettes, began sponsoring Cubs and White Sox games on WGN, while other tobacco companies sponsored score and highlight shows on the NBC Red Network and local stations. Lorillard developed baseball excursions to the Windy City for fans within a 250-mile radius after announcer Bob Elson received thousands of letters from fans asking him to buy them tickets for Sunday and holiday games in Chicago.[54] Big tobacco became big sponsors of baseball after World War II, until it was banned from the airwaves by federal legislation in 1971.

As the 1930s drew to a close, the last radio holdouts, the three New York clubs, finally succumbed to the aural medium. In December 1938, General Mills and Socony-Vacuum, joined by Proctor & Gamble, signed the Dodgers for both home and away games. The new president and general manager of the Dodgers, Larry MacPhail, a radio supporter, made the team the first in New York to sign once the five-year radio band lapsed. Then in January 1939, the Yankees and Giants signed with the same three sponsors for the broadcasting of their home games, excluding Sundays, over WABC.[55] Other advertisers interested in the Gotham baseball breakthrough included P. Lorillard, American Tobacco, Kellogg, Atlantic Refining, and Coca-Cola.[56] While shut out of the New York market, Atlantic Refining doubled down on baseball for the 1939 season, sponsoring over eighteen hundred games on thirty-nine stations in the East and South at a cost of about $600,000.[57] The number of General Mills' baseball stations dropped slightly, but the company still expected to spend much more than $1 million because of additional New York team sponsorships. General Mills replaced its growing Chicago announcers' conference with regional meetings in Cincinnati, Dallas, Atlanta, Tacoma, San Francisco, and New York.[58] Perhaps responding to criticisms of excessive commercialization, General Mills planned to limit commercials to four per game, with the announcer permitted to "ad lib briefs on the product at any time, using his own discretion."[59]

Commercial Era Established

As night games became more common and as television developed, breakfast-cereal makers moved their commercials from baseball to daytime after-school and Saturday-morning television programs. By the late 1940s, advertisers were using baseball and other sports to target adult working-class males who could use their increasing leisure time to listen and later watch baseball during summer evenings and weekend days. Petroleum companies and tire makers remained strong supporters of baseball broadcasts. Later, they were joined by auto manufacturers and related businesses. World War II taught a generation of young males about the virtues of cigarettes and alcohol. While the National Association of Broadcasters still forbade its members from hocking hard liquor, beer was advertised. In the postwar years, breweries became the leading sponsors of baseball broadcasts. Tobacco products also became a major supporter.

Although General Mills ultimately abandoned baseball for more target-audience-appropriate advertising venues, it played a crucial role in the history of baseball on the radio. It was the corporate force that moved baseball owners, split for more than a decade over radio, to accept the medium. For some owners, radio remained a necessary evil and a drain on attendance; for others, it was a promotional powerhouse that enriched their coffers with a second, increasingly robust, revenue stream. While the National League never became "a breakfast food league,"[60] as president Ford Frick once worried, baseball on the radio became a standard piece of every Major League and most Minor League franchises. The press box made room for a permanent broadcast booth.

For radio networks, the baseball problem—stations preempting daytime network programming for local games and thus irritating network sponsors—gradually faded away. As the number of U.S. radio stations exploded after World War II, baseball found a home on the many new independent, non-network-affiliated stations. In addition, when the game embraced night baseball and network radio ceded the prime-time evening hours to television, radio network programming no longer conflicted with baseball. The problem reemerged briefly in the late 1940s and early 1950s in the new medium of television. Baseball was broadcast widely on network stations until the expansion of network prime-time and daytime programming pushed it to independent stations or weekend afternoons.

By the start of World War II, the commercialization of radio was nearly complete. While baseball officials, journalists, and many listeners complained about the increasingly advertising-saturated broadcasts, the pattern of commercials at the end of each inning and commercial "blurbs" during the play-by-play became established practice. In 1953 Frick, now baseball commissioner, counted 106 advertising messages in a one-hour-fifty-eight-minute game he recorded. The commissioner grumbled, "Nothing is 'baseball' any more. If it's a home run that's been hit, it isn't a 'baseball' home run but a '_____' home run."[61] While the commissioner's complaints might have garnered some attention, he had no "best interests of the game" power that could override team contracts with sponsors and stations. By 1953 Frick was reflecting the bygone era when he had worked in radio. In those days, the medium's captains feared public outcry and government intervention if they pushed the commercial envelope too far. But that time had passed. For baseball broadcasts and the rest of radio programming, the advertising genie was out of the bottle. And that aggressive imp forced owners to accept radio as a full partner.

Part II

The Age of Acceptance,
1937–60

7   Re-Creating Baseball

During much of the early history of baseball on the radio, the re-creation of Major League Baseball games was common practice. Although that practice ended nearly sixty years ago, the games invented from fragmentary telegraph information are fondly remembered and widely recounted in the national pastime's lore. Re-creations are also one of the few topics in the history of baseball broadcasts that have enjoyed scholarly attention.[1] For older fans, re-creations recall a simpler era when there was no interleague play, no designated hitter, no free agents, no TV, no fantasy teams, and only sixteen real ones—baseball the way Abner Doubleday invented it, if he had actually invented it.

Adding to the myth surrounding re-creations are stories of sucker bets won by barroom sharpies. Although with many variations, the basic story involves betting on what will happen next at a ball game on the radio. The con knows that the radio broadcast is a re-creation; the sucker does not. The con also knows what has already happened on the field, courtesy of information relayed in a live broadcast from the ballpark or Morse code heard in the background of the re-created gamecast. With this advanced knowledge, he becomes unerringly clairvoyant and a bit richer. Red Barber claimed that such stories involving his broadcasts must have been false because he allowed no delay between receiving the telegraphic information and calling the game.[2] But re-creators were often a half inning, or more, behind the wire, so the re-creation con was a real possibility.

At the heart of re-creation is *creation*. It is shaped by the fertile imagination of the announcer, who envisions the myriad details absent from the telegraph reports. The announcer receives little more than the basic "scorecard" information of the game, plus balls and strikes. The rest he must invent. But also at the heart of re-creation is deception. Re-creation announcers ran on a continuum from the more or less factual to the blatantly fictional. The factual side was anchored by Barber, who always wanted the audience to know they were hearing an oral report on events actually taking place elsewhere. Barber wanted no sound effects and based his creation on the typical patterns of player behavior he had observed at Ebbets Field. He told Curt Smith, "I couldn't go for that dishonesty. To me, the audience should know the truth. So what I did was intentionally arrange for the sounds of the wire service to be in close proximity to the mike. At home, you heard the dots and dashes—the sounds of the operating receiver typing away. I wanted the sounds to be heard—nobody was going to con the fans."[3]

On the fictional side was Gordon McLendon, who is fondly remembered for creating dramatic accounts of the game action in his Dallas radio studio that were far better than the real thing reported from the ballpark. McLendon rarely did games from the park, and he never observed any single team on a regular basis. His imagination was bound neither by memory nor direct observation; he was free to invent.

But even when there were appropriate disclaimers and no sound effects, the factual reporting incorporated fictional elements. According to Red Barber, on a pitched ball, the wire sent "S1C" for "strike one called" and "B1L" for "ball one low."[4] Was strike one called a heater thrown right down Broadway, an overhand curve that broke sharply over the outside corner of the plate, or any one of dozens of other possibilities? Was ball one low, bounced in the dirt, or nipping at the bottom of the strike zone? Was the DP (double play) a short-to-second-to-first routine or was the first baseman nearly pulled off the bag? At the ballpark, the announcer could report what he saw with his eyes. In the studio, he had only his mind's eye. It was impossible for the announcer to report the facts when he did not know them. On the other hand, who expects literal truth from a witness absent from the scene?

Even the journalistically committed Barber had to create much of what he said on the basis of his knowledge of the game and its players. In *The Broadcasters*, Barber explains how he might use his experience to re-create an at bat of the notoriously slow-footed Cincinnati Reds catcher Ernie Lombardi. From the telegraphed words "Lombardi up," Barber would set up his at bat:

> I saw Lombardi from the many times I had studied him, and from seeing him mentally, I spoke audibly—"The next batter is Old Schnozz, Ernie Lombardi . . . a big towering, right-handed batter . . . he takes his stance with his back foot close to the catcher . . . he is the only fellow in the big leagues who uses an interlocking finger grip. . . . Lom is hitting against a seven-man outfield . . . he is the slowest runner in the league, so all four infielders are playing back on the outfield grass . . . the defense is around into left . . . he always pulls the ball. How he won the batting title last year when he never gets a leg hit, I'll never know." . . . I announced what Lombardi did from what I knew he was doing . . . and I did this for every player in the league. When a new man came in the league, I carefully, mentally photographed him. I used my eyes against the days in the studio when I would be unable to use them.[5]

Barber used the sketchy Western Union account of the game action to create a vision of how those actions might have unfolded on the basis of his Mensa memory of the players and their previous performance.

This chapter attempts to answer the journalist's six questions about re-creations: what, when, why, who, how, and where. What were the various types of re-creations used over the years, and when were they used? When did they start, and when did they end? Why were re-creations needed? Who were the practitioners of the art? How were the re-creations constructed? Where were they performed? The review takes us from the very first flash broadcasts of game action in the early 1920s to end of MLB re-creations in the mid-1950s.

What Is a Re-Creation?

Strictly speaking, the one kind of call of a baseball game that is *not* a re-creation is when the announcer observes the action on the field directly and broadcasts an oral account of that action as soon as it happens. Whenever an announcer calls a game that is based on information other than real-time observation by the announcer, he is re-creating the experience of the live broadcast. The live broadcast requires an announcer at the ballpark with a microphone connected to a radio transmitter. A re-creation requires information relayed from the ballpark that can serve as the basis of an announcer's call. While WJZ in Newark, New Jersey, is often credited with the first broadcast of a World Series in 1921, the announcer, Thomas Cowan, was not at the Polo Grounds to call the game but dependent on information observed at the ballpark and related to him by telephone. Thus, radio's first World Series games were also among its first re-creations. There is also some evidence that Harold Arlin used information relayed from Forbes Field to re-create a game on the radio two days before his historic first live broadcast on August 5, 1921.[6]

While Western Union telegraph wires were the most common means of transmitting information from the ballpark to an announcer at a distant radio station, any means of instantaneous communication would suffice. A voice call on a telephone or shortwave radio transmitter could relay the details of the game. In the late 1940s, the legendary sports re-creator Gordon McLendon used rooftop observers to gather game information through binoculars and relate it to his Dallas studio by telephone. At ballparks that allowed patrons to exit and reenter the park, a spotter would write down summaries of the action, leave the stadium at the end of an inning, phone it into the station, and reenter for the next inning. Other observers allegedly wrote down the game action on slips of paper that were dropped from the stands into the hands of confederates who would relay the message to the station.

Most re-creators used Western Union's "Paragraph One" service, a pitch-by-pitch account of the game that was available to any interested takers. The service took its name from the initial paragraph of the FCC Tariff 216 covering the rates and condition of sports play-by-play over the telegraph. The FCC rules provided rates for eight baseball services, including "Paragraph Two," half-inning reports, and "Paragraph Three," end-of-inning reports.[7] Western Union paid baseball owners for the rights to send the information, and initially, the owners imposed no restrictions on who could receive it. Newspapers could use the accounts for evening or special-edition reports on the day's games. In the early 1920s, radio stations began broadcasting summaries after the end of each half inning, calling them "flash" broadcasts. But it was not long before announcers began to supply reports as soon as the information was relayed, simulating the call of a live game. Unrestricted, Western Union's "Paragraph One" could make any station in the country a "voice" of any Major League team. Some broadcasters, such as WHO in Des Moines or the Liberty Broadcasting System in its first years, did only re-creations, never setting foot inside a big league park.

When Were Re-Creations Used?

The "when" question has two time foci: the years that stations used re-creations and the time of day that re-creations were broadcast. Re-creations were used for almost all Major League road games broadcast before 1945. In the heat of a September pennant race, teams might broadcast a few road games from their host's ballpark, and opening-day road games might also receive live treatment. But the rest of the road competitions were re-creations, if they were broadcast at all. Teams needed the permission of the host team to use Western Union wire for re-creations. The strongly antiradio New York–area franchises usually denied such requests. But after their five-year ban on broadcasts was lifted in 1939, the Gotham trio, led by Brooklyn Dodgers president and general manager Larry MacPhail, gradually began to warm up to radio. In 1946 MacPhail, now leading the New York Yankees, made the team the first franchise to eschew re-creations and broadcast all of its road games live. For the next decade, more and more MLB teams switched to live broadcasts of road games, as sponsors became more willing to cover the announcers' travel costs and AT&T line charges. In 1955 the Pittsburgh Pirates were the last team to go live from the road.[8]

While most re-creations were aired during the live games, the delay between the game action and its re-creation by an announcer varied greatly. Announcers were often far behind the action on the field. The action must take place, be observed, typically translated into Morse code, transmitted over telegraph wires, decoded by a telegraphic operator at the other end, given to the announcer, and finally, re-created. Since the audience had no other access to the game, the announcer was under no pressure to make the call as quickly as possible. Announcers were often substantially behind the game action, and these delays did not even account for interruptions produced by the all-too-frequent telegraphic equipment breakdowns.

At times, the re-creations would take place long after the game was completed. Radio-adverse owners might not allow broadcasts during a day game but permit re-creations that evening to help promote the team and establish a radio presence. In the evening, stations also would offer re-creations of live game broadcasts aired earlier that day, allowing an "encore" presentation of the game in an era when recordings were expensive and less common. In 1936 the Chicago Cubs sponsored encore re-creations of its games on WIND to increase the promotional benefits of radio. The team hired Hal Berger from KNX in Los Angeles to give the hour-long prime-time re-creations. Cubs owner Philip K. Wrigley hoped "through these evening rebroadcasts to interest a lot of people in baseball who don't pay much attention to the sport at present."[9] North Dakota station WDAY even found an audience for late-night re-re-creations of Northern League Fargo-Moorhead Twins games. The station re-created 5 p.m. Twins games that same evening at 10:15. Despite an early-to-bed, early-to-rise culture, "folks out here wanted their baseball so sincerely that they gave concrete evidence of sitting up nights and listening."[10]

Why Were Re-Creations Used?

Re-creations saved sponsors and broadcast stations money. Travel costs, including hotel, meals, transportation, and announcers' time, were obvious savings. In an era when radio ad budgets were much more modest, sponsors could not easily absorb these costs. Less obvious but more substantial was the considerable cost of AT&T's line charges. In addition to very high toll-call charges, AT&T charged stations $4 per watt of power as a license fee, with a minimum fee of $500 and a maximum of $3,000. Broadcasters often used much-cheaper telegraph service for all of their long-distance information needs. For a single baseball game, Western Union charged stations only $27.50 in 1949.[11]

Travel costs and line charges were saved by all re-creators, but some stations used re-creations to overcome teams' objections to broadcasts and to avoid any broadcast rights fees charged by team owners. Owners could easily control access to their stadium, preventing live broadcasts, but controlling Western Union reports or game information observed from nearby rooftops or pirated from other broadcast stations was more difficult. As we will see, these "bootleg" broadcasts were intensely condemned by the owners and ultimately led to court action of historic significance.

Who Did Re-Creations?

For Western Union, what the broadcasting of baseball gave with one hand it took away with the other. The re-creation of games and presentation of scores and highlights by stations across the country brought Western Union new telegraph customers during the regular season. But the World Series was a different matter. By the mid-1920s, when World Series games could be heard in much of the country by live radio broadcast, the market for Western Union's game summaries was drying up. In 1920 Western Union's revenue from both leagues totaled $122,000, and it jumped to $205,000 by 1926. But the World Series portion of that revenue declined from $66,000 in 1922 to $34,000 in 1927.[12] Western Union, sensing that the World Series revenues would not return, went to the owners to improve its regular-season revenues.

In the mid-1920s, Major League Baseball's contract with Western Union forbade it from distributing inning summaries during the game in the city in which the contest was held. The owners were afraid that if more and more fans could receive the inning summaries in theaters or other public displays, attendance at the games would suffer. At the joint meeting of the Major Leagues in December 1928, Western Union, citing stagnant revenue from Major League Baseball, asked the owners to lift the ban, at least when the games were being broadcast locally. Broadcasted games reached far more potential costumers than telegraphic transmissions did, even if the latter were displayed publicly. Western Union's representative requested, "If the broadcasting is to continue, we should like to have the same equal, free footing with broadcasters in the matter of describing in our way the games no matter where they are played."[13] Several owners saw an opportunity to eliminate all broadcasts and moved to do so, but Bill Veeck Sr., president of the Chicago Cubs, argued successfully that teams should continue to control radio broadcasts from their home parks. The owners did vote to allow Western Union to sell play-by-play information from the ballparks to all takers, if the game was broadcast.

Since Western Union made a small profit from each station sale, it was motivated to increase the number of stations re-creating games. The stations received desirable and relatively cheap programming, needing only an announcer and a wire operator to create the broadcast. Conversely, teams got little from the re-creations made outside their control. Western Union gave the leagues only 10 percent of its revenues from the Major League game feeds, so increasing circulation provided little additional revenue. However, teams could still exert some control over Western Union's actions through their contract with the company. For example, the New York teams forbid stations from the visiting team's market from re-creating games using Western Union feeds from their stadiums. Thus, the Gotham blackout extended to all other Major League markets. Western Union and news services could be controlled, but there were other ways to get game information.

By the mid-1930s the demand for Major League broadcasts was creating a "black market" in baseball broadcast. At the July 1936 American League owners' meeting, league lawyer Joseph C. Hostetler outlined three ways "bootleggers" could obtain the information needed for a re-creation:

"One is though a short wave set[;] you can detect that. Now there is a radio broadcast set, short wave, the batteries of which will go in a belt around a man's body, and the loudspeaker of which isn't much bigger that a silver dollar, and he can talk into it from some place in your park. . . . Another method they use is to listen to somebody's broadcast. The third way is to have somebody come into the park and go out and telephone every half-inning just what happened."[14]

Hostetler was confident that bootleggers using shortwave sets and stadium pay phones could be detected and controlled, but using other broadcasts as the source for re-creations was more troubling. Hostetler found evidence that WMCA was re-creating Boston and Philadelphia games for the New York market for baseball megasponsor General Mills. Hostetler told the owners that the only sure way to beat the bootleggers was to offer live broadcasts of the game: "The worst that can happen to you, in my judgment, is that you are forced to broadcast, those of you who aren't. I do not believe there is any bootleg broadcast that can successfully compete with an authorized broadcast. . . . The purpose of this New York thing is to force Ruppert [the Yankees' owner] to broadcast."[15]

At issue was owners' control of their teams' broadcast. The owners wanted to use their hold over Western Union's wire rights to games to limit re-creations. In 1937 a conflict between the Tigers and WJBK of Detroit erupted, with Western Union caught in the middle. Western Union refused WJBK's request for play-by-play reports of Tigers road games, a service it had provided to the station since 1933. WJBK accused Western Union of "unjust discrimination" because it continued to provide the reports to other stations. The station argued that Western Union was a common carrier and as such was obligated to provide the reports to all paying customers, voiding Western Union's agreement with MLB. The station filed mandamus proceedings in federal court and brought a formal complaint to the FCC. It also got the cooperation of a sympathetic representative who rattled the congressional saber by proposing a congressional investigation of baseball over the matter.[16]

When WJBK proceeded to offer the re-creations using information from "undisclosed sources," American League president William Harridge requested an FCC investigation of WJBK, arguing that the station's actions were "not only contrary to the honest business practices of licensed stations, but also in violation of the Communications Act of 1934 and the provisions of Rule 177 of the rules and regulations of the Commission with reference to rebroadcasting." WJBK responded that it had "never obtained information for its broadcasts in any manner that violates FCC rules nor will it ever do so."[17] The AL action appeared to work, as WJBK abruptly dropped its FCC case against Western Union in September 1937.[18]

Although of considerable concern to owners, bootleggers were only a small player in the re-creation business. Most re-creations were of road contests, produced by the same stations that provided live coverage of home games. The same announcer was used, and the broadcast was during the same time period as the actual game. In this era, most baseball announcers also covered a variety of other sports and entertainment programming for the station and needed to be at their home stations to complete those tasks. The constant travel that is the bane of modern announcers, not to mention players, coaches, and managers, was not part of the job. Most baseball announcers preferred it that way. According to the *Sporting News*, before 1946, "99 percent of road broadcasts were done through re-creations."[19] Minor League teams continued to use re-creations long after the Major Leagues had abandoned them in the mid-1950s. Again, the main reason was to save the announcers' travel costs and line charges.[20]

How Were They Done?

While re-creations could be made from any source of information about the game action, most of them involved a tightly coordinated relationship among a station, a baseball announcer, and at least two telegraph operators. Baseball owners were initially suspicious of Western Union's presence at the ballpark, just as they were to be of radio's and television's entry into the game. If the game action could be transmitted to public display boards at newspaper offices and opera houses, who would want to pay to come to the game? In 1872 the Cleveland franchise barred the telegraph from its ballpark, forcing a Western Union employee to climb a tree outside the ballpark to record the score each half inning.[21] Substitute radio or television for the telegraph, and you extend owners' suspicion of mass communication another ninety years. But by the age of radio, Western Union reports were the norm. The telegraph company negotiated a contract with baseball owners to provide information during contests to clients who were acceptable to the owners. The leagues received 10 percent of Western Union's take, which was evenly divided among the owners. As we will see in chapter 9, Texan Gordon McLendon exploited this nominal fee structure to develop a national radio network founded on Major League Baseball game re-creations.

Although described in many sources, the most complete account of the re-creation process appears in J. Steven Smethers and Lee Jolliffe's *Journal of Radio Studies* examination of the partnership between Western Union and broadcasters in producing re-creations.[22] The researchers interviewed ten telegraph operators and twelve announcers who had re-created sports events.

Despite Western Union's monopoly on commercial telegraphic services in the United States from 1851 to 1979, its charges for game information were very reasonable, especially compared to AT&T voice line charges. Western Union operators were stationed at Major and Minor League parks throughout the country, sending Morse code, dots-and-dashes descriptions of the game using a "bug," a semiautomatic transmission key. The bug produced dots by a right press and dashes by a left press of the key. Transmission was quicker than the traditional telegraph key because there was no need to press it for each dot or dash. Holding the key to the right would produce multiple dots, and to the left, multiple dashes. Morse code was also improved in 1879 with the addition of an abbreviated code for six thousand common terms. By the early 1930s, teleprinters were being used to print incoming messages on half-inch-wide strips of paper. The teleprinter had a typewriter-like keyboard and could be used to send and receive messages. Telegraph operators now needed only to be good typists. However, the teleprinter was expensive, required high-quality lines, and was subject to breakdown.

Thus, the old-fashioned Morse equipment often provided backup or even primary service in more remote areas.

Although the press-box operator primarily sent messages, he could also be sent messages from any receiving stations. The receiving operator could break in with his own key. This allowed for clarifications or corrections. However, since several receiving operators might want the press-box operator's attention at the same time, the transmissions could be hard to follow. Red Barber described how break-ins could create chaos: "On a big game with many points hooked together, the sending operator at the ball park would get furious if stations began breaking in on him . . . and so would I, standing in an empty studio, waiting for the play while some guy in Iowa chattered away, to be followed by a fellow in Alabama asking for a repeat, and then a man from Indiana would break in."[23]

The press-box operator's knowledge of baseball and willingness to provide detail was also important in producing an accurate re-creation. One operator might send only the words "fly ball out" to describe an outfield play, while a more meticulous one might type "fly ball to gap in left center, caught by CF," providing the announcer with enough detail to re-create the play. Journalistic announcers such as Barber wanted as much detail as possible to enhance the accuracy of their reporting. On the other hand, more authorial announcers such as Gordon McLendon needed only the essential results to provide a "factual frame" for their creative improvisations.

When the telegraphic signals broke down, as they frequently did, the split between journalists and authors became most pronounced. Barber would simply tell the audience that there was a technical breakdown, provide the scores across the leagues, and play some music to fill the time. McLendon would let his imagination run free, creating a story about a dog escaping onto the field, hotly pursued by a groundskeeper with a net or an outfielder with quick feet and a large glove. Authorial announcers also might summon up a fast-breaking rainstorm that would conveniently end just when the telegraph starting clicking again. Shorter delays could be handled by a sequence of foul balls, numbering ten or more at times, followed by erupting showers if the wire was not restored quickly.

To reduce keystrokes, operators would develop abbreviations that were quickly learned by the receiving announcers. Smethers and Jolliffe offer one example of how an operator might speed up the transmission by sending abbreviations in Morse code:

JAMES UP—BATS LEFT

B1	LO OS
S1	C
S2	S
B2	HI IS
F1	BACK TO RF FENCE
B3	LOW IN DIRT
S3	C.

"B1" meant that "ball one" was called by the umpire, while "LO OS" meant the ball was low and outside. The designation "S1 C" simply meant strike one was called, while "S2 S" meant the batter swung at the ball for his second strike.[24]

These abbreviations made it possible for operators to include more game details and shorten the time between the action on the field and its re-creation at the station.

While some announcers, including Barber, played it straight, others used elaborate effects to simulate sounds. Working after World War II, when portable recording equipment was becoming more common, McLendon insisted there be recordings of stadium sounds and performances of the national anthem at each ballpark from which he re-created games. The recordings "authenticated" his re-creations and evoked the unique atmosphere for each location. McLendon also had several varieties of crowd sounds cued on different turntables to simulate different fan reactions. The stadium echo heard during public-address announcements came from the men's room across from McLendon's studio. Baseball re-creators often had their own means of producing baseball's most distinctive sound, the crack of the bat, but it usually was produced by hitting a stick with a hammer or another stick.

While McLendon and many other re-creators were seeking stadium verisimilitude, some only wanted to enhance the entertainment value of their broadcasts. Pirates announcer Rosey Rowswell and his assistants created perhaps the most imaginative of these fanciful sounds as part of his elaborate home run call. For most of the re-created games, Rowswell used no sound effects, relying on his colorful catchphrases. He would shout "doozie marooney" for an extra-base hit or announce that "the bases are FOB," or "full of Bucs," for bases loaded. He was also known for his vivid stream-of-conscious descriptions based on the wire feeds. But Rosey's home run call—"Get upstairs, Aunt Minnie, raise the window! Here she comes!"—begged for audio enhancement. After the sound of shattering glass, number-two announcer Bob Prince would drop a dumbwaiter's tray holding nuts, bolts, ball bearings, and bells. Rowswell would bellow, "Oh, that's too bad. She tripped over a garden hose! Poor Aunt Minnie! She didn't make it again!"[25]

Where Were Re-Creations Performed?

Most re-creations took place at one of the originating station's broadcast studios. But unlike live broadcasts, which originated from the home team's press box or later its broadcast booth, re-creations could be launched from any location with a phone connection to the station's transmitter. These remote broadcasts offered more flamboyant re-creators the opportunity to apply some stagecraft to their work. Jack Graney, the former Cleveland Indians outfielder turned announcer, launched his meticulous re-creations from a local auto dealer's showroom. According to the long-time Tribe announcer Jimmy Dudley, "Only a plane of glass separated Jack from customers wandering in and out."[26] Graney was considered a master at re-creations, although they worried him. According to Ted Patterson, the author of *The Golden Voice of Baseball*, "Graney perfected recreations into a highly precise art form. He said he had an advantage over broadcasters in other cities because he had played in and was quite familiar with every American League park. When a telegrapher handed him a note saying a ball had just been hit off the scoreboard in Detroit, Graney knew exactly where the spot was located because he had bounced off the same wall numerous times during his playing days." But Graney also saw re-creations as "a dizzy job" and would "wake up in the middle of the night in a nervous fright" over mistakes he might have made, knowing that he would "get letters."[27]

The announcer who most fully exploited the theatrical potential of baseball re-creations was Arch McDonald of the Washington Senators. The DC team was a stalwart member of the antiradio camp in the 1920s and 1930s, waiting until 1938 to allow regular home-game broadcasts. But team owner Clark Griffith did see the promotional and revenue value of road-game re-creations. Starting in 1934 under the sponsorship of Peoples Drug stores, Senators road games became a Washington mainstay. For four years, re-creations were the whole baseball show for McDonald, and his sponsor provided a very public place for his performance.

From the second floor of a Peoples Drug store three blocks from the White House, McDonald's remote broadcasts of Senators games drew afternoon crowds of fans and curious strollers. According to the *Washington Post* sportswriter Shirley Povich, "When Arch did re-creations, all the little boy [in him] came out. . . . He'd be up on the second floor, you know with the crowd noise and the taped bells going off. People would crowd around the store on the sidewalk and, as he broadcast, sweating up a storm, they'd roar."[28]

The McDonald baseball show became so popular that in 1935 Peoples Drug stores built a studio dubbed the "Radio Grill" in the drugstore's basement. The studio had bleachers on all four sides of the broadcast booth, holding an average of three hundred fans.[29] McDonald would call the game from the middle, with a Western Union operator at his side. According to McDonald's son, Arch Jr., "People would stand in line to come in, have a seat, and watch dad and the Senators roll." Working the frequently capacity studio crowd, McDonald used a gong to signal each of the not-too-frequent Senators hits—one stroke for a single, two for a double, three for a triple, and four for a home run. Over the years, many fans told Arch McDonald Jr., "Man it's the best show in town."[30] Attracting customers to the drugstore was part of the plan. Peoples Drug's director of promotion, Julian W. Pollard, reported in *Broadcasting* that "hundreds of people come to the radio grill to see the broadcasts put on and of course buy merchandise while they are there."[31]

A Bygone Era

In retrospect, re-creations exemplified the formative stage of the sport-media relationship in the United States. In the 1920s, 1930s, and 1940s, radio developed into an effective and profitable advertising medium but was still a distant third to newspapers and motion pictures as a commercial enterprise. Television became the dominant media industry by the 1950s, but radio was an undervalued medium in the age of baseball re-creations. As a result, sponsors generally were unwilling to underwrite the cost of live road games. AT&T's monopoly over long-distance telephone and most of the telephone industry kept voice transmission fees very high. Re-creations of road games enabled stations to air a team's entire schedule, making baseball a nearly everyday, albeit seasonal, program, rather than one interrupted by frequent road trips. At the same time, the reluctance of some owners to allow broadcasts created a "black market" for baseball broadcasts. Any station with access to the game's batter-by-batter results could become a baseball broadcaster. Access to the ballpark was not required. In short, re-creations empowered aggressive stations to create inexpensive and highly desirable radio programming that could be aired during a game or even time shifted to the evening hours, when more listeners were available. It also enabled a generation of announcers to hone their craft and, much to their glee, to avoid road trips and see their family every day. As the radio medium matured, as rights fees increased, and as stations, teams, and advertisers demanded a better radio product, re-creations receded into baseball history. While re-creations were certainly central to the history of baseball on the radio, it was the owners' final acceptance of the medium that ushered in its zenith.

1. (*top*) While some critics questioned the accuracy of Graham McNamee's reporting, he became radio's first celebrity sportscaster.

2. (*bottom*) Graham McNamee at an early World Series broadcast.

3. Bob Prince with Harold Arlin, baseball's first play-by-play announcer.

4. Cubs owner William Wrigley. To Bill Veeck Sr., Wrigley was "as great a salesman as ever trod the earth."

5. (*top*) Quin Ryan, WGN's first voice of the Cubs and White Sox.

6. (*bottom*) Harry Caray (*left*) with his Griesedieck Brothers beer team, near the beginning of his Hall of Fame career.

7. A young Mel Allen shows how simple radio could be.

8. (*opposite top*) Yankees owner Jacob Ruppert and Joe DiMaggio. When you had Ruth, Gehrig, and DiMaggio you did not need radio.

9. (*opposite bottom*) Bill Veeck Sr. was always selling the virtues of radio and looking to the future.

10. (*above*) Kenesaw Landis could pitch some pain to announcers and their networks.

11. (*top*) If Judge Landis was ever spit on by a player, he told announcers it was their job "to simply report the event."

12. (*bottom*) Beantown scribes resented Ted Husing's constant chatter; Judge Landis resented his criticisms.

13. Landis rejected and then later accepted Jack Graney, an ex-player, in the World Series booth.

14. Bob Elson at the Mutual microphone. In 1939 the upstart network changed the World Series radio rules.

15. A "portable" radio at League Park.

16. The "Barber of Flatbush" works his magic. Red Barber at the WOR microphone.

17. Bob Prince (*back*) and Rosey Rowswell (*front right*) add live sound effects to their re-creations.

18. Red Barber in his Cincinnati days.

19. Gordon McLendon, a youthful "Old Scotchman."

20. Happy Chandler upped World Series rights.

21. The Hall of Famer Lindsey Nelson learned the art of re-creations from Gordon McLendon.

22. (*top*) Vin Scully with all the tools of the trade.

23. (*bottom*) Bowie Kuhn with Montie Irvin, looking for a better radio deal.

24. Ernie Harwell was scooped up by CBS Radio.

25. (*top*) Red Barber valued on-field research.

26. (*bottom*) Several Major League teams have immortalized beloved announcers in bronze. This statue of the late Harry Caray rising from the fans is located in front of Wrigley Field's bleachers. Courtesy of James R. Walker.

8 Baseball Reluctantly Embraces Radio

Road game re-creations gave the remaining reluctant MLB owners a means of exploiting the promotional power of radio without risking the home park product. But the golden age of baseball broadcasts really begins with the owners' final capitulation to radio interests. Although over a decade had passed since the first regular-season broadcasts of home games in Chicago, Major League owners were still split over radio in 1936. Passionately proradio voices came from the Windy City—especially the Cubs—as well as from Detroit, Cincinnati, Cleveland, and Boston. The New York, Philadelphia, Washington DC, Pittsburgh, and St. Louis teams were still resisting regular-season broadcasts. As we saw in chapter 6, major national advertisers, including General Mills, Kellogg, Mobil Oil (Socony-Vacuum), and Atlantic Refining, were forcing baseball's hand. The radio debates seemed endless. National League president Ford Frick, introducing yet another radio discussion, lamented, "The subject matter is this question of radio, which has been coming up, more or less dogging our footsteps for a good many years."[1]

In the last half of the 1930s, radio made its final push, and the remaining laggards reluctantly embraced the now well-established aural medium. The American and National Leagues successfully fought off stations pirating their games. Networks, to protect their daytime sponsors, pressured their affiliates to drop afternoon baseball. Coverage of both home and away games became the norm. A few teams began to follow the model of the Boston regional network and offer their games to additional stations in their territory. Although radio's major benefit to teams was its promotional power, more teams began charging stations and sponsors for broadcast rights. Broadcasts rights became a steady stream of additional income. Following the Minor Leagues' lead, Major League owners gradually moved to offering a few night baseball games. World War II slowed the development of both night baseball and radio coverage, but the long baseball-radio war came to an end. By the 1950s, weekday baseball became predominantly an evening event, giving radio a bankable product to offer in its fight with television for the nighttime audience.

"We Never Had Any Appreciation of the Value of This Thing"

While the owners remained clearly divided on the worth or harm of radio coverage, they gradually began to focus more on the value of their broadcast product and how they might protect their ownership rights for radio, even as television loomed on the horizon. Owners were beginning to understand that radio rights had value beyond promotion, that they must act to ensure those rights, and that the public wanted baseball on the radio. That public demand spurred advertisers to spend more dollars sponsoring broadcasts and gave interested legislators a reason to challenge an owner's right to refuse to broadcast. Both the National and American Leagues made radio a major topic at their 1936 meetings.

American League owners focused intensely on radio issues at their July 6 meeting in Boston. The major issue was team control over radio rights and infringement from General Mills–sponsored re-creations of Boston and Philadelphia games on WMCA in New York. Although wire services could be controlled to reduced unauthorized broadcasts, the owners reviewed the various ways their games might be "bootlegged" and how they could cheaply record and monitor such broadcasts using Dictaphone equipment. Even legitimate stations presented problems. Higher-powered stations paid more for broadcasts rights but also strayed into neighboring Minor League markets. Stations could not reduce their power just for the baseball broadcasts because distant listeners would complain to the FCC. According to American League lawyer Joseph

C. Hostetler, "If they ever allowed a big station, which is relied upon by some fellow out in the mountains in his sheep ranch, to cut the power down so that for one program he couldn't get it when he wanted to, there would be so much kick . . . they would be afraid to do it."[2] Looking for greater control than that offered by broadcast stations, the owners even discussed the potential for "wired radio," a five-channel system to be delivered over electric power lines. Hostetler tried to persuade the owners that this technology would be better than broadcast radio: "[It] can not only control the city where it goes, but their substations, their power stations, you see. In other words, they don't just put it on the air to fly all over, everywhere. They can control where it is to go, and what it is to be used for. And they can absolutely control it."[3]

But wired or cable radio never became a reality in the United States. Owners would have to work the legal system to protect their radio rights. And they would have to change their own attitudes to realize the financial benefits of the medium.

Later in the July 1936 meeting, AL owners began to discuss the value of their broadcasts. Noting that most teams sold their rights to a station or group owner such as John Shepard of the Yankee Network, some AL owners and officials began to question if they were undervaluing their product. This concern is reflected in the following exchange between Hostetler, Edward T. Collins of the Red Sox, Ed Barrow of the Yankees, and L. C. McEvoy of the Browns:

Mr. Hostetler: You see, here you have been selling the broadcast, the rights to a station.

Mr. Collins: Yes, the Shepard Stores.

Mr. Hostetler: Then that station goes out and sells it to whoever they want to.

Mr. Barrow: They farm it out.

Mr. Hostetler: Sure. Now whether you are going to change that technique some day, I mean whether you are going to sell it to the ultimate consumer and let him arrange with the station, or how you are going to do it, time alone will tell.

Mr. Collins: Well, it is dollars to doughnuts if we sell it to the Shepard Stores they are making more out of it, because they sell it to the sponsor.

Mr. Hostetler: I'll say! We are nowhere near getting for ourselves what we should.

Mr. McEvoy: We never had any appreciation of the value of this thing.

Mr. Hostetler: No. The truth is that I don't think we have ever really appreciated what we have got.[4]

Even radio hater Ed Barrow, general manager of the Yankees, thought owners underestimated the value of their radio product. "Any club that sells the broadcast for less than a thousand dollars a game is cheating itself right now. It is worth that if it is worth a nickel."[5] Hostetler argued forcefully that baseball was a great radio program. The game offered six months of attractive two-hour-per-day programming, had little tune-out, and gave sponsors at least eighteen natural commercial breaks that did not interrupt the natural flow of a program, as they would for a music concert. Hostetler suggested that owners would get more money from radio if they clearly established their control over team broadcasts. The American League owners approved unanimously a contract "to show that they have all agreed that ownership [of radio rights] is in the club in whose park the game is played."[6] However, the agreement was short-term. It could be voided after December 31, 1936. The purpose of the short-term agreement was to establish a precedent for owners' control over radio rights that could be used in future court cases.

By the next AL owners meeting in November 1936, however, the owners' commitment to a common contract had waned. With the authorization of AL president Will Harridge, Hostetler had contacted NL president Ford Frick and learned that the senior circuit was considering developing its own approach to contracts. Hostetler emphasized that the contract developed by the league forced sponsors and stations to "to stand with [the league] in defending any extension of that broadcast."[7] In the context of General Mills' sponsorship of Boston and Philadelphia games on New York station WMCA the previous year, Hostetler wanted to ensure that in the future sponsors would work with teams and their stations to prevent any rebroadcast of games in or outside the team's market. After an off-the-record discussion of broadcast plans for 1937 that revealed considerable variations in broadcast contracts, Hostetler concluded that a uniform broadcasting contract for standardizing the sale of broadcast rights was unfeasible: "I mean some of you want to give a broadcasting contract that is exclusive. Others want to give it non-exclusive. Some want to give exclusive for home games and open for out-of-town games. . . . Some of them want them with sliding scales and some of them want them flat, so that I do not think the paper that was mailed to you ten days or two weeks ago is feasible as a standard form of contract."[8]

Hostetler did urge owners to send their contracts to Harridge for review. Controlling rebroadcasts of games was important, he said, because "once this broadcasting thing grows to where you can begin to see what is in it I think you are going to want to sell broadcasting rights in other cities."[9]

At the December 1936 meeting of the American League owners, they approved the creation of a broadcast department to monitor broadcast contracts. The position was offered to L. C. McEvoy, the former business manager of the St. Louis Browns. The idea of a broadcast czar for all of baseball, not just for the American League, had been floated at a Montreal meeting the previous week with representatives from General Mills, the American League, the National League, the International League, and the American Association. Sponsors even offered to pay the broadcast czar's salary.[10] But cooperation among the leagues was difficult to finesse. The owners also discussed the challenge of controlling Western Union's feeds. Although direct purchase of service by stations could be contractually controlled, Western Union sold the service to pool rooms and other concerns that might leak the game information to broadcast bootleggers.

Concurrent with the American League heads, the National League owners were also meeting in New York in December 1936. They wanted to know how much each of them was making from radio. Cardinals owner Sam Breadon revealed that he received a total of $16,000 from two stations in the previous year but was unsure if it was better to grant exclusive rights to one station or to sell to several different stations. Cubs owner Philip K. Wrigley reported that the Chicago teams charged stations from $2,000 to $7500 on the basis of their power and hours of operation, producing $21,000 in additional revenue for each team. Representing the Cincinnati Reds, Warren Giles reported that the team sold the rights to Socony-Vacuum for $25,000, allowing the sponsor to negotiate with stations over broadcast fees. After Sunday contests and road games against the New York clubs were eliminated, the club granted rights to 120 games for the 1937 season. The Phillies received $20,000 for a single station that had the right to sublet the games to its sister station. Although the team received no compensation, some Phillies games were rebroadcast into the radio-dark New York market.[11]

NL president Frick noted Commissioner Landis's concerns about station power and the possible penetration of Major League broadcasts into Minor League territories. Frick also pushed for the development of a standard radio contract that would establish each club's legal claim to broadcast rights, as the American League had already done. This would make the negotiation of broadcast rights a team matter rather than a league concern. In the coming television era, this "balkanized" approach handicapped MLB in negotiating with television networks to maximize the value of its network contracts. It also added to the revenue disparity among clubs because large-market clubs could demand more for their local broadcast rights than small-market clubs. Vast differences in television rights still remain the single most important factor differentiating teams' revenues and their players' salaries.

At their 1937 winter meeting, the National League owners reviewed a new standard contract and recorded in their minutes, each team's radio negotiations. The league had authorized Nathan L. Miller, the former Republican governor of New York, to develop a standard contract that teams could use as a model in their negotiations. Miller offered two contract versions: one for a team and sponsor and one for a team and broadcaster. While President Frick noted that these were merely templates, he did emphasize the importance of provisions in both contracts that would require sponsors to cooperate with clubs in controlling information about the games and thus assisting the National League in limiting bootleg broadcasts.

The rest of the radio discussion was devoted to each club's negotiations with sponsors for broadcast rights. Robert Quinn of the Boston Braves advised playing one sponsor against another to maximize rights fees, proudly reviewing how he had been able to move the rights fees from $15,000 to $35,000. The NL owners discussed the virtue of multiple versus single-station coverage. Warren Giles of the Cincinnati Reds reported that he took less money so that the team's games could be carried on both Reds owner Powel Crosley's WSAI and the *Cincinnati Post*'s WCPO. Giles believed the publicity generated by extending goodwill toward a major community newspaper was worth much more than a few additional rights dollars.

Quinn suggested that teams might do better if the league negotiated as a unit, suggesting the teams might get $50,000 apiece if they worked together. This comment prompted Leo Bondy of the New York Giants to drop the biggest bombshell of the meeting, telling the other owners that his team had turned down $100,000 for rights to the team's 1937 broadcasts. A shocked Branch Rickey blurted out, "You turned down $100,000?"[12] Bondy's bomb quickly defused talk of working cooperatively. It was probably clear to everyone that the New York teams, once they finally embraced radio, would make much more from their rights than other teams. They would not likely be willing to take a "one size fits all" contract even if it benefited most of the other clubs. The balkanization of radio, and later television, rights was under way.

Controlling Radio Rights

The definitive battle over broadcast rights ownership was waged in radio-abhorrent Pittsburgh, where station KQV had perfected a better way to steal Pirates games. According to the *Sporting News*, KQV stationed its announcers behind a second-story window in a house next to Forbes Field. The station was also using authorized and sponsored KDKA re-creations of road games as the source of information for its own re-creations. When the Pirates learned of the pirating of Forbes Field games, the team put up a large canvas to block the bootlegger's view. But when fans at the park complained, the team removed the tarp. While the "tarp era" was brief, KQV's actions produced a permanent shift in the Buccos' radio policy. Road games had been re-created since the start of the season, but the Pirates were one of the few remaining home-game holdouts. In July 1938, the team contracted with KDKA and WWSW to carry all home games, except on Sundays and holidays. Sporting a perfect attendance record at Pirates home games since 1906, Rosey Roswell became the team's first regular radio announcer.[13] KQV claimed a victory for the listener, having pushed the Pirates to finally authorize home-game radio. Conceding that KQV had forced the team's hand, Pirates president William E. Benswanger acknowledged, "Local fans are entitled to receive a first-class play-by-play description of the games from Forbes Field."[14] But the Pirates were far from done with KQV.

On July 6, 1938, the team, joined by its sponsors General Mills and Socony-Vacuum Oil, filed a $100,000 damage suit in federal court against KQV, claiming the station's broadcasts were unauthorized.[15] The $100,000 damage claim was partially punitive, as rights fees from the authorized KDKA-sponsored broadcasts were only about half of that amount.[16] KQV maintained that it had the right to use information gained from vantage points outside the stadium to broadcast the games. The Pirates argued, "Forbes Field is so situated that no person outside the field or grandstand can observe enough of the action of games to give an accurate and comprehensive description 'such as is being broadcast by KQV.'" The lifting of information from KDKA, based on that station's rights to exclusive Western Union accounts of the away-game action, was another matter. General Mills and Socony-Vacuum maintained that they had paid for exclusive rights to broadcast the games and that KQV's competing broadcasts significantly reduced the value of their rights. KQV agreed to discontinue road-game re-creations based on KDKA's accounts.

In August 1938, federal judge F. P. Schoonmaker granted the Pirates and their broadcast sponsors a preliminary injunction, stopping KQV's broadcasts. According to the terms of the injunction, KDV could no longer broadcast play-by-play accounts of any game before it ended, could not interfere with General Mills' and Socony-Vacuum's broadcast privileges, and could not rebroadcast KDKA descriptions of the contests. KQV was also required to post a $10,000 bond.[17] Two months later, the ban was made permanent. The damages were limited to the plaintiffs' costs.[18]

While the Pirates and their sponsors were certainly relieved to see the end of the KQV broadcasts, the most important outcome of the case applied to all Major League teams and by extension to all professional sports franchises. A federal court had established clearly that teams had property rights to accounts of the games in their ballparks during game time. Judge Schoonmaker, using the finest legalese, wrote, "The right, title and interest in and to the baseball games played within the parks of members of the National League, including Pittsburgh, including the property right in and the sole right of, disseminating, news, reports, descriptions, or accounts of games played in such parks, during the playing thereof, is vested exclusively in such members." Pittsburgh and the National League 1, KQV 0. Schoonmaker justified the ruling on the grounds that usurping this property right also directly harmed the teams and their sponsors and enriched the appropriator. Pirates 2, Predators 0. KQV's actions also deceived the public: Judge Schoonmaker also concluded that "the action, threatened action and practice of the defendant constitute a fraud on the public."[19] Buccos 3, Bootleggers 0. Finally, Schoonmaker determined that KQV had violated the Communications Act of 1934. Such a violation could potentially cost KQV its license to broadcast.

The Pirates and MLB's victory was complete. Game broadcasts were no longer viewed by the federal courts as a public service but as a property right that could be fully exploited by the team. In the short run, the profits from broadcast rights were just sprinkles on the icing of the MLB revenue cake. In 1942 broadcasting rights for baseball's most successful franchise, the New York Yankees, was only $75,000, or about 5.7 percent of the team's income.[20] But as the decades rolled on, electronic-media revenues became as significant as ballpark attendance. In 1963 radio-TV rights were $13.5 million. By 1983 the figure zoomed to $152.7 million. By the end of the millennium, rights approached a half a billion dollars.[21] In December 2011, the Texas Rangers and the Los Angles Angels of Anaheim signed twenty-year TV-rights agreements with Fox Sports for around $3 billion each.[22] For baseball's bottom line, *The Pittsburgh Athletic Company et al. v. KQV Broadcasting Company* of 1938 may well have been the most consequential court case in baseball history.

The Crown Jewel: The New York Ban Ends

With the West and New England already in the radio camp, the mid-1930s saw the eastern holdouts begin to accept the aural medium. The Washington Senators were the first to relent, offering re-creations of road games in 1934. Announcer Arch McDonald was brought to DC from Chattanooga, Tennessee, and his popular re-creations helped create a demand for live baseball broadcasts in the nation's capital. By 1938 pressure from fans and sponsors pushed the Senators to offer home-game broadcasts as well. Due north in Philadelphia, the Phillies and Athletics began regular-season broadcasts in 1936 under the sponsorship of General Mills. The company commissioned a survey of Philly fans that it believed showed the value of radio in promoting attendance, although Athletics owner John Shibe believed otherwise. Across the state in Pittsburgh, the Pirates were pushed by the their sponsor, Atlantic Refining, and rival station KQV to expand their road broadcasts and include home games starting in July 1938. Only three Gotham teams, the Dodgers, the Giants, and the Yankees, bound by their 1934 agreement, continued to blackball baseball broadcasts. But that agreement was expiring, and the Dodgers were bringing in new management. Prophetically, the theme of the 1939 New York World's Fair was "The World of Tomorrow." And that tomorrow would finally include baseball on the radio.

The first Gotham franchise to embrace the future was, not surprisingly, Brooklyn—the one with the newest leadership. Initially Larry MacPhail had been wary of radio as general manager of the Cincinnati Reds, but the popularity of the broadcasts by Red Barber on owner

Powel Crosley's WLW/WSAI and Harry Hartman on WCPO won MacPhail over to radio. Along with night games, MacPhail saw radio as part of the world of baseball. According to Barber, MacPhail learned that radio could teach women about baseball and that the medium could turn "a game played by two teams into a contest involving interesting personalities who had hopes, fears, families, troubles, blue or brown eyes."[23] In December 1938, at the Minor League meetings in New Orleans, MacPhail announced that both home (live) and away (re-creation) games would be sponsored by General Mills, Socony-Vacuum Oil, and Proctor & Gamble for a fee of $1,000 a game, totaling over $150,000 for the year.[24] The station and announcer were not revealed, but in short order WOR and WHN became the home of the Dodgers, and Barber followed MacPhail from the Queen City to Flatbush. Barber actually was hired by General Mills and assigned to the Dodgers broadcasts. The stations broadcast twenty exhibition games before the regular season started on April 18.

Within a month of the Dodgers announcement, the Yankees and Giants made it known that they would finally join the new radio reality. The teams chose to work together, offering only the home games of each club, giving their sponsors live broadcasts on most days. Sunday games would be excluded from the package. The Giants anticipated $150,000 in rights fees, while the world-champion Yankees expected $175,000–$200,000. Both teams remained skeptical of any positive impact of radio on attendance. Yankee owner Jacob Ruppert saw the games as "a gift to shut-ins, rather than as an asset to his team."[25] On January 25, 1939, the teams announced that Dodgers sponsors General Mills, Socony-Vacuum Oil, and Proctor & Gamble would sponsor the home broadcasts on WABC (later WCBS), the CBS-owned station in New York.

The sponsors hired Arch McDonald away from WJSV and the Washington Senators to cover both teams. Although he reportedly never applied for the position, McDonald was selected over six-hundred-plus applicants. In addition to the home contests, McDonald would call nine preseason games and hosted a ten-minute *Baseball Preview* program before each game.[26] A creative "phrasemaker," McDonald was the first to call Joe DiMaggio the "Yankee Clipper." But he tended to use "his few good phrases over and over," according to Barber. McDonald's country style and "corn-pone expressions" were also a poor match for sophisticated Gotham.[27] After a year, McDonald returned to the Senators, where he remained until 1956. His departure opened the door for Mel Allen; Allen and Barber were eventually the first announcers elected to the Baseball Hall of Fame.

Noting the "growing influence of air lines on the national pastime," the *Sporting News* concluded, "The addition of the three greater New York clubs to the list [of radio clubs] is the most important single development of the season."[28] However, despite the influx of Major League games, Minor League broadcasts by Earl Harper continued in New York. WNEW carried the Minor League Newark Bears and Jersey City Giants games, sponsored by Atlantic Refining and General Mills.[29]

The First Regular-Season Networks

In the 1920s and 1930s, the predominant broadcast model for Major League teams focused on authorized distribution of the games by local stations. Most teams used two or more stations to maximize exposure of their product in their home markets. Out-of-market coverage typically was limited to the broadcast range of these stations. In an era when few small communities had local stations, long-distance listening to major-market AM stations was common. Some big-market stations branded themselves regionally. For example, WLS in Chicago called itself the "Prairie Farmer Station" and targeted rural listeners throughout the Midwest. For Major League teams, out-of-market broadcasts had advantages and disadvantages. On the downside, this coverage often produced conflicts with neighboring Major and Minor League teams. Minor League teams complained that the nearest Major League club was poaching their fans. Sunday attendance was especially hurt by weekend family trips to big league games. On the upside, the radio game encouraged distant fans to attend games on weekends and holidays, and when the collection of rights fees became standard, those additional listeners could help increase a team's radio dollars. Teams focused on using high-powered stations because regional team networks were difficult to build, particularly in view of AT&T's steep fees for connecting lines between the flagship and networked stations.

During the first decades of baseball on the radio, there were two major exceptions to the local station(s) model: New England networks that carried the games of the Boston franchises and Michigan's regional network that featured Detroit Tigers regular-season games.

The Yankee and Colonial Networks

Probably the most aggressive regional broadcaster of the era was John Shepard III, owner of the Yankee and Colonial Networks of New England.[30] Shepard was also a difficult network partner. Tired of rankling with the obstinate Shepard, in April 1936, CBS dropped his WNAC in Boston from the network in a nine-word telegram that said simply, "The Lord is my Shepard I shall not want."[31] Starting with two stations, one in Boston (WNAC) and the other in Providence, Rhode Island (WEAN), both housed in family-owned department stores, Shepard began to network the stations in 1928. He quickly added more stations from the region, launching the Yankee Network in 1930 and the companion Colonial Network in 1936.

New England provided a nearly perfect situation for a regional network. With a strong regional identity dating from the colonial period, New England wanted provincially focused programming. It also had more radio households and higher household incomes than other regions in the United States. The region's mountainous terrain made distant AM reception difficult. Radio service came from numerous smaller community stations, and national networks had little interest in affiliating with these small-market voices. Compared to the rest of the country, New England was also geographically compact, reducing the cost of AT&T's long lines. Shepard's networks focused on developing sponsored programming in the mornings and afternoons, times typically filled by networks with unsponsored sustaining programs. This gave Shepard additional revenues from time slots that most stations gave away. But his programming needed to be attractive and relatively inexpensive.

Baseball and other sports programming fit the needs of Shepard's Yankee Network. Boston offered two teams that could provide a live home broadcast most days during the summer. Shepard also loved baseball, and the game gave him programming with a strong regional appeal. The regional interest in the Red Sox, especially, would increase with regular-season exposure. Expenses were limited to an announcer, Fred Hoey; an engineer; and the AT&T long lines needed to connect stations. Initially, the Boston teams got no rights fees; they were happy to use the broadcasts as team promotions. Shepard began carrying Red Sox and Braves games in 1926 on WNAC and including them in the Yankee Network's programming when it began in 1928. By September 1932, the home games of Boston's Major League teams were carried on eleven New England stations on the Yankee Network.[32] By 1938 the Boston Major League games had moved to Shepard's fourteen-station Colonial Network.[33] By 1942 the number of Colonial Network stations carrying baseball grew to nineteen.[34]

Regional networks were not limited to New England. In January 1933, the Michigan Radio Network began operation. The network's most famous contribution to radio history was *The Lone Ranger*, produced at flagship station WXYZ. *The Lone Ranger* and WXYZ later became cornerstones of the national Mutual Broadcasting System. As with Shepard's New England–based networks, the Michigan Radio Network linked stations that were geographically close and looking for popular regional programming. Unlike Shepard's operation, which had exclusive rights to team broadcasts in Boston, Detroit station WXYZ provided Harry Heilmann's coverage of Tigers contests only to stations outside the city. WXYZ did not carry the broadcasts but produced them for the Michigan Radio Network. WWJ's Tigers broadcasts, called by Ty Tyson, controlled the city. While WWJ also provided nearby coverage, the signal propagation of AM radio during daytime was limited, even for a fifty-thousand-watt station such as WWJ. Thus, Tyson was the Tigers' voice in Detroit and surrounding communities, but for the rest of the state, it was Heilmann. Like the Yankee and Colonial Networks in New England, the Michigan Radio Network linked medium-market stations to provide excellent regional coverage of the Wolverine State. By 1936, when most teams had one or two local stations carrying their games, the Michigan Radio Network had outlets for baseball in five Michigan communities: Battle Creek, Bay City, Flint, Grand Rapids, Jackson, and Kalamazoo.[35] The number of stations taking WXYZ's Tigers feed grew to seven by 1939.[36] After Tyson retired in 1942, the two Tigers broadcasts merged, and Heilmann became the voice of the Tigers until his death in 1951.

While the Yankee and Colonial Networks and the Michigan Radio Network were the largest regional Major League Baseball broadcasters, other clubs offered broadcasts to a few satellite stations in the 1930s. The Cincinnati Reds sent Red Barber's WSAI broadcasts to WHIO in Dayton. In 1938 the St. Louis Cardinals radio network was launched; it emerged as the model for team networking in the 1950s. General Mills sponsored Cardinals games over a six-station Iowa network that included three Iowa communities—Des Moines, Cedar Rapids, and Shenandoah—as well as stations in Yankton, South Dakota and Lincoln, Nebraska. In addition, stations in Columbia and Jefferson City, Missouri, aired the home games of both St. Louis teams. Also, in 1938 the Philadelphia Athletics' sponsor, Atlantic Richfield, began feeding broadcasts to nine lower-powered stations in Pennsylvania, New Jersey, and Delaware.[37] A year later, the Phillies joined Atlantic's baseball network. As both the number of radio stations and the owners' acceptance of the medium grew, Major League–city broadcasters became the flagship stations for fledgling team networks. The growth of team networks also raised the ire of the Minor Leagues, which resented Major League invasion of their territories. After World War II, the team network expansion hit its full stride, producing a golden age for Major League Baseball on the radio. The Minor Leagues sought relief from the broadcast invasion, first from the Majors and ultimately from Congress.

The War Years

The Second World War starved the consumer electronics industries, as resources and research were focused on the war effort. Television and FM radio, two media set for vigorous growth, were especially hard hit.

New station construction was halted, the program schedules of operating stations minimized, and the manufacture of new receivers severely curtailed. For the established medium of AM radio, the war years still were profitable but creatively stagnant. Paper shortages reduced the available space for print advertising, pushing more advertisers into the ether. While production of many consumer products—automobiles, appliances, housing—were greatly reduced, sponsors had even more funds to devote to radio advertising because of "ten-cent advertising" dollars. Because excess profits from government war contracts were taxed at 90 percent during the war and advertising was viewed as a legitimate business expense, some of the generous profits made from military contracts could be shifted to advertising at a cost of only ten cents on the dollar. While not "dollars to donuts" in 1940s prices, it was very close, and radio advertising proliferated during the war. The portion of the total advertising pie eaten by radio jumped from 12 percent in 1941 to 18 percent in 1945.[38] While advertising demand was high, the Major League product on the field took a hit.

On January 14, 1942, Commissioner Landis wrote President Franklin D. Roosevelt asking him if baseball should be suspended for the duration of the war. The president replied to him the very next day in what has become known as the "green light" letter:

> I honestly feel that it would be best for the country to keep baseball going. There will be fewer people unemployed and everybody will work longer hours and harder than ever before. And that means that they ought to have a chance for recreation and for taking their minds off their work even more than before. Baseball provides a recreation which does not last over two hours or two hours and a half, and which can be got for very little cost. . . . Here is another way of looking at it—if 300 teams use 5,000 or 6,000 players, these players are a definite recreational asset to at least 20,000,000 of their fellow citizens—and that in my judgment is thoroughly worthwhile.[39]

Roosevelt's letter saved Major League Baseball from a wartime hiatus, but it did not prevent many of its best players from enlisting or being drafted. With stars such as Joe DiMaggio, Ted Williams, Bob Feller, Hank Greenberg, and many others in military uniform, the quality of Major League play resembled the high Minors at best. While it was still the only big league ball around, MLB attendance declined 23 percent from about 9,700,000 in 1941 to about 7,465,000 in 1943.

Radio coverage during the war remained at near prewar levels. But there were some notable gains and losses. The most notable loss actually started before the United States entered the war. After General Mills' contract with the Yankees and Giants expired in 1940, the teams could not find sponsorship on WABC at their prices. So for 1941, there were no live Yankees broadcasts, only Giants games against the Dodgers for Giants fans. Baseball-mad New Yorkers read descriptions of Joe DiMaggio's forty-one-game hitting streak in the papers. In 1942 the teams returned to the air on WOR but were off the ether again in 1943. In 1944 they returned to radio and have remained ever since.[40] With Mel Allen now in the armed forces, Gillette–sponsored Yankees and Giants games on WINS were called by Al Schacht and Don Dunphy in 1944 and by Bill Slater and Dunphy the next year. In 1946 the Yankees and Giants broadcasts were split: WINS carried the Yankees live, both home and road contests, while WMCA did live home and road re-creations of Giants games. Mel Allen returned to WINS's Yankees mike with Russ Hodges at his side. The future voice of the Cubs, Jack Brickhouse, and Steve Ellis took over the Giants games on WMCA for one year.

During the war, some teams reduced broadcast coverage. Between 1944 and 1945, the Philadelphia Phillies and Athletics network contracted significantly, losing seven of eleven stations.[41] The war took a toll on Chicago's multistation approach to radio broadcasts. By 1944 only WJJD carried the Cubs, and only WIND carried the White Sox.[42]

Still, the war years triggered some positive developments for baseball on the radio. Atlantic Richfield developed a five-station western Pennsylvania network for the Pittsburgh Pirates broadcasts from flagship station WWSM. Rosey Rowswell's calls now had outlets in New Castle, Uniontown, Butler, Johnstown, and Altoona, Pennsylvania.[43] In 1943 the Pirates' network expanded to eight stations.[44] Though forced to make some wartime adjustments, baseball on the radio remained a staple during warm-weather months. Emerging team networks set the stage for a postwar baseball explosion.

The Dawn of Night Baseball

Almost as an afterthought in the "green light" letter, President Roosevelt asked owners to increase the number of games played under the lights. The commander in chief added to the end of his fourth paragraph, "And, incidentally, I hope that night games can be extended because it gives an opportunity to the day shift to see a game occasionally."[45] The remark indicated that even the president was aware that Major League Baseball's owners had dragged their feet for a decade on the issue of night baseball. In a nine-to-five workaday world, the evening hours are any entertainment medium's prime time. Movie attendance is greatest during the evening. Most live theater and vaudeville shows are evening affairs. During radio's golden age, its prime time was the twilight hours. But the games of the Major Leagues were daylight bound long after the technology for night baseball was readily available. Moreover, the Minor Leagues had proven the commercial potential of weeknight baseball.

The potential impact of night games on radio broadcasts was clear. Radio helped sell the game to new fans, including women and children, but it was losing much of its primary male target audience during the daytime hours of the workweek. Although some men could listen on the job, most missed the live weekday broadcasts, settling for evening radio scoreboard shows or perhaps re-creations of an earlier game. As a result, cereal makers, targeting children and their mothers, were the leading sponsors of baseball broadcasts. While some sponsors, such as Atlantic Richfield and Texaco, targeted men, most sponsors selling traditionally male goods—beer, tobacco, and automobiles and related products—ignored weekday daytime baseball broadcasts for weekend sports or prime-time programs. Evening games would open the door for many more potential baseball sponsors, increasing competition among advertisers for a large but still fixed number of baseball games. Both owners and stations would profit from the increased demand.

However, the potential boost in radio rights was dwarfed by the potential boost in attendance. The Great Depression struck Major League Baseball like a fastball to the bean. Attendance collapsed, dropping from about 10.1 million in 1930 to 6.1 million in 1933.[46] Despite the capital costs of stadium lighting, shifting to weekday night games seemed one sure way to bring more fans to the park. But owners resisted. In good times, the owners could ignore the nighttime revenue potential of their ballparks. For instance, they turned down an offer from Edsel Ford, the president of the Ford Motor Company, to capitalize on their parks during the evening hours. In 1930 Ford approached National League owners with a secret plan to use their stadiums at night. He would install lights and give the owners a cut of the gross revenues. When pressed by suspicious owners for more details, Ford finally unveiled his plan; he envisioned professional skeet-shooting competitions packing Major League ballparks during the evening hours! The owners, citing other stadium contractual commitments, declined Ford's "better idea."[47] Despite a sharp decrease in attendance in the 1930s, Major League owners seemed set on ignoring the potential bonanza in radio rights fees and box office that night baseball could produce.

Night baseball was hardly a new idea. *Baseball Magazine* reported that games under the lights were tried as early as 1894 in Houston, Texas, and 1886 in Wilmington, Delaware.[48] By 1931, as the Great Depression gripped the nation, the Minor Leagues, hoping to minimize attendance losses, began moving games to more convenient times. At least fourteen teams representing fourteen different Minor Leagues planned to install lights for night games.[49] By 1937 George Trautman, president of the American Association, reported that night games "increased attendance in cities of our circuit that have adopted the game, by as much as 40 to 50 per cent."[50]

Gradually, Major League owners' attitudes changed, first in the National League. For the 1935 season, the NL owners approved a maximum of seven night games per city. On May 24, 1935, at Crosley Field, the Cincinnati Reds hosted the first Major League night game. With President Roosevelt throwing the switch to turn on the lights and new NL president Ford Frick tossing the first ball in front of 20,433 fans, the Reds beat the visiting Phillies, 2–1.[51] A week later, the Reds played the second Major League game under the lights, this time against the Pirates. The Reds played seven night games that summer, with an average attendance of 17,713, while the day-game attendance for the season averaged 4,632.[52]

Some NL owners, however, remained unconvinced. The Giants' Charles Stoneham, concerned about potential injuries because of reduced visibility, refused to play night games. While the National League at least experimented with night baseball, the junior circuit was solidly opposed. At the American League owners' meeting in July 1936, president Will Harridge surveyed owners and found they were unanimously against night baseball for the 1937 season, with influential Yankee president Ed Barrow adding, "I hope forever."[53] According to Red Barber, Barrow was "a man of enormous force and stubbornness" who also was "utterly opposed to radio."[54]

The next year, the president of the Cleveland Indians, Alva Bradley, who had a new eighty-thousand-seat Municipal Stadium to fill, pushed for night games. The league, however, adopted merely a resolution allowing night games only if a team "could show financial cause—the dire necessity for this move."[55] But by the end of the 1938 AL meeting, Bradley, supported by Connie Mack, succeeded in convincing four other AL owners to allow seven night games per team. *Baseball Magazine* reported that Bradley and Mack won over Senators owner Clark Griffith by refusing a waiver on Zeke Bonura, allowing Griffith to sell the first baseman for more money to the National League Giants.[56]

While Bonura may have inadvertently helped the cause of night baseball, it was the economic reality of night games that gradually converted Major League owners. The number of night games for each team was limited to seven in the early 1940s, but the number of American League night games increased from twenty-one in 1939 to two hundred in 1948, representing about a third of the total regular-season contests.[57] As the number of night games continued to rise in both leagues, radio sponsorship shifted from cereal companies to brewers and cigarette makers, with continuing support from oil companies. Baseball on the radio became a prime-time product, setting the stage for a postwar gamecast explosion. With the displacement of World War II receding, the dominant era for baseball on the radio lay just ahead.

9 An Explosion in
National Coverage

While many histories of radio characterize the 1930s and 1940s as the medium's "golden age," the greatest expansion in radio's coverage of the national pastime occurred in the 1950s and 1960s, followed by a second growth spurt in the 1980s (see appendix).[1] Although all teams were broadcasting regular-season games by 1939, the average franchise used only five stations in 1939 and only twelve stations by 1948. But three years later in 1951, the number had doubled. By 1961 the figure was thirty; it reached forty-three by 1970 and leveled off at forty-five by 1981.

But team network stations were not the only source of baseball's postwar broadcast growth. The emergence of daily games on the Liberty Broadcasting System in 1947 and Mutual in 1950 brought even more stations to the MLB table. *Radio Daily* reported that 183 stations were signed up for big league baseball at the start of the 1949 season, an increase of about 30 from 1948 and about 70 from 1947.[2] The reliable industry source *Sponsor* put the 1949 figure at about 200 for the Major Leagues, but when Minor League and local teams were included, nearly a thousand of the country's more than 2,600 stations were carrying baseball.[3] Beer was the dominant big league sponsor, with seven different breweries represented among team broadcasts. But Atlantic Refining was the biggest single supporter of Major League broadcasts, sponsoring multiple teams.[4] Audience ratings could be astounding. According to *Sponsor*, WCOP in Cincinnati achieved a 61 share (percentage of the audience listening to radio during game time) for the Sunday-afternoon Reds games and a 48 share for the Saturday-afternoon games.[5] The late 1940s and early 1950s, the period most often associated with the beginning of radio's decline, was really the beginning of broadcast baseball's zenith.

Why Did Team Networks Expand?

The reasons for this expansion in team networks after World War II are rooted in the changing dynamics of the radio industry and changes in MLB's radio policy sparked by a Department of Justice inquiry. Most significantly, the number of radio stations in the United States grew dramatically in two phases. First the growth of AM radio stations, which had be stunted by the Great Depression and materials restrictions during the war, exploded after 1945. In only five years, the number of stations more than doubled from 948 in 1946 to 2,086 in 1950. By 1960 there were 3,456 commercial AM stations, and by 1970 there were 4,292. In 1991 AM stations reached an all-time peak of 4,987. After the war, MLB found that many new stations all across the AM dial were hungry for big-time programming with an established audience. The second growth spurt came from FM's four-decade expansion. FM grew from 688 struggling stations in 1960 to 5,766 commercial stations in 2000, giving the FM radio industry dominance over AM.[6] FM's growth not only provided many more outlets for both Major and Minor League Baseball; its superior sound-transmission qualities took much of the music programming away from AM outlets. This created more demand on AM stations for voice-based programming, including baseball broadcasts. In the postwar decades, the number of MLB teams also nearly doubled from sixteen to thirty, but the number of commercial radio stations grew by a factor of ten.

As the number of stations grew, so did the number of hours that stations needed to program. In 1946, 90 percent of radio stations were affiliated with a network, and those networks provided programming throughout the daytime and evening hours.[7] In the early 1950s, as television expanded, the networks began to turn back large parts of their schedule to affiliates for local programming. In the 1930s, networks and their affiliates frequently battled over clearance (carriage) of network daytime programs because local stations wanted to carry Major or Minor League Baseball instead. By 1960 those conflicts were over. Except for hourly news and special features, golden-age radio networks—NBC, CBS, ABC, and MBS—had all but vanished as program suppliers.[8] While syndicators and specialized networks did offer some alternative programming, most radio stations in the United States needed to fill most of their own program hours. The formula of music, disc-jockey patter, commercials, news, and jingles filled most of this time on most stations, but baseball and other sports broadcasts provided attractive, low-cost options for many stations. This was especially common during the evening hours, when most audiences abandoned radio for prime-time television. Small- and medium-market stations could fill six months a year with original, unpredictable, and habit-forming programming that was a staple of American culture. A 1960s Chevrolet advertising jingle captured the connection. In the United States, it was "baseball, apple pie, and Chevrolet."

A third factor in the growth of team radio networks was the expansion of AT&T's radio service in the 1950s. From the beginning of regular-season game coverage in the 1920s until after the World War II, road games were rarely broadcast because of the substantial costs of the phone lines needed to connect announcers at road ballparks to their flagship stations. The same costly lines were needed to interconnect satellite stations to the flagship voice. Between 1936 and 1939, the FCC reviewed AT&T's charges, "resulting in a limited rate reduction."[9] After the war, as AT&T's network capacity increased, audio line charges were less than one tenth the cost of television connections, making regional radio networks a viable option for teams.[10]

While more stations meant more demand for MLB product and falling AT&T line charges reduced delivery costs, it was action by the Department of Justice that forced MLB to revise its restrictive radio policy. MLB had a long-standing policy of protecting the Minor League teams from competing broadcasts. In December 1946, as part of a broader agreement to restrict Major League invasion of Minor League territory,[11] MLB adopted Rule 1(d), which severely restricted team broadcasts beyond a fifty-mile radius of the team's home park. Subsection 2 of Rule 1(d) stated, "No Major League club shall consent to or authorize a broadcast or telecast (including rebroadcast or network broadcast) of any of its games to be made from a station outside its 'home territory' and within the 'home territory' of any other baseball club, Major or Minor, without the consent of such other baseball club."[12] This meant that any complaining Major or Minor League team could tell any other Major League team to remove any broadcasts of its games from stations within a fifty-mile radius of the complaining team's home park. The restriction applied regardless of when the broadcast aired, even if it was a different time from the Minor League team's game or when the Minor League team was on the road. The rule clearly restricted the development of team networks without the consent of the Minor League teams affected. The Department of Justice "was informed that many baseball clubs used this veto power to completely to prevent the broadcast in their home territories of baseball games played by other clubs."[13] Teams also used their veto power to demand payment from stations for permission to broadcast out-of-market games or to grant exclusive rights for broadcast of Major League games to a particular radio station or sponsor in their territory.

Even when the Minor League team was owned by the Major League club and within the fifty-mile territory of the Major League team, the Minor League team would sometimes seek protection. For example, the October 24, 1939, minutes of the New York Yankees' Board of Directors meeting include a request by George Weiss, board member and future Yankees GM, that the team compensate its Newark Minor League club for any negative effects on attendance coming from the Major League club's broadcasting contract.[14] In 1948 the Department of Justice began to investigate alleged monopolistic practices by MLB, and by late 1949, the Majors amended Rule 1(d), making it possible for teams to expand their networks into Minor League territories.[15]

Team Differences in Radio Expansion

The rapidly changing radio industry and MLB's evolving radio policy were only part of the postwar story. The varying patterns of radio adoption by MLB teams in the postwar era are the other part. While AT&T's line rates may have been similar for MLB teams, network expansion varied greatly by team. At the top of the postwar heap were the St. Louis Cardinals, with an average of seventy-three stations in their network for the years 1948 to 1959. The Cardinals nearly doubled their nearest rivals, the Boston Red Sox and Milwaukee Braves (for 1953–59), which had a thirty-eight-station average. Besides these three, the top-ten franchises in average stations included the Tigers (thirty-seven), Reds (thirty-seven), Kansas City Athletics (thirty-five for 1955–59), Indians (thirty-three), Cubs (twenty-six), White Sox (twenty-six), and Pirates (twenty-two). The Yankees had a limited network after the war but averaged thirty-three stations from 1954 to 1959. The teams with the fewest stations included five teams that relocated in the postwar era: the Brooklyn Dodgers (six for 1948–57),[16] New York Giants (nine for 1948–57), St. Louis Browns (fourteen for 1948–53), Washington Senators (sixteen), and Philadelphia Athletics (seventeen for 1948–54). In general, mid-American franchises with some distance from other MLB cities developed substantial networks, while coastal cities and those with nearby competitors had more modest networks.

A comparison of the team network haves and have-nots shows that relocating franchises, many of which were financially strapped, developed smaller networks, while most stable franchises had substantial networks. The Boston Braves franchise, long packaged with the Red Sox's substantial New England network, was a notable exception. The smaller-network teams also tended to be in coastal cities with nearby franchises (New York, Philadelphia, Washington DC, Los Angeles, San Francisco), while dominant networks were surrounded with territory for expansion: St. Louis and Kansas City in the Midwest and Boston in New England. In addition, two large-radio-network franchises, the Milwaukee Braves and Kansas City Royals, also restricted televised games, after experiencing attendance declines blamed by owners on TV overexposure at their prior East Coast homes.

The St. Louis Cardinals Network

The model for vigorous postwar radio-network expansion is the St. Louis Cardinals. The Redbirds came out of the war with a modest 7-station network in 1946, but as MLB rules began to loosen, the Cardinals expanded rapidly to 43 stations in 1948, 73 in 1950, and 92 in 1954, representing a fifteenfold increase in less than a decade. The network's rate of increase slowed but continued, reaching its peak of 131 stations in 1989. During its postwar decade of explosive growth, the Cardinals radio network had no Major League competition in the western and southern United States, making more than half of America its potential home territory.

From 1945 to 1969, the club also benefited from the skill and enthusiasm of one of the country's most popular baseball announcers, Harry Caray. Building on the popularity of Dizzy Dean, Cardinals broadcaster from 1941 to 1946, Caray's fan-centered broadcasts built a legendary following in much of America outside the Northeast. Caray's popular broadcasts on a growing Cardinals network created Redbird fans throughout the Midwest and South, despite some fairly lackluster teams. As Cubs owner William Wrigley predicted in the 1920s, radio promoted baseball, bringing new fans to the ballpark to see the game in person. Changes in postwar America helped bring those radio-honed fans to Sportsman's Park in St. Louis.

More cars and expanding roadways transported distant fans to the ballpark, especially for weekend contests. While there were few large cities in the Cardinals' radio reach, there were many smaller ones and thousands of small towns in America's heartland. With the family car now a staple of American life, more leisure time after the end of overtime war shifts, and growing families to entertain, baseball fans within driving distance could heed the call of Caray and other MLB baseball announcers to enjoy a day at the old ballpark.

While often accepted as a given for the Cardinals, the link between radio expansion and game attendance also has been empirically established. In one study, researchers correlated the number of stations in each of the sixteen MLB franchise networks to each team's attendance from 1936 to 1958.[17] They also controlled for four other factors that could also affect team attendance: the number of wins per season, the population in the franchise city, the number of competing MLB teams in that city, and the general health of the economy as measured by per capita yearly income. Even after controlling for these confounding factors, the researchers found a significant correlation ($r = .20$) between the number of stations in the network and team attendance. This relationship accounted for four per cent of the variation in game attendance. While a correlational study of this type does not establish that a larger radio network caused better attendance—more popular teams might simply have attracted more stations to their networks—it does show that network size and attendance were positively connected.

Although important, the raw number of stations in a team's network does not account for all of the variation in the strength of a team's radio presence. The power and reach of the team's flagship station, as well as the power and market size of each station in that network, is as significant as the number of stations. In addition, established and popular radio voices were likely to draw more fans to the broadcasts and to promote the teams more effectively. It is also likely that a combination of several positive factors—a winning team, a strong network, a popular announcer, record-chasing players—might have an even greater effect in combination than in isolation. Nonetheless, there was a positive relationship between the development of extensive radio networks and the general level of success of MLB teams during the age of acceptance of baseball on the radio.

National Networks: A Not-So-Old Scotchman

The postwar expansion of team networks was gradual and received little national attention. But the development of the Liberty Broadcasting System, a new national radio network with baseball and other sports at its heart, provoked strong reaction from the baseball establishment. The creative center of the Liberty Broadcasting System was Gordon McLendon, the son of a wealthy Texas businessman, B. R. McLendon. Less than enthusiastic at the prospect of becoming a Harvard-educated lawyer, the younger McLendon was drawn to the creative potential of radio as it awoke from its World War II stagnation. He started at a hundred-watt station in Palestine, Texas, but by late 1947, with his father's financial backing, he had opened KLIF in Dallas, a city about to begin a dramatic postwar transformation. The challenge of competing against established stations in the rapidly growing market was a perfect match for McLendon's creative bent. While McLendon was able to attract some big-name talent— Tommy Dorsey, Gene Autry—little of KLIF's initial programming was memorable until he began to tap his own legendary skill as a sports announcer.[18] The self-dubbed "Old Scotchman," only twenty-six at the time, took the craft of game re-creations and turned it into an art. Sitting in KLIF's studio at the Cliff Towers Hotel in Dallas, McLendon reinvented the long-used practice of re-creating football and baseball contests from Western Union wire highlights of the games. McLendon's first re-creation, a Detroit Lions–Chicago Cardinals NFL contest, coincided with KLIF's inaugural day, November 9, 1947. Baseball re-creations followed that spring.[19]

While the re-creation rights to NFL games were cheap and easily obtained, MLB was a different story. Baseball owners did not want to compete with their own developing team networks. In addition, the Minors had an agreement with MLB to restrict team broadcasts within fifty miles of a Minor League park. KLIF was only a short distance from Rebel Stadium, home of the Texas League's Dallas Rebels. Western Union would not transmit game information to KLIF without MLB's consent, forcing McLendon to become, in the words of the *New York Times*, "a modern-day Texas outlaw." The Old Scotchman procured an AT&T teletype line and someone to listen to Mel Allen's account of the Yankees games on WINS, while reporting the game action to him in Dallas. McLendon's re-creation of Allen's live broadcast made it to the ether with only a ten-second delay.[20] Later, McLendon stationed binocular-equipped observers on rooftops near MLB ballparks to gather the game data.[21] Although the re-creations seemed to skirt copyright law, McLendon's position was that the team's rights to the facts of the game ended after their initial broadcasts and that he was simply using information already made public on broadcasts or observed from outside the ballpark. Whether club owners were unsure of their legal ground or thought it not worth the trouble to stop one Dallas radio station, they chose not to fight. For the 1948 season, MLB sold McLendon the rights to Western Union's wire service with reports from Major League parks, and at "a very reasonable fee" of $500 per month, which was paid to the Dallas Minor League team as compensation for allowing the broadcasts.[22]

McLendon's baseball re-creations did not remain a one-station pony for very long. A competitor in nearby Denison, Texas, who was losing his afternoon audience to McLendon's re-creations, asked if he could join the baseball party. The same request came for other nearby small-market stations and then from larger-market broadcasters. McLendon's grassroots baseball network spread to stations in neighboring states: Louisiana, Oklahoma, Arkansas, Mississippi, and Colorado, totaling about forty stations by early 1949.[23] Baseball was America's game in 1948. However, since St. Louis was both the game's most southern and most western franchise, regular-season games were unavailable to stations in most of the United States. Even in the franchise-rich East and Midwest, MLB team networks were restricted to a fifty-mile radius of their home park. As the Baseball Hall of Fame broadcaster Lindsey Nelson, one of McLendon's early sports announcers, observed, "Whoever brings baseball to these folks on the radio—people, remember, panting to follow big-league games—is going to make a whale of a lot of money."[24] Also, with established radio networks, except for Mutual, shifting their resources to television, these new stations were desperate for network programming, even if only for a few hours a day during the baseball season. McLendon was meeting a market-driven need by providing low-cost, popular programming for the bumper crop of postwar AM radio stations in small-town America. And he was reaping a handsome reward for his efforts.

At first primarily a sports network, the Liberty Broadcasting System (LBS) expanded rapidly in the Southwest, in the South, and on the West Coast, offering a hyperaccelerated version of the U.S. population shift in the second half of the twentieth century. By February 1950, LBS could not offer the programming variety or national reach of CBS, NBC, or ABC, but it was a booming regional network of 150 stations that appeared to be kidnapping the national pastime's over-the-air presence.[25] The Not-So-Old Scotchman's unplanned network was rapidly becoming a major radio player and major headache for Major League Baseball.

Revising Rule 1(d): A Fight for Access

While MLB was certainly concerned about the expanding role of LBS in airing the national pastime, it was more concerned about the U.S. Justice Department's investigation of MLB's broadcast policies. The game had long been protected by the 1922 federal baseball decision that Major League Baseball was not interstate commerce and thus was not subject to federal antitrust law. The emergence of a much more powerful federal government in the 1930s and 1940s made a reassessment of the 1922 decision a looming possibility. The government's intervention came shortly after the creation of Rule 1(d) in 1946.

In 1947 an Arlington, Virginia, radio station was denied permission to carry a Dodgers-Giants game by Washington Senators owner Clark Griffith because the competing broadcast reduced the value of his franchise's broadcast rights.[26] The station complained to the Department of Justice, and by 1949 nine other station owners, including Gordon McLendon, were involved. At the center of the complaint was MLB's Rule 1(d), adopted in December 1946, banning game broadcasts "in any city without the consent of all major and minor league clubs in that city and within 50 miles."[27] MLB, anticipating the postwar growth in radio and television, wanted to limit any possible negative effect on attendance while appeasing its Minor League allies' even stronger concern about the destructive impact of local broadcasts of MLB games on their own gate. The dispute was the start of a twelve-year fight with the Department of Justice and the U.S. Congress over MLB's control of broadcast rights. The struggle finally ended with the passage of the Sports Broadcasting Act of 1961, which codified the right of professional sports leagues to sell their broadcast rights collectively. But in 1949 McLendon's LBS was bumping heads with Minor League owners in some major markets—Los Angeles, New Orleans, Memphis—over permission for LBS affiliates to carry his popular MLB re-creations.

While organized baseball argued that Rule 1(d) protected the Minors, Justice Department officials saw it as a restraint of trade that denied millions of Americans broadcasts of Major League games that they had long wanted. Attorney General J. Howard McGrath summarized the government's position, emphasizing that the public and broadcasters had a right to baseball: "Baseball is accurately referred to as the Great American Game. It is also an important commercial enterprise upon which thousands of Americans depend for their livelihood. Both the fans who desire to hear or see baseball broadcasts or telecasts, and the businessmen engaged directly or indirectly in bringing these broadcasts and telecasts to the public, are entitled to freedom from unreasonable restraints."[28]

The Department of Justice's interest in Rule 1(d) also threatened MLB's overriding antitrust exemption. Commissioner Happy Chandler, sensing that the Department of Justice would press the case and that MLB might lose more than just Rule1(d), worked to hold the government at bay.

After meetings with Department of Justice officials in the spring of 1949, Chandler tried to dispel the issue by clarifying the meaning of Rule 1(d) for owners in a seven-legal-page, single-spaced letter. While preserving the rule for the moment, Chandler made it clear that teams could only limit the broadcast of other clubs into their territory to protect their team from intrusion, not to profit from their power to control out-of-market broadcasts. In particular, a Major or Minor League team did not have for other teams' broadcasts

    (a) Any property right whatever in the local or other broadcast or telecast of Major League games;

    (b) Any right to grant any radio station or sponsor the exclusive right to the local or other broadcast or telecast of Major League games;

(c) Any right to select the particular radio or television station or stations which are to broadcast or telecast the Major League games locally or elsewhere;

(d) Any right to select the commercial sponsor, if any, of the local or other broadcast or telecast of Major League games.[29]

The commissioner then provided detailed hypothetical examples of exactly what stations could and could not do under Rule 1(d). The letter also made it clear that the power or number of stations carrying the game within a Major League team's territory was not relevant. Within its territory, an MLB team could broadcast games over multiple stations, including fifty-thousand-watt AM stations capable of covering nearly half the country at night.[30]

After further meetings with the Department of Justice in the summer of 1949, Chandler realized that educating team owners would not be enough. In October 1949, Commissioner Chandler informed Major League owners of the changes to Rule 1(d), sending them three documents: a copy of the new Rule 1(d), his written interpretation of the rule, and most significantly, a press release from the Department of Justice stating that it was "suspending further action in its investigation of alleged restraints in the broadcasting and telecasting of Major League baseball games."[31] The Rule 1(d) section on radio (i.e., broadcasting) now stated,

Each Major League club shall have the exclusive right freely to authorize a broadcast (including rebroadcast and network broadcast) of games played in its home park, except that a Major League club shall not authorize a broadcast of such games to be made from a station located outside its home territory and within the home territory of another Major or Minor League club during the time that such other club is playing a home game, unless such other club has prior thereto consented to the broadcast of said game or of any game of another Major League club during such time from a station located within its home territory.[32]

While somewhat shrouded in legalese, the new rule meant that instead of Minor League teams banning all out-of-market games at all times, teams could only object to games broadcast from transmitters within a fifty-mile radius of their home parks *during their home games.*

The rule also specified that game time began thirty minutes before the game and extended for three and a half hours for a single game and five and a half hours for a doubleheader. In addition, the revised Rule 1(d) specifically forbid Major and Minor League clubs from giving consent for an out-of-market broadcast of another club's game to specific stations or sponsors (usually for a fee paid by that station or sponsor). "No club giving such consent shall be entitled to limit its consent to any particular station or sponsor."[33] In a subsequent letter to all Major and Minor League teams, Chandler laid down the punishment for teams that tried to limit or sell their consent: the possible loss of Rule 1(d)'s protection for the remainder of the season, opening the door to unlimited out-of-market broadcasts.[34]

The commissioner followed up the October announcement with an extensive six-and-a-quarter-legal-page, single-spaced letter providing detailed explanation of the revised Rule 1(d), including several hypothetical examples. For example,

> A Major League club desires to authorize the broadcast of one of its afternoon games from a station located outside its home territory and within the home territories of four clubs—Daleville, Easytown, Foxburg, and Georgetown, all Minor League club [*sic*]. Daleville and Easytown are both playing afternoon home games during the time of the proposed broadcast, Foxburg is playing a night home game on the same day, and Georgetown is playing an away-from-home game but is broadcasting and telecasting it from stations in its home territory.

> ANSWER: The Major League club must obtain the consent of both the Daleville and Easytown clubs before it authorizes the broadcast. It need not obtain the consent of either the Foxburg or Georgetown clubs.[35]

The Department of Justice now accepted that most restrictive parts of Rule 1(d) had been purged, noting, "Under the revised rules each Major League Club is free to determine whether or not rights to broadcast or telecast its games shall be granted or sold at any time and in any area, without reference to any other club, Major or Minor, except during the time the other club is actually playing a game in its home park."[36]

In essence, Minor League teams could control direct competition that might affect their home gate, but from now on, broadcasters were free to air games at other times. Since both day and night MLB games were plentiful in this era, McLendon's Liberty Broadcasting System could offer its affiliates a day or night contest. The affiliates then could select the game that did not compete with any scheduled home game in their market. Most affiliates could schedule at least one LBS "game of the day" most days. The new certainty of a steady supply of Major League games lit the LBS baseball rocket.

McLendon Re-Creates Baseball

While radio re-creations of sporting events began in the 1920s, Gordon McLendon is widely acknowledged as the master of the art. McLendon blended his own language talents and interest in history with the evolving audio-production techniques of the late 1940s to re-create not only current baseball and football contests but historic boxing bouts, tennis matches, baseball games, and football contests, as part of his "Great Days in Sports," which could be used to cover MLB rainouts.

The baseball radio announcer is in near total control of the game. The audience only knows what he tells them based on his observation and analysis of the on-field events. But the baseball re-creator has even more control since the on-field events are only the most basic elements transferred by the Western Union operator. The announcer invents the rest. From these descriptive fragments, McLendon could apply his "natural creative ability" and bring "a flair, an excitement and a sense of reality to [re-creations] that became legendary among listeners and fellow announcers alike."[37] McLendon's re-creations often were more popular than competing game broadcasts from skilled professionals at the ball-park. McLendon believed his radio re-creations were superior to the video version of the national pastime.

> I was able to paint a picture there. No picture that is shown on tele-vision could be possibly as vivid as the picture I painted in my own mind of a baseball game. . . . Players were far bigger than life, and Ebbets Field, even though there were 3,000 people there if you were actually broadcasting from the field, was always in my mind's eye crowded with 35,000 people. The walls were a thousand feet tall that those home runs were hit [over]. So, I could take and in the re-creations spin from my own imagination . . . a far more vivid picture than any that I could have ever painted from the baseball park itself.[38]

While Gordon McLendon brought a baritone voice, "an effective vocal delivery and a mastery of the English language," he also made use of writers to create similes that he could appear to invent during the broad-cast. A player with a hit was as "happy as a cow in a Quaker Oats factory," and teams on a losing streak were "colder than an igloo's basement."[39] While the occasional authored phrase would contribute, McLendon's control of the mike and his announcing stamina were legendary. A Western Union telegrapher, a lone engineer, and he would produce a doubleheader, seven hours of baseball. McLendon was both announcer and color, supplying all of the verbal content. The engineer added sound effects from three or more turntables. Crowd noise came in three forms: general crowd sounds when the on-field action was limited, more intense crowd response for a base hit, and a jump in crowd excitement when the ball left the park. To assure authenticity, McLendon recorded crowd sounds from most of the Major League parks, matching the crowd effects to the re-created game's actual park. Mixed in with the authentic crowd noises was the occasional vendor calling out a sponsor's name, courtesy of a continuous tape loop—the Old Scotchman's version of product placement. Sound effects were added to simulate game conditions: a recorded thunder clap during a rain delay or the public-address announcer produced by a live announcer calling from the restroom near-est to McLendon's mike. Radio baseball's primal sound effect—the crack of the bat—was produced, after considerable experimentation, by "strik-ing a baseball bat near its handle with a 'nickel pencil.'"[40] Since the engineer was isolated from McLendon, McLendon would use hand signals to tell the engineer what would unfold.

As for all radio sports re-creators, McLendon's greatest challenge occurred during the all-too-frequent interruptions of Western Union feeds. When the break happened, the announcer usually had no idea how much time he would need to cover: a few seconds, a few minutes, or an hour. For short interruptions, a few invented foul balls would do the trick. But longer gaps needed more creative cover; a dog running onto the field, an argument at home plate, a fight in the stands provided open-ended texts that could fill thirty minutes in the imaginary world of the baseball re-creation. According to Lindsey Nelson, LBS's shoestring operation would do games live from the park only one week a month, relying on re-creations for the other three weeks.[41]

National Dreams

By June 1950, LBS had contracted for a minimum of 210 games to be networked to over 241 stations in thirty-three states.[42] WMGM in New York City gave LBS entry into the Northeast, affording it national expo-sure. The seven hours of daily programming were dominated by baseball, but more content was needed, much more after the baseball season con-cluded. LBS developed six daily newscasts, a radio minstrel show (*Liberty Minstrels*), other variety shows, a crossword-puzzle-based quiz show, and *Disc Jockey Roundtable*, which sampled the work of DJs from around the United States. McLendon was ready to challenge the network big boys. On October 2, 1950, LBS became America's fifth national radio network, joining ABC, CBS, MBS, and NBC.[43] At the end of the year, LBS offered sixteen hours of programming, and by August 1951, it claimed 431 affiliates. The LBS radio rocket was taking off fast, but it lacked legal control over its most popular product, descriptions of Major

League Baseball games. Much as Minor League Baseball overexpanded after the war and suffered a sudden contraction, LBS fell quickly—but not without some help from Major League Baseball.

Major League Baseball Takes Control

While Major and Minor League team owners complained that LBS was hurting attendance, McLendon found a sympathetic audience for his side of the debate at the 1951 convention of the National Association of Broadcasters. In his address, titled "What Is the Effect of Major League Broadcasts on Attendance in Minor League Cities?," McLendon pointed out that broadcasts of Major League games in Minor League territories in 1948 and 1949 had coincided with record Minor League attendance. Only in 1950 did Minor League attendance drop from its all-time high. Was the slide from its high mark a radio effect or just the result of "bad management, poor weather, increased local competition from softball and sandlot ball, television, poor baseball clubs, runaway races?"[44] At the conference, McLendon argued that the decline was part of a more general decline in entertainment expenditures. Movie-theater attendance had declined 25 percent and MLB attendance 15 percent, proving that the Minor League drop of 17 percent in attendance was simply part of a larger trend. He cited numerous factors that contributed to the decline in entertainment revenue: increased installment buying of televisions, the Korean War, the natural decline that follows any upsurge in attendance, bad weather in spring and early summer, increased entertainment competition (especially from television), management apathy, and over-expansion of Minor League Baseball into communities too small to support a team.[45] McLendon argued that LBS actually softened the decline in Minor League attendance by promoting the Minor Leagues. McLendon applauded his afternoon broadcasts of MLB games for hyping Minor League games and telling listeners "about the thrilling play in the minor leagues and [urging] them to go out that night and see their local club in action."[46] McLendon also provided testimonials from many small-market radio stations on the positive effects of baseball broadcasts on attendance.

The problem for McLendon was that Major League owners could not control most of the factors that he believed were hurting Minor League attendance, but they could control their broadcast rights. With the Justice Department forcing a loosening of MLB's out-of-market radio policy, the league joined forces with a much-better-established network competitor, the Mutual Broadcasting System (MBS), its long-standing World Series and All-Star Game partner. In 1950 Mutual was well established, with 543 stations, many in LBS's strongholds: the South, Southwest, and West. Mutual offered its *Game of the Day* live, no re-creations, Monday through Saturday afternoon to over 350 affiliates. The investment in live baseball was costly, an estimated $4 million to cover production and network time, but the product was first-class.[47] Mutual's baseball pedigree and MLB's full support conferred instant credibility. The focus on day games reduced clearance issues with local teams because Minor League teams played more night games. No Sunday *Game of the Day* broadcasts meant no competition with the Minors on their biggest payday of the week.

A Fast Fall with an Assist from MLB

To strangle the upstart LBS, MLB upped its rights fees to LBS from a pittance of $1,000 per season in 1949 to over $225,000 by 1951. Only three MLB teams—the Dodgers, Reds, and White Sox—were under contract for the 1952 season and willing to let LBS in their parks. The other clubs refused to do business with McLendon's fifth network. LBS also lost an important baseball sponsor, Falstaff Brewing Company.[48] The brewer remained heavily invested in team networks in the Midwest and brought Dizzy Dean to television for a "Game of the Week," first on ABC (1953) and later on CBS (1955). Western Union now hit LBS with a gut punch, refusing, at the urging of MLB, to sell the play-by-play game descriptions that the network needed for its re-creations. On February 21, 1952, McLendon counterpunched, filing a $12 million suit against MLB commissioner Ford Frick, NL president Warren Giles, and AL president William Harridge. Once Western Union refused LBS game descriptions, it also was included in the suit.[49] With baseball season at hand, Chicago federal district court judge John P. Barnes refused LBS's motion for a restraining order that would force Western Union to sell game descriptions to the network. Barnes concluded that owners had property rights to the descriptions of their games, they had the right to restrict access to anyone who would provide those descriptions, and their contract with Western Union allowed them to restrict the company from providing accounts to any entity they had not approved.[50]

Faced with a severely compromised product and strong competition from MBS, LBS was quickly losing its hold over baseball. And without baseball, the good ship Liberty was adrift. As Lindsey Nelson, one of McLendon's star pupils, put it, "Without the product Liberty had been founded on, how could there be any Liberty? It was all over, curtains."[51] Despite an influx of $1 million (a $400,000 investment and a $600,000 loan) from the independent oil man Hugh Roy Cullen in 1951, LBS reduced programming from sixteen to eight hours a day on May 6, 1952, and then suspended operations on May 15.[52] McLendon, ignoring his own questionable business decision in overexpanding Liberty, blamed the government for the network's failure in his last LBS blast. He roared, "Tonight, as a direct result of the United States Government's failure to enforce our laws against monopoly, the Liberty Broadcasting System must suspend operations."[53] McLendon also attacked MLB's leaders: "These men at the top of baseball, posing as a public institution, propose to deny broadcasts of this great game of baseball to the blind, the aged, the sick, the disabled veterans and the people at large." The owners "have decided that you may hear baseball, when we tell you, where we tell you and how we tell you."[54] The trial date for McLendon's case against MLB was delayed repeatedly and finally set for April 18, 1955. On January 10, 1955, organized baseball offered to settle out of court for $200,000. Will Harridge, American League president, while admitting no wrongdoing, lamented, "The cost of preparing and trying such a long case will be very expensive and winning the case will cost us more than the proposed settlement." Harridge also noted that Rule 1(d) by that time had been eliminated by MLB, so there was no need to continue to defend the rule.[55] Although McLendon was pleased that MLB offered some compensation, he found the amount too small. However, LBS's creditors finally accepted the offer.[56]

In retrospect, McLendon's case showed just how tenuous MLB's hold over its rights were. Despite an antitrust exemption provided by the 1922 Supreme Court decision, the popularity of baseball and its perceived status as a public trust made any broadcast-access decision by the game's leaders subject to political pressure from either Congress or the Department of Justice. MLB, fearing the loss of its antitrust exemption, made concessions on its broadcast policy. The public wanted Major League Baseball on the radio, and stations had a rising need for the national pastime's six months of daily programming. The popularity of baseball on the Liberty Broadcasting System had forced MLB's hand. Owners responded by expanding dramatically radio's reach on a major national network, Mutual, while also expanding their own team networks. The Minor Leagues continued to pressure MLB to protect their local markets from radio and the growing menace of televised baseball. Colorado's Senator "Big Ed" Johnson, also president of the Western Baseball League, called a much-publicized Senate Commerce Subcommittee hearing in 1953.[57] At the hearings, Commissioner Frick accused the Justice Department of forcing MLB into "eating its young" by not allowing teams to restrict their broadcasts adequately. After Johnson's hearings produced no change, the Minor Leagues continued to push for broadcast restrictions. MLB did nothing, and Commissioner Frick continued to blame the Justice Department, telling the Minors that the "rug was pulled out from under [MLB]" by the agency's probes.[58] By 1952 the baseball radio horse was out of the corral, and no amount of wishing would force its return.

The Rise of Mutual's *Game of the Day*

After the fall of Liberty, Mutual had the national *Game of the Day* to itself. Beginning with a Red Sox–Yankees contest on April 18, 1950, Mutual broadcast at least ten games from each American League park and also broadcast from every National League park.[59] The live broadcasts meant no more wire-service interruptions and the addition of player and manager interviews before or after the game. The ballpark sounds would be live, not recorded. At first, Mutual asked its affiliates to find sponsors for the *Game of the Day*. By August 1950, the network had 387 local stations airing the broadcasts, supported by about three thousand sponsors. Once MBS grabbed the Falstaff beer sponsorship from LBS, local sponsorship decreased.[60]

For the first five years, the Mutual's *Game of the Day* lead voice was the beefy Al Helfer, who had worked for all three New York–area clubs during the 1940s. Over his half decade on Mutual, "Brother Al" logged about four million air miles. In *Voices of the Game*, Curt Smith offers a small sampling of Helfer's hectic schedule: "In St. Louis for a Monday game, Helfer might dart to Cincinnati on a Tuesday, then to Wrigley Field for a 2:30 'Ladies Day Special,' then to Detroit and Fenway Park and Yankee Stadium before, finally, on Sunday, sighting rest. For six days a week, twenty-five weeks a year, he boarded a plane once or twice a day."[61]

Every year Helfer went on a season-long road trip, but the *Game of the Day* granted him a place in millions of American homes. From 1950 to 1954, for most fans outside the northeastern United States, Helfer was "the authoritative voice of baseball." Once, after catching a foul ball at Cleveland's Municipal Stadium, Helfer offered to give it to the first fan who wrote to ask for it. He received fifty-two hundred written requests for one very ordinary baseball.[62] In 1952 at least one of Helfer's broadcasts made its way into 65 percent of U.S. households.[63]

Helfer was joined by Dizzy Dean for the 1951 and 1952 Mutual broadcasts, although at least one source suggests that the two did not get along. According to Curt Smith, the two announcers "called each other 'bastard,' argued between innings, and refused to share a plane."[64] Dean, of course, reached his announcer zenith as the top dog on CBS-TV's *Game of the Week*, but Mutual gave "Ol' Diz" his first regular national exposure. Mutual's *Game of the Day* employed many more first-rate announcers during the Eisenhower decade, including Van Patrick, Gene Elston, Buddy Blattner, and Bob Wolff.

By the early 1960s, the expansion of Major League Baseball into the South and West and the continued growth of team networks made national radio gamecasts less viable. In 1961 the new Los Angeles Angels began a twenty-two-station network, and in 1962 the Houston Colt 45s contributed a fourteen-station network. In addition, Mutual had far fewer MLB day games to choose from than when the *Game of the Day* started in 1950, making it harder to find appealing matchups.[65] Anticipating the changing MLB landscape and struggling with finding stations, Mutual dropped the *Game of the Day* after the 1960 season. Daily national, regular-season games faded from the scene until a rebirth on the CBS radio network in 1976.

The end of the Second World War is often seen as the beginning of the end of radio's golden age and the beginning of television's ascendancy. However, for baseball on the radio, both nationally and locally, it was the true golden age. Fearing a drag on attendance caused by over-exposure on TV, owners who relocated teams in the 1950s restricted the number of televised games in their new markets, but they expanded radio coverage after the Department of Justice forced MLB to reduce broadcast restrictions. Other owners followed suit, and team radio networks flourished, while most clubs limited telecasts to weekend games. Although nationally televised weekend games grew in importance during the 1950s, with Saturday and/or Sunday games on all three networks by 1960, even these games were "blacked out" in television markets with Major League teams. Daily television broadcasts of regular-season games were limited in most markets outside New York and Chicago. In the precable era, most Major League markets had only a few stations, and at least three of the available commercial stations were ABC, CBS, or NBC affiliates. Thus, markets with MLB teams often lacked enough independent stations to provide weekday slots for televised games. Before the rise of cable television in the 1980s, the average TV viewer lived in a baseball-deprived market. To follow one's home team, one would need to "see" the game on the radio. And with national coverage from Mutual and team coverage on hundreds of radio stations, virtually every one of America's homes and most of its cars could follow the national pastime on a daily basis. For most Americans during these three decades after World War II, the long baseball season was an aural experience. The home team's announcers were lively uncles who moved in each spring, promising to stay until the silence of autumn's first frost.

Part III

The Television Years,
1961–Present

10 Radio in the Age of Television

As television replaced radio as the center of family entertainment, radio diversified and adapted to its position as a secondary medium. Baseball on the radio moved in a similar direction but at slower pace. MLB owners' limits on regular-season television coverage created a window of opportunity for baseball on radio. Radio maintained a prominent position in the coverage of regular-season baseball games until cable-television coverage of Major League Baseball on regional sports networks became common in the late 1980s.

By the mid-1950s, the structures for radio's coverage of Major League Baseball had emerged. The World Series, and later an ever-expanding number of playoff rounds, was covered by radio, but that coverage became less and less significant to baseball fans as television became the sport's dominant medium. As early as 1951, television rights to the World Series were over six times those for radio ($975,000 versus $150,000).[1] The radio versions of the game's premier contests provided merely an alternative for those who were forced from their TV sets. MLB's long delay in moving the World Series games to prime time—the first World Series night game was in 1971—meant that the radio audience of workers, students, and drivers was somewhat inflated. Nonetheless, the World Series memories from the 1950s on, for most fans, are video images. However, regular-season baseball was a whole other ballgame.

The national distribution system for radio expanded rapidly starting after the Second World War. While national networks declined, regional team networks grew swiftly. Radio's growth spurt was not shared by television. After a freeze on all new station licenses from 1948 to 1952, the FCC issued new television allocation tables as part of its "Sixth Report and Order." The VHF (very high frequency) and UHF (ultra high frequency) station allotments, distributed across the country with more future stations allocated to more populous areas, provided a blueprint for the development of a national over-the-air broadcast television system.[2] VHF service on channels 2–13 was established before the freeze on new station applications. All televisions were able to receive signals from VHF stations. The newly created UHF channels required an additional tuner and antenna for existing sets. Thus, existing VHF stations had both a significant head start and a clear technological advantage over their UHF rivals. As a result, few UHF stations were built until after passage of the All Channel Receiver Act of 1962, which required all televisions sold in the United States to have a UHF tuner starting in 1964. Even then it took many more years before UHF-equipped televisions replaced existing VHF-only sets. For the 1950s, 1960s, and 1970s, most American households outside large metropolitan areas had access to only a few stations. Due to this limitation, coupled with baseball owners' worries about the negative effect of television exposure on game attendance, relatively few fans of the national pastime saw weekday games outside Chicago and New York.

The standard team approach during this era was to limit games to weekend afternoon contests, favoring away games over home games. The Saturday-Sunday approach to TV games worked well for most stations, since they were offered limited, if any, network weekend-afternoon programming during the baseball season. Most importantly, there was no conflict with network prime-time programming. For the baseball teams, weekend television exposure provided weekly promotion of the product without too much damage to the live gate. From 1949 to 1981, the average MLB team televised about forty-six games, less than 30 percent of their schedule. To ensure that the video version could not compromise home attendance, many teams televised only road games. For example, the St. Louis Cardinals averaged thirty-two televised games per year from 1949 to 1981, but thirty of them were road games. The Pittsburgh

Pirates, Houston Astros, and San Diego Padres were even more cautious, televising only road games.[3] In the 1980s, the expansion of ESPN and the development of regional sports networks allowed cable television to offer more regular-season games. With the development first of satellite and then of Internet distribution in the 1990s, the video version of the national pastime was virtually universal for all regular- and postseason contests.

Steady Growth of Team Networks

The baseball radio story was very different from its television story. While television was still limited, the mean number of stations in MLB team networks grew from thirty-three in 1958 to forty-two in 1968 to fifty-four in 1988. Despite the proliferation of television channels increasingly carrying MLB games, MLB team radio networks peaked at an average fifty-five stations in 1992. It was not until the growth of regional sports networks and a new Internet-based distribution system now competing with broadcast radio that the number of stations in an average team network declined to forty-two in 2001. But earlier, newer franchises in the expansion era—after 1960—were especially aggressive in developing extensive radio networks.

By the beginning of the expansion era, team owners saw radio as a powerful promotional tool that could develop new fans in cities and regions that, after decades of franchise stagnation, were finally getting Major League ball. The conventional wisdom was that radio sold the product, while television gave it away. Radio expansion was all to the good, and new MLB owners were good to go. While the St. Louis Cardinals had been the radio leader in the 1950s, newer franchises copied their radio model and assembled networks even larger than the Cardinals' radio juggernaut. The Atlanta Braves occupied the South, averaging ninety-eight stations in their network between 1966 and 2000. Nearly as expansive as the Braves, the Kansas City Royals maintained an average of ninety-four stations from 1969 to 2000. Other expansion teams with large station averages from their inceptions to 2000 included the Milwaukee Brewers (fifty-six), Minnesota Twins (fifty-four), Colorado

Rockies (fifty-four), Montreal Expos (forty-five), and Toronto Blue Jays (thirty-nine). These teams also benefited from expansive territory surrounding their franchises. Relocated or expansion teams moving to the coast encountered an ocean constricting their radio territory and thus acquired far fewer stations in their networks: San Francisco Giants (sixteen), Los Angeles Dodgers (twenty-two), Los Angles Angels at Anaheim (nineteen), Oakland Athletics (sixteen), Miami Marlins (twenty), Seattle Mariners (twenty-three), and Tampa Bay Rays (sixteen).[4]

Baseball broadcasts provided a forum where local and regional advertisers could associate their products and services with both strong national (Major League Baseball) and local (the area franchise) identities. Team announcers, through their everyday presence, became family friends and very effective pitchmen. Smaller stations on team networks offered affordable spots to small, local-community businesses that could not possibly afford television ads. Since baseball was the summer's game, those products consumed in greater quantities during the hot months— beer, outdoor food products, gasoline, and auto parts—were eager radio sponsors. Even some national advertisers shifted focus to radio from television, which they found too expensive. In 1977 Champion Spark Plug, stung by the rising cost of TV advertising, moved all of its baseball support to radio broadcasts in twenty MLB cities, citing "very positive feedback from [its] use of local baseball radio over the last few years."[5]

Since the early 1950s, television has provided the lion's share of national broadcast rights fees. For instance, during the 1977 season, network television rights, shared equally among MLB clubs, averaged about $900,000 per team. On the other hand, each club would earn less than $3,000 from the $75,000 paid by CBS Radio for rights to the All-Star Game and postseason. While national radio rights fees rose dramatically in the 1980s, television rights fees increased even more. But the split between rights for local television and radio presented a different picture.

In 1992 *Broadcasting* began separating the local rights fees for broadcast TV, cable TV, and radio in its annual preview of the baseball season.[6] The difference between local radio and broadcast TV rights were sometimes modest, especially for teams with expansive radio networks and smaller TV markets. For example, in 1992 the Cincinnati Reds received $4 million for their local broadcast TV rights and $3 million for their radio rights, the St. Louis Cardinals received $6 million for TV rights and $4.5 million for radio rights, and the Kansas City Royals received $3.5 from broadcast TV and $2 million from radio.

These TV–radio ratios, however, were exceptions to the rule. Because of vastly larger television markets and more scheduled games, the Los Angeles Dodgers earned $11 million for TV and $3 million for radio, and the Boston Red Sox earned $15 million for TV and $4 million for radio. The New York Mets reported $15–$20 million for TV and $5 million for radio. Broadcast-only TV rights for the Yankees were not reported, but the team earned $40.5 million for cable-TV rights, compared to $5 million for radio. For the fifteen MLB teams reporting both broadcast TV and radio rights, the average figures were $6.84 million for TV and $2.72 million for radio. On average, radio rights generated about 40 percent of the local broadcast TV figure. For the twelve teams with broadcast TV, cable TV, and radio rights listed, radio rights were about 27 percent of the total TV (broadcast and cable) rights. While television had clearly eclipsed radio, the amount that teams generated from their extensive networks was hardly trivial. For a generation of mid-twentieth-century baseball fans, the power of baseball on the radio was palpable.

MLB's Radio Generation

The rich aural coverage of Major League Baseball in the 1950s, 1960s, and 1970s created a generation of radio lovers. Because of the scarcity of regular-season games on television, the postwar baby-boom generation grew up with baseball on the radio. Many of the boomer generation later argued the superiority of radio over the increasingly popular video medium. Curt Smith begins his 623-page celebration of baseball announcers, *Voices of the Game*, with a nostalgic remembrance: "Listening to the woven quilt of baseball on the radio, I retreated to the announcers of my sleepy, sheltered childhood—back to the welcome beckoners of a thousand afternoons. Their voices, more than two decades later, were part of me; they have settled on my consciousness. They formed as much of the web of baseball as did my first fielder's mitt, small and brown and fragile."[7] Twenty years later, Eldon L. Ham, comparing baseball to other, faster-paced sports, saw that baseball's deliberate pacing made the game simply "quintessential radio."[8]

In 1969 the *New York Times* profiled the heartbreak of a baby-boomer Cubs fan from Muncie, Indiana, who followed his team on WGN radio. As the summer wore on, the Cubs raised hopes for the NL East title, only to collapse in the late-summer sun. For the Muncie lad, listening to the Cubs on WGN was a family tradition encompassing three generations. According to his mother, the boy would not go anywhere without his transistor radio: "He takes it into the bathroom, out in the yard, into his room when he's studying. During the school year, he's supposed to go to bed at 9:30, but one night he even snuck the radio under his pillow."[9] When his radio's batteries ran down, he would retire to the family car with his blanket and peanut-butter-and-jelly sandwiches to experience each moment of the Cubs' fading dream. The young Muncie fan was one among 350,000 to 400,000 Cubs listeners spread over eight Midwest states: Illinois, Wisconsin, Minnesota, Iowa, Missouri, Indiana, Ohio, and Michigan. The *Times'* piece captured the magical connection between radio and listener before television commandeered the game. Many young men and women of that generation have similar memories of baseball on the radio.

The radio generation found in the aural medium a liberation for the imagination. Television in the 1950s shrunk black-and-white sluggers to the size of a twelve-inch screen; on radio they could be colorful giants, larger than life. The center fielder running full speed and leaping to snatch the ball just as it was about to clear the fence would soar forever in the listener's mind. But on TV, with the limited camera lens of the era, the catch was scarcely visible. And there was no replaying the magic moment, since instant replay only gradually came to the video game in 1960s and 1970s. But the radio announcer could reprise the play again and again, producing his own verbal highlight reel.

Tony Silvia's recollections in *Baseball over the Air* exemplify the active role that the black-and-white-television generation played in nostalgically re-creating the experience of baseball on the radio: "Baseball on the radio, it seemed to me . . . was never played in 'black and white,' but in a world of nuance, where color becomes a participatory act on the part of the listener, as each of us fill in the pauses and silences with our own unique vision of what the distant park looked like, how the batter stood, the strain of the windup, the stretch, the pitch, and the swing."[10] Silvia's active listeners construct their unique radio texts. While contemporary televised baseball offers endless replays of every seemingly significant moment, radio listeners, guided by play-by-play and color announcers, create their own unique versions of those moments, providing their own instant replays.

In a 1990 *New York Times* article, the radio personality Jonathan Schwartz also lauds the radio gamecast's ability to create radio replays far more "intimate" than television's repetitious reruns of every significant play, concluding that the baseball announcer's relationship with the listener is "not unlike the magic of books, that special arrangement between author and reader."[11]

Schwartz begins his tribute to baseball on the radio with Vin Scully's amazing, spontaneous description of a single play from one of his CBS Radio Network World Series broadcasts:

> Gibson has his lead off first. The pitch to Scioscia is lined deep to left center. Bonds and Van Slyke are racing back, racing, racing, and it's Van Slyke who makes a stumbling, remarkable catch, falling to the warning track but holding the ball! Gibson, around second, is in trouble. Van Slyke is up and throws a strike to Jay Bell who whirls, and with crucial accuracy duplicates Van Slyke's perfect peg, to double up Gibson by a wide and humiliating four or five feet! Scioscia hit the ball as wide and as deep as the August sky and has come away with only the dust of a double play to show for it!

Scully offers listeners not just Bell's accurate throw but one "with crucial accuracy" duplicating "Van Slyke's perfect peg." Scioscia struck not just a hard hit but one "as wide and deep as the August sky," producing not just two outs but "the dust of a double play." For Schwartz, "Scully, the most literate of narrators, has televised a moment of baseball on the radio."[12]

The positive vibrations for the radio game are not limited to researchers and radio hosts. The literary have penned their praise as well. One of the most popular American authors of the baby-boom generation, John Grisham, conjured the baseball radio spirit in his nostalgic 2001 novel *A Painted House*. Grisham captures the daily ritual of Harry Caray's call of Cardinals games, religiously performed by an Arkansas farm family. He locates the daily routine on the front porch, where the family would tune in Caray's play-by-play of the Redbirds. While his mother and grandmother completed their chores, "any loose ends of dinner gossip would be wrapped up," and "of course, the crops were fretted over." The patriarch's little GE radio, purchased in Boston, allowed access to the beloved Cardinals. Grisham reports that the family "seldom missed a game."[13]

Grisham captures four essential characteristics of regular-season baseball broadcasts: their everyday presence, their celebration of a revered announcer, their worship of a favorite team, and their integration into the tapestry of ordinary life. The family received a daily visit from a trusted guide when it took time to "tend to baseball."

Another son of the South, Willie Morris, featured the romance of baseball on the radio in his coming-of-age memoir *North toward Home*. The broadcast of Gordon McLendon on the Liberty Broadcasting System offered a bridge from Morris's observation of country hardball in the South to his Major League–city dreams. Morris would follow two games, the one in front of him and the one from his radio, which brought him, his father and his friends "the rising inflections of a baseball announcer called the Old Scotchman." The combination of the two contests "merged and rolled across the bumpy outfield and gully into the woods" and "seemed perfectly natural to everyone there."[14]

Morris later discovered that McLendon's inflections were part fiction and part fact when he encountered a competing broadcast that was several innings ahead of the Old Scotchman's re-creation. But like many McLendon fans, Morris found that "the Scotchman's, in fact, struck [him] as more poetic than the one [he] had heard first." Through McLendon's prose, Morris "could hear the roar of the crowd, the crack of the bat, and the Scotchman's precise description of foul balls that fell into the crowd, the gestures of the base coaches, and the expression on the face of a small boy who was eating a lemon popsicle in a box seat behind first base."[15] Perhaps it is not surprising that a great writer of fiction should appreciate the work of Gordon McLendon, the most creative re-creator of baseball broadcasts.

A postwar generation of writers and researchers raised on baseball on the radio offers an appealing aesthetic argument for the aural version of the national pastime. With language gifts of their own, they are uniquely situated to appreciate the baseball announcer's verbal art. While baseball on the radio continues into its tenth decade, the generations that followed the boomers have experienced the game primarily through television. During their youths, the video version of the game has constantly improved, adding the center-field camera shot, color, instant replay, better lenses, enhanced graphics, and high definition as the decades have rolled on. Technological advances have totally transformed televised baseball in the twenty-first century from the primitive TV game experienced by boomers in the 1950s. On the other hand, the radio gamecast is much the same. The boomer generation raised on radio may often repeat the "baseball is better on the radio" mantra, but most fans and advertisers moved onto the video medium long ago. While baseball on the radio is no longer the primary way Americans enjoy the sport, it continues to offer the game to fans at times when television cannot: in the car, during a jog, at the beach, or even at work when the job does not require full attention. In the 1970s, one of the first radio networks to broadcast the game nationally saw a new opportunity for baseball on the radio.

CBS Radio Brings Back National Broadcasts

In 1976 CBS Radio jumped back into the baseball picture for the first time since it last covered the World Series in 1938. While NBC had offered World Series and All-Star Game coverage as part of its contract with

MLB, it was losing interest in the radio broadcasts. Richard M. Brescia, then senior vice president of CBS Radio, stated that changes at NBC made the radio version of baseball's crown jewels available to other suitors. "They had gone to a new format on their radio network, all news, and in '75 they decided that sports were interruptive, that it didn't fit in with what they were trying to do. . . . They literally abandoned baseball."[16] NBC surprised baseball commissioner Bowie Kuhn, informing him late in the negotiation process that it was no longer interested in the radio versions of the All-Star Game and the World Series.

Not wanting to lose national radio exposure, Kuhn contacted CBS and offered it a separate and very attractive radio deal. "They wouldn't charge us much for the fees, but would we please do it," Brescia recalled.[17] The CBS Radio executive, who had worked for Mutual during its *Game of the Day* years, believed that baseball on the radio was not a broadcast throwaway but a superior product. "We felt baseball could thrive on network radio, as it hadn't always on network TV, because this was the medium created by God for the game."[18]

CBS's four-year deal with MLB, signed in 1975, was for $300,000, or $75,000 per season, not even a good tip on MLB's $92,800,000 four-year television tab, split by NBC and ABC. Clearly, by the mid-1970s, television was the electronic media's sports king. However, CBS Radio had affiliates in all MLB cities, except Montreal, and its 250 affiliates reached 92 percent of the U.S. population. CBS Radio also provided full coverage of the League Championship Series. Unlike NBC, where the television coverage was of prime importance, CBS Radio privileged its radio-only offerings. In its first year, CBS promoted its baseball broadcasts with full-page ads in *Time*, *Sports Illustrated*, and the *Sporting News* and promos on its NFL broadcasts. Although MLB team networks could continue to broadcast their teams' postseason games, CBS Radio would be the national voice of Major League Baseball.[19] Early sponsors included Kelly-Springfield, Anheuser-Bush, Airborne Freight, and Amana Refrigeration.[20]

Since the CBS contract covered only the All-Star Game and the postseason, the network could court the game's best regular-season announcers for its national broadcasts. Starting with the Cardinals' legendary play-by-play man Jack Buck on the network's All-Star Game broadcast in 1976, CBS employed a pantheon of baseball announcers in its first decade, including the Hall of Fame announcers Ernie Harwell, Jerry Coleman, and Vin Scully. The Hall of Fame player Ralph Kiner and the future National League president Bill White also called games for CBS Radio. According to the CBS executive Richard Brescia, the network preferred excellence to fame: "We didn't just look for names who *happened* to broadcast baseball. We exerted tremendous care, and we went for guys who had great baseball credentials, who we felt could help our broadcasts—guys who know *baseball*, have a sensitivity and love for it, and could transmit that love so that listeners feel it, share it."[21] CBS also knew how to seize and exploit an opportunity. When the Detroit Tigers' team president, the former University of Michigan coaching legend Bo Schembechler, foolishly dismissed announcer Ernie Harwell, after thirty-two seasons covering the Tigers, Harwell was snapped up by CBS in 1992 for its "Game of the Week." The Tigers quickly came to their senses and hired Harwell away from CBS after his one year with the network's weekly game.

Commissioner Bowie Kuhn believed that the deal with CBS "should be excellent for both" MLB and CBS. "Even more important, the vast facilities of the CBS Radio Network will make the All-Star Game and all Championship events available to so many fans."[22] The commissioner was not overlooking the promotional value of radio, but the $75,000-per-year rights fees appear to have been a bargain for the network. For the 1978 season, CBS was selling forty-four one-minute-spot packages for $184,000.[23] By the end of the contract, the *Sporting News* reported that CBS Radio was selling an undisclosed number of packages of forty-four one-minute spots, covering the postseason and All-Star Game, for $205,000.[24]

The network claimed, "Baseball has been a consistent sell-out . . . over the last several years with a wide range of advertisers being attracted by the cost efficiency of radio." Citing a network-sponsored survey by Opinion Research Corporation, CBS said 48 million adults listened to one or more of the World Series games. Richard M. Brescia, senior vice president of CBS Radio, argued, "The Yankees weren't the only winners in the World Series. . . . Our affiliates benefitted from great listener interest in our broadcasts . . . and, you could say our advertisers joined the winners' circle too."[25] The next year, CBS reported that 47 million different adult listeners heard an average of 3.3 of the 7-game 1979 World Series.[26] The All-Star Game also drew substantial numbers, an average of 21.5 million adult listeners from 1976 to 1986.[27]

The CBS Radio deal was negotiated at the same time that ABC began sharing half of the MLB national television package with NBC. NBC would televise Saturday and ABC Monday-night regular-season games. The networks would alternate televising either the World Series or the All-Star Game and League Championship Series. In the mid-1970s, committing to ABC Sports meant committing to its biggest star: Howard Cosell. Before joining ABC's postseason baseball coverage in 1976, Cosell had ripped the game in the *Chicago Tribune Magazine*. "The game is too dull—it's that simple. . . . One must realize that baseball is no longer the national pastime. To say so is sheer pretension."[28] The baseball press was not amused. Cosell was a "blight on the national pastime" and triggered a "roar of disapproval."[29] One critic quipped that Cosell doing baseball was like Bob Hope attending an antiwar rally.[30] Although Bowie Kuhn lobbied to have Cosell booted from the telecasts and even tried to get NBC to take over the entire TV package, ABC Sports' premier announcer was there to stay.

CBS Radio sought to cash in on Middle America's little love–mostly hate, relationship with "Humble Howard." For both its MLB package and NFL Monday-night games, CBS promoted itself as the Cosell alternative, urging Cosell's viewers to mute their sound and listen to Jack Buck and the rest of the CBS crew while viewing the video. Cosell was a hard-edged eastern elitist, a crusty New York rye to Buck's soft midwestern white bread. And most of America still preferred sliced white. After soliciting reader responses to *Monday Night Football*'s competing radio and TV announcers, the *Sporting News* claimed that 90 percent of respondents preferred Jack Buck and Hank Stram to Cosell and his

ABC booth buddies. One fan captured the widespread disdain for Cosell's appropriation of baseball: "The only sound worse than Cosell blathering about football is Cosell blathering about baseball, especially during the playoffs and Series."[31] After Cosell left the ABC baseball telecasts, Jack Craig, a sports-TV columnist for the *Sporting News*, lamented that Cosell's departure left "CBS Radio with no one to kick around on promotions of its coverage of the same prime-time games."[32] When CBS took over the national MLB TV contract in 1990, Jack Buck parlayed his radio popularity into a new role as CBS's lead television play-by-play announcer.

MLB's first CBS Radio deal generated promotion for the sport but little profit for its owners, only about $75,000 per year. However, the network continued to expand its coverage and develop new sales packages. In 1980 it included a five-segment preseason special hosted by Curt Gowdy. For the postseason, CBS offered advertisers a "maximum/minimum package" consisting of fifty thirty-second spots for a fee of $230,000. Advertisers buying the package would receive exposure on division playoffs, league championships, postseason specials, and the first four World Series games. If the Series went more than four games, additional spots came at no extra cost.[33] By 1981 the price for a single spot on the All-Star Game or World Series rose to between $20,000 and $25,000. One spot produced enough revenue to pay for almost one-third of MLB's total radio rights fees. CBS's bargain became a windfall.[34]

After watching CBS profit handsomely from MLB's product, Commissioner Kuhn made a course correction on radio rights fees. CBS would pay more than $2 million a year for the worldwide (except for Canada) radio rights to MLB's All-Star Game and postseason for 1982 and 1983, representing a twenty-seven-fold increase.[35] While TV rights were still billed like the main meal, the radio gratuity was no longer an embarrassment.

The Return of the Game of the Week

In December 1983, *Broadcasting* reported that, after initially agreeing to a one-year deal for the 1984 season, MLB and CBS Radio came to terms on an additional five-year, $32 million deal that would keep the Major Leagues on CBS through the 1989 season. The nearly $6.4-million-per-year deal was a more than threefold increase over the 1982–83 deal. CBS outbid both NBC and ABC for the radio rights.[36] But it took almost a year for the full extent of the package to be known. CBS waited until the "height of interest" at the end of the 1984 baseball season to surprise its affiliates with a new game-of-the-week package, the first on radio in thirty years. While the 1984 season included the All-Star Game and postseason, starting in 1985, CBS Radio would broadcast regular-season games to a national audience for the first time since Mutual's *Game of the Day* ended after the 1960 season.[37] The 1985 schedule included two Saturday games (day and night) for twenty weeks, beginning on Memorial Day weekend. After two years, the regular-season games would start the first week of the MLB season. The contract also allowed for coverage of late-season weekday games with playoff impact.

To promote the new series internally and bring local station managers aboard, CBS sent engraved baseball bats to its affiliates.[38] Advertisers could choose to sponsor a summer package, consisting of the game of the week and the All-Star Game, or a fall package, including the league championships and World Series, or both packages. The network claimed that the regular-season games attracted new advertisers, including some "youth-oriented summer advertisers." Advertisers buying both packages included Anheuser-Busch, Honda, Big A Auto Parts Stores, and Safeco Insurance. The summer-only advertiser Jaymar-Ruby's Sansabelt stretch pants cleverly bought spots that aired during the "seventh-inning stretch."[39]

While the broadcast audience for televised baseball was sometimes stigmatized as "the rural, low-income, the elderly, grade school graduates,"[40] evidence was emerging that CBS Radio's baseball audience offered a different profile. Separate studies by two radio-representative firms, Interep and CBS Radio Representatives, found that listeners to Major League baseball were more upscale than previously thought. Interep found that over 25 percent of men who listened to baseball were college graduates at a time when about 20 percent of the population had a four-year degree. More than a quarter (27.6 percent) had household incomes of $50,000 or more, compared to the medium U.S. household income of $25,000. Nearly two-thirds (63 percent) were aged twenty-five to fifty-four, an age group eagerly sought by advertisers. The CBS study found that 46 percent of baseball listeners were in white-collar jobs, and 23 percent were in professional or management positions; 36 percent of listeners had household incomes over $40,000.[41]

By the end of the contract in 1989, 265 CBS affiliates carried the games, and the network had added coverage of the Baseball Hall of Fame induction ceremonies. In addition, the radio veteran John Rooney hosted a series of sixteen two-minute baseball reports. CBS also continued to feature local team announcers during the "hometown" fifth inning. The 1989 CBS announcing team included Johnny Bench, Steve Busby, Jerry Coleman, Gene Elston, Steve Garvey, Jim Hunter, and Dick Stockton.[42] While Bowie Kuhn had sold the national radio rights for a pittance in 1975, he did leave incoming commissioner Peter Ueberroth with a much healthier financial and promotional radio package. In March 1989, CBS Radio announced details of its next contract with MLB, making it clear that Ueberroth and his team could do even better.

The four-year deal running from the 1990 through the 1993 seasons bumped national radio rights fees to $50 million. The average of $12.5 million per year nearly doubled the rights fees from MLB's pervious CBS contract. As Ueberroth had with the $1.1 billon national television contract with CBS, he had established a new standard for radio rights. The contract called for continuation of CBS's radio coverage of twenty-six Saturday "Game of the Week" broadcasts, the All-Star Game, the League Championship Series, and of course, the World Series. For the additional money, CBS added twenty Sunday-night games and four holiday games: opening day, Memorial Day, July Fourth, and Labor Day. John Rooney and Jerry Coleman would man the Sunday-night booth. CBS would also have the right to broadcast any late-season games affecting the pennant races or division tiebreakers. Additional programming included All-Star Game and World Series specials and a weekly talk show hosted by Brent Musburger. CBS's plan to expand radio coverage was applauded by Bryan Burns, MLB's senior vice president of broadcasting: "Inventory was our biggest consideration, we wanted to expand the package. It makes us better on radio now than ever before." Demonstrating MLB's increasing interest in controlling its international presence the new contract, while expanding Spanish-language coverage, excluded worldwide radio rights, except for Mexico and Canada.[43]

Rights Correction

CBS Radio's final contract with MLB extended through the 1997 season, before the network turned over the national baseball broadcasts to the new sports-radio king, ESPN Radio. The six-year deal was for $50.5 million, about the same as the previous four-year contract, but the annual value represented about a 35 percent decrease. At the same time, MLB and ESPN signed a new $255 million, six-year national cable-TV deal, representing a 56 percent decline from their previous $390 million, four-year agreement.[44] The reduction in radio and cable rights was part of a general decline in national baseball rights fees after the disastrous CBS-TV/MLB $1.06 billion contract for the 1990–94 seasons that lost over half a billion dollars.[45] While the decline in radio rights fees was significant, it did not provoke the radical change that was to come to TV.

The baseball losses sustained by CBS-TV suppressed the interest of broadcast television networks in MLB's product, leading to the formation of the Baseball Network in 1993, a joint venture of MLB, ABC, and NBC. With the Baseball Network, MLB received no rights fees but 87.5 percent of the advertising revenues. History was nearly repeating itself. In 1934 Commissioner Landis sold the radio rights to the World Series directly to an advertiser, the Ford Motor Company. The radio networks were then paid by Ford to carry the broadcasts. In the new arrangement, MLB was responsible for time sales, while the networks provided production and distribution.[46] The networks assumed much less risk, since they paid no upfront rights fees. While some analysts hailed the new structure as the wave of the future, each team could expect about $6 million less than it received under the previous deal with CBS. But it would get much worse. In August 1994, after months of futile negotiations with the Players Association, the owners called a lockout that would end the season. The lockout caused the first cancellation of a World Series in ninety years and continued into the 1995 season. The radical structural shift that was the Baseball Network lasted only two years. In 1995 MLB signed a new five-year TV deal with Fox and NBC, splitting the national broadcast-TV contract.

TV Takes Control

While radio gradually was supplanted by television as the country's primary means of experiencing Major League Baseball in the decades following World War II, the aural medium continued to offer every regular-season game of every Major League team. Team radio networks continued to expand throughout most of the last half of the twentieth century. The Major League version of the national pastime was available to more listeners than ever before. In the 1970s and 1980s, CBS Radio brought back national broadcasts of Major League Baseball: first the postseason and All-Star Game and then weekly regular-season contests. The broadcasts were a financial and critical success and provided baseball with exposure on an additional national network. But as television viewing choices expanded with the growth of cable networks, more and more games were available on the video medium. Fans were listening less and watching more.

Beginning in the 1980s, as regional sports networks began to offer full television coverage of regular-season games, radio no longer held a monopoly on the electronic transmission of daily contests. For youthful boomers, radio was the means to follow a favorite team each summer day. Baseball announcers became family friends and the national pastime on the radio a cherished memory. Many fans from that generation continue to argue that baseball on the radio is a richer experience than any that can be produced by television. For the generations to follow, baseball on television would be the star attraction, with radio receiving only second billing. Despite TV's increasing importance, a new generation of play-by-play announcers and color analysts would prefect the radio craft entrusted to them by their golden-age mentors.

11 The Modern Baseball Announcer

The stories of legendary mike men have been well documented by other writers, especially Curt Smith, who, starting in the 1980s, recorded extensive interviews with many of the golden-age announcers. No comprehensive history of these voices will be attempted in this modest chapter. Instead, it examines how the job of the baseball announcer evolved from an additional chore for radio announcers into a full-time occupation with a fifty-plus-year life span. I offer commentary from the Hall of Fame announcers Red Barber and Vin Scully and two contemporary voices from major markets: Charley Steiner and Pat Hughes. While the competitive realities of broadcasting baseball have changed, the craft of calling the game has enduring qualities, reflected in the intergenerational conversation that follows. However, we start with a snapshot from the golden age of baseball on the radio, when television was still a novelty. The source is a graduate-school thesis completed by a practicing broadcaster and based on his survey of working professionals.

In 1950, as baseball on the radio was approaching its peak, a master's student at the Pennsylvania State College, Milton Jerome Bergstein, surveyed twenty-five sports broadcasters, including Bill Stern and Marty Glickman, about how they covered various games.[1] Bergstein devoted a chapter to the baseball broadcasts. The year 1950 was perhaps the pinnacle of baseball broadcasting, with about a thousand stations carrying live Major League games. At the time, hundreds of small-town stations broadcast local Minor League, American Legion, or even Little League games. At these stations, the gamecast was just one of many assignments.

Bergstein offered advice to fledgling sports broadcasters of many different sports, including football, basketball, boxing, and wrestling. Unlike the Floyd Gibbons School in 1930 (see chapter 3), which focused on broad topics, Bergstein homed in on the specific recommendations for a successful baseball broadcast.

Solid preparation was a must for any aspiring baseball broadcaster, starting with a sound knowledge of baseball's complicated rules. For Bergstein, this commenced with a thorough review of the rule book. "No broadcaster can hope to turn in a creditable performance without a sound knowledge of the rules of the game."[2] He noted that in baseball the announcer is far from the action, and umpires do not usually signal to fans what has happened on the field, as officials do in other sports when there are penalties or breaks in the action. The broadcaster must know what rules are being enforced and must be able to draw from memory quickly the appropriate information. The broadcaster also "should be completely familiar with all available information and statistics concerning that particular player and his record."[3] In the pre-personal-computer era, Bergstein recommended the preparation of a regularly updated index card for each player. Relying on fallible human memory was not endorsed. Broadcasters also needed to keep up with their own club's statistics, perhaps even summarizing the stats themselves.

Unlike other sports in which the offense dictates the action and receives the announcer's initial focus, baseball features offense and defense on each play, and the broadcaster must report on them equally. When the batter steps into the box, the announcer needed to describe his every move. "The broadcaster should note every swing, steps into and out of the batter's box, the batter's search for signs." Then the commentary should switch to the pitcher. "What kind of pitching motion is he using? What type of pitch is he throwing? Is it a strike or a ball?" After the ball is put in play, three questions must be answered until the action stops: "Where is the ball? Where is the base-runner? Where are the other runners who were on base when the ball was hit?"[4] Bergstein then provided his readers with two examples of poor calls and one of a good call from the same moment of action. In his model call, the announcer answered "all of the offensive and defensive questions which a good broadcaster must answer."[5] Bergstein concluded by offering four points for any future baseball broadcaster to remember: "Study and absorb the rules of the game. Strive for a working baseball vocabulary. Develop a workable and efficient system for keeping individual and team statistics. Call every detail of offensive and defensive action."[6]

Baseball Announcing: A Conversation over Time

While Bergstein's brief review of baseball broadcasting technique provides a useful entry, it is only a tantalizing introduction. For Bergstein, the commentary from working announcers was limited to short responses to just a few questions. For a more complete analysis of baseball broadcasting craft, we need to rely on more complete commentary from experts. To organize the rest of this chapter, I borrow an approach that the famed baseball analyst, historian, and writer Bill James employed in his overview of Major League Baseball managers from 1870. James identifies three managerial families: the Connie Mack, Branch Rickey, and Ned Hanlon families. Near the beginning of his managerial history, James shows how the then-contemporary, now-retired managers Tony LaRussa and Lou Piniella could trace their lineage from themselves to their managerial mentor to the mentor's mentor to the mentor's mentor's mentor and so forth.[7] James offers a variety of routes for each manager, but his controlling idea is that players observe their managers and internalize many of their approaches to the game, much as children learn how to be an adult by observing their parents. The same can be said about baseball announcers.

What follows is a continuing conversation about the craft of baseball announcing, running from Red Barber through Vin Scully and then to Charley Steiner and Pat Hughes. The chapter illustrates how the craft that developed in the golden age of baseball broadcasting shapes the work of today's announcers. The Connie Mack, Branch Rickey, or Ned Hanlon in our analysis is Red Barber. While Barber was not among the nascent announcers covered in chapter 3, who invented the craft, he was probably the first nationally recognized baseball announcer, and he established a standard of excellence that is still lauded by today's announcers. As Pat Hughes, the voice of the Chicago Cubs, put it, Red Barber "is simply the most influential play-by-play man in the history of the country, and nobody else is even close."[8]

Barber's professional history is well documented both by himself and by other historians. He started in radio reading agricultural reports at the University of Florida radio station WRUF. He gained fame and local acclaim calling football games at the university. An audition landed him a position as staff announcer at WLW and WSAI in Cincinnati in 1934. Both stations were owned by the industrialist Powell Crosley. Baseball was just one of Barber's many announcing chores. Barber's first call of a Major League game was also the first MLB game he ever saw. The twenty-something redhead held his own against the local Cincinnati favorite Harry Hartman during the 1930s. If he had stayed in the Queen City, he likely would have become a regional but not a national celebrity. But Barber had ambition. In 1936 Barber sought a national position at NBC, interviewing with the network in New York. His work in both baseball and football broadcasts impressed network executives, but they also found him "a little too much of a prima donna."[9] National network fame would wait until 1946, when Barber joined CBS and later created its *College Football Roundup*. However, Barber had already moved to a much larger local stage.

The year 1939 was a big one for Barber. Larry MacPhail moved from the Reds' front office to become president and general manager of the Brooklyn Dodgers. While MacPhail had been initially skeptical of radio, he now saw it as critical to his franchise's position in a three-team market. MacPhail brought Barber to Brooklyn, where he became the "Barber of Flatbush." As the first voice of the Dodgers, he gained national fame, becoming the gold standard of the journalistic approach to baseball announcing. In the late 1940s, Barber moved from radio to television and in 1954 to the New York Yankees. But his legend was established in Brooklyn and on the radio.

Vin Scully was Barber's announcer offspring. He joined Red on the Dodgers announcing team in 1950 and inherited Red's position as lead announcer with Barber's move to the Yankees. In *The Broadcasters*, Barber even refers to Scully as the "son" he never had. When Scully was given the World Series assignment in 1953 after a dispute between Barber and Dodgers owner Water O'Malley, Barber absolved his protégé and gave him his blessing in replacing him at the mike. "Vince you didn't have a thing to do with my resigning the Series. . . . In fact, my boy—you are welcome to my scorebook, . . . my pencils, . . . my egg timer. If you will let me, I'll come to the booth and give you a rubdown before you take the air."[10] Barber first hired Scully in 1950 to help with the CBS *College Football Roundup*. When Barber called Scully to offer him the position, Scully was out; his mother answered the call and took a message. She told the future Hall of Fame broadcaster that *Red Skelton* had called about a job. Scully called his first college football game from the freezing roof of Fenway Park because there was no booth set up for the game. When Barber learned of Scully's stoic effort, he was impressed by the young announcer's resolve. "He didn't even tell me about the lousy conditions when I saw him the following Monday, I had to find out from other people."[11] On opening day 1950, the twenty-two-year-old Scully joined Barber and Connie Desmond in the somewhat-warmer Brooklyn Dodgers broadcast booth, despite never having completed an inning of baseball play-by-play.

Scully readily acknowledged his debt to Barber. In a June 1971 letter to Barber thanking him for a copy of his latest book, Scully said, "I have never forgotten how much I owe you for your faith in me and for the fact that you cared what happened to me." He also thanked Barber for his "lead" that prompted Scully to negotiate "12 carefully selected road games off so as to avoid prolonged separation from the family." Scully closed his letter to Barber with, "I send you a man's love for another man and a fond kiss for Mrs. B. . . . Keep writing and living and loving."[12]

However, in terms of both longevity and critical acclaim, Scully out-shined his pater announcer. In 2014 Scully completed his sixty-fifth season announcing Dodgers games. With each new call, he breaks his own record for the number of games broadcast by one announcer for one team. Inducted into the Baseball Hall of Fame in 1982, Scully has called twenty-five World Series, twelve All-Star Games, twenty-five no-hitters, and three perfect games.[13] Even at eighty-five, he is widely acclaimed as one of the best in the business (see chapter 10 for an example of Scully's verbal artistry). Curt Smith rates him as the number-one all-time baseball broadcaster. Pat Hughes views Scully as "the best at what he does, the most poetic, the most lyrical, the smoothest, the most knowledgeable, the smartest" and says, "he still works his tail off every single day." Hughes also hears "little traces of the influence of Red Barber on every Vin Scully broadcast to this day."

Barber trained and supported the young Scully. Scully in turn influenced the next generation of broadcasters, including Pat Hughes and Charley Steiner. The former Yankees and current Los Angeles Dodgers radio play-by-play announcer Charley Steiner recalled listening as a child on Long Island to the still-young Vin Scully. Upon hearing Scully, the crowd, the crack of the bat, and the peanut vendors, Steiner recalls, "I was like the old RCA-Victor dog," and "from that moment I knew what I wanted to do when I grew up. I wanted to be the announcer for the Brooklyn Dodgers, and they *moved* six months later." Hughes grew up in the San Francisco Bay area but was still quite familiar with the voice of the rival Dodgers. Like many other announcers, Hughes heard Scully on national television when he called the World Series for NBC.

Starting with Red Barber, moving to Vin Scully and then to Pat Hughes and Charley Steiner, these three generations of announcers have covered all but the earliest years of baseball on the radio. The remainder of this chapter examines how each of them faced some of the most important challenges confronting the men and women in the booth. Those challenges include calling the game professionally, balancing the announcer's role of promoter and reporter, working with a partner, and surviving and prospering during the long baseball season.

Calling the Game

The mechanics of calling a baseball game on the radio have changed only slightly over time. Television coverage is far more complex, and the director's choice of camera shot tends to lead the announcer's call. The vastly expanded instant replay and graphic support in television make the announcer's work even more complex. The radio world is simpler, but the announcer bears primary responsibility for a successful broadcast. For Red Barber in the golden age of baseball on the radio, the announcer needed only a "scorebook, record books, four or five sharp pencils, egg timer, and the commercials."[14] The sands of the egg timer ran from top to bottom every three minutes, reminding Barber to give the game score, so that people just tuning in would not be in the dark. Contemporary announcers have added more sources of instant information, provided by a laptop-equipped associate producer. Announcers also can receive inquiries from fans by text, by email, or through social media. But announcers are often too busy to use computers during the game. Pat Hughes is amazed that some younger announcers can email and use Twitter during the game; he cannot imagine doing it himself, although his assistants do. For Barber, in a simpler time, the mechanics of announcing were relatively unimportant. Instead, the "Barber of Flatbush" focused on six "serving-men": preparation, evaluation, concentration, curiosity, impartiality, and imperturbability.[15]

Preparation and Evaluation

In an eleven-page chapter in *The Broadcasters*, Barber elaborates on each of his six "serving-men." "Preparation" begins with studying "our magnificent language." Announcers should read as much as they can about baseball "for professional background and for depth and insight." Skimming many books is better than closely reading only a few, because "an educated man is one who knows where to find information." Barber then lists several standard references of the era, such as *The National League Green Book* and *The American League Red Book*. Reading the sports sections of morning papers is essential, pausing to take mental notes when needed. Barber suggests arriving two hours before the game to allow time to interview the manager, coaches, and players, as available, to obtain the latest information position by position. He cautions against obtaining "off the record" information, noting that during the heat of a broadcast, it is difficult to remember what can be used and what cannot. He prefers never to hear off-record comments at all, observing the obvious: "What you don't know you can't say."[16] Preparation includes getting to the booth at least half an hour before the game and always making a stop at the men's room before arriving at the booth. During a long ball game, "the rising of the inner tide is not conducive to broadcasting serenity."[17]

Barber viewed solid preparation as part of his professional responsibility. Vin Scully shares his mentor's belief in the value of preparation but is driven by a more primal motive than professionalism: fear. "I'm always secretly afraid of going out and sounding like a horse's fanny, which is one reason why I prepare. I prepare out of fear. Sir Laurence Olivier was asked what makes a great actor and he said, 'The humility to prepare and confidence to bring it off.' Believe me, I'm loaded with the humility to prepare."[18]

For Charley Steiner, preparation is one of the key elements distinguishing a good broadcast from a bad one. Morning preparation requires at least an hour researching and reading about the previous day's events on the Internet, then arriving at the ballpark at about 3:30 p.m. for a 7:10 game. He "schmoozes" with the players, coaches, and managers of both teams, collecting anecdotes that "humanize" the participants: "so that in a given moment somewhere in back of the rolodex of my brain, I can pick out that nugget." Pat Hughes also believes in preparation but focuses on what is happening around Major League Baseball, rather than statistical observations. He references the late, great Ernie Harwell, who reminded him that the more statistics you use, the less each means. Hughes also feels that spring-training broadcasts are a necessary part of an announcer's preparation for the long baseball season.

In addressing the crucial role of "evaluation," Barber recommends reviewing the coming broadcast with the engineer, giving a sound check, arranging materials for easy access, and then just "five to ten minutes to sit quietly and bring today's game into working focus." It will be "the last calm before the competitive storm." The announcer needs to set the stage for each game, providing a "headline" that makes the game significant and perhaps unique: "Is first place at stake? Is a pitcher going for this twentieth win? Is a winning streak up for grabs? Is a player trying to hit his sixty-first home run? Is a rookie making his first appearance?"[19]

Concentration

"Concentration" during the long game remains a major challenge for even experienced baseball broadcasters. In Barber's day, concentration was limited to two to three hours. Today, announcers must focus for three to four hours most games. The fear of failure is always present and concentration a means to overcome it. "Any one word, or group of two or three words, can be a public error or a public embarrassment. There is no eraser on a microphone, . . . no rewrite man on the news desk."[20] The announcer's concentration must survive in a noisy environment with engineers, associate announcers, statisticians, and advertising-agency representatives in the background.

"Professional concentration" means that the announcer "has schooled his mind to stay at attention during the game." His speech comes naturally; "he hasn't the time to sustain artificial speech or vocal tempo."[21] Great hitters cannot articulate how they do what they do; they just "see the ball and hit the ball." Great announcers often cannot explain how they "talk the talk." Steiner also believes that the announcer's personal style is part of his natural expression. "All you can do is only be you, and you hope that is going to be good enough. And if it's not, you can't be anybody else, so then it's not going to be good enough." As an announcer, Steiner needs to "paint the picture as accurately" as he can. He is concerned that younger radio announcers, raised on television, do not offer precise descriptions of the action. "'Here's a pitch, it's two and two.' Well, where was the pitch? Where is the defense aligned? Is it cloudy? Where's the crowd? Those are the nuances I don't hear." The Dodgers announcer also thinks that baseball requires an "unbelievable amount of focus and concentration." The voices of the game are "on stage, and there is no safety net. You're tap dancing on the tight wire the entire game."

Curiosity, Impartiality, and Imperturbability

For Barber, "curiosity," "impartiality," and "imperturbability" are related. "The announcer should not care how the game comes out, but he must be interested—curious—as to how it will go." "Curiosity" is rooted in the repeated application of a one-word question, Why? "For every move on the field, there is a reason, a why it was attempted, a why it failed, a why it worked."[22] The broadcaster seeks answers to the why questions from all knowledgeable sources, because listeners want to know. He does not guess why; he asks. In satisfying his curiosity, the broadcaster becomes an informed commentator and generates considerable content to fill the many pauses in action that are, some fans would say, part of the charm of baseball.

On the issue of "impartiality," Barber is an outlier. Trained by Judge Landis to report what he saw and not to offer opinions about it (see chapter 5), Barber believed that the fan "does not want to know what the announcer wants to see happen, but what he actually sees." It is not his right "to care, to root, to anguish, to rejoice—these are the rights of the fan. They are not the rights of the professional announcer, any more than they are of the umpire."[23] The yoking of announcers' impartiality to umpires' objectivity is stunning. Umpires are responsible for the integrity of the game as it is played; announcers only entertain fans and sell products. But for Barber, the announcer is responsible for the integrity of the game's representation in the larger world. In *The Broadcasters*, Barber remembered with pride that a New York writer once reported to him a Brooklyn cabbie's complaint: "That Barber—he's too fair."[24]

The need for accurate reporting means that the announcer must also be "imperturbable." At the most tense moments, the announcer needs to be in control: "When the stakes are big, when the climax is exciting, or the turn of events is stunning with its surprise—like Bobby Thomson hitting that home run off Ralph Branca in that play-off game in 1951 at the Polo Grounds—that is when the listener, who can't see for himself, needs so desperately to know, and to know with detailed exactitude, what is going on. The man at the microphone needs to report, needs to announce the ball, needs not to be swayed as the crowd in the park is swayed."[25] For Barber, Russ Hodges's famous "the Giants win the pennant" refrain after the Thomson blast may not hit the mark. It tells the audience what happened but not how or why. Nonetheless, modern announcers agree that the broadcaster must remain focused during the most critical times and make the historic calls. Steiner remembered his call of Aaron Boone's walk-off home run in Game Seven of the 2003 American League Championship. With the commercial running long, Steiner thought this could be baseball's "Heidi Bowl," but he was back on the air just in time to call Boone's homer. In the back of his mind, he knew this call would be for the ages, and when it was over, he said "I was just glad I didn't screw it up."

While Barber's understudy Scully shares his mentor's point of view on overt partisanship, most announcers believe they must reflect some of their audience's joy and sorrows while accurately describing what is taking place on the field. Steiner, because of his background in news, sees himself as more of a reporter than an entertainer, but he understands that both roles are part of the equation. "There are moments when you apply your sense of humor." For Hughes, a sense of humor is an important instrument in the announcer's toolbox, particularly when there is time to fill between plays. "You should have fun. . . . Baseball is not World War III." But Hughes also cautions that humor should not be forced or offensive.

Most contemporary announcers recognize that some of the game's greatest broadcasters rooted for the their teams. Harry Caray was a fan in the broadcast booth and occasionally in the outfield stands. The Pirates' Bob Prince was a classic "homer," wearing his partisanship on his sleeve. Mel Allen, who entered the Baseball Hall of Fame with Barber as the Hall's first broadcaster inductees, believed a team's announcer could be "partisan" but should not be "prejudiced." He should root for his team but still must report what is happening on the field fairly and accurately. Hughes concurs. The baseball announcer is not a journalist but a team's employee or a station's employee approved by the team. If you are going to be the voice of a team, "you really are an extension of the public-relations department of the ball club." However, Hughes believes the announcer has a clear responsibility for accurate, honest, and fair reporting. "When Sammy Sosa was hitting sixty home runs every year, I felt if he misses the cutoff man when he is playing right field and allows the batter to get to second base, I don't care if he is hitting a hundred home runs a year; that's the way I have to report it. Sosa missed the cutoff man, so Albert Pujols is now at second base and the double play is no longer in order." For today's Major League announcers, the era of the pure reporter has passed, and partisanship is now assumed. However, accurately reporting both the team's triumphs and its tribulations is still crucial for the announcer's craft.

Adding Color: Working with a Partner

Barber worked most of his radio broadcasts alone, and his protégé Scully continues to work by himself today. A few other contemporary announcers, notably Bob Uecker and Marty Brennaman, also work solo. But for most announcers, working with a color analyst is standard operating procedure, and developing a strong rapport with their daily companion is essential. The standard approach is for the play-by-by announcer to be a professional broadcaster and the color analyst a retired player. Many ex-players also have become excellent play-by-play announcers on radio and television, including early greats such as Jack Graney, Waite Hoyt, Dizzy Dean, and Joe Garagiola and contemporary legends such as Bob Uecker, Hawk Harrelson, and the late Jerry Coleman. Today former players are an accepted part of the booth, but in earlier years they faced stinging criticism.

Barber was particularly critical of Phil Rizzuto early in the Hall of Fame shortstop's announcing career. Barber thought Rizzuto was weak in both concentration and preparation. Barber was also angry that he was forced to fire Jim Woods, whom he saw as a competent professional announcer, because the sponsor, Ballantine beer, insisted on Rizzuto, who "had never done one inning of play-by-play."[26] Scully shared his mentor's distain for some ex-players, telling Barber in a letter, "I got into a terrific argument with NBC about the way they hire announcers for the World Series. . . . The NBC battle had to do with a matter of Principle. I am not a big fan of retired JOCKS who retire to the booth."[27]

On the other hand, Hughes, an award-winning professional announcer, cherishes his relationships with player-analysts. Hughes even coauthored a book-length tribute to his late longtime partner, Ron Santo.[28] For Hughes, maintaining an excellent working relationship with a partner is "like a marriage really; you always have to think about the other person no matter what you do," building "an environment that is pleasant for the other person. . . . You try to create karma, you try to do things for them, you try to be unselfish." Good on-air chemistry between partners is something that must "evolve." Not all partners will have it. When good chemistry happens, it is the product of good fortune and hard work.

While the announcer may prefer calling a game solo if it has a lot of action and a good pace, Hughes says that over the long season, "it's great having a good partner." However, you have to "give the other person space" and "let them make their points." Hughes wants to make sure that his partner gets the opportunity to make his comments. He tells his partner, "At the end of this broadcast, I want you to feel like you had every opportunity to say what you wanted to say, period." While some announcing teams may employ cues to let each other know when one wants to speak, Hughes prefers to use eye contact or letting his "voice trail out to let the other person know, 'okay, it's your turn.'" He will also address his partner by name, inviting a direct comment on a play or player. To bring in his recent partner, Keith Moreland, Hughes might inquire, "Well, Keith, why weren't the Cubs able to turn that double play?"

Challenges of a Long Game and a Long Season

For the contemporary baseball announcer, longer is not necessarily better. The season is 162 games, plus many additional spring-training contests. Although veteran announcers earn a few games off, most call the full schedule. Announcers in the Barber era typically called a two-hour game. The typical three-hour modern contest has increased the announcer's pressure-filled broadcast time by 50 percent. While much of that additional time comes from commercials, the games also take longer. Modern batters are schooled in the value of "working the count" to see better pitches, wear out starting pitchers, and gather walks. In this environment, the typical three-hour game can "quickly" become a four-hour one. Hughes treasures the one inning off he gets each game, a privilege earned after nine years with no innings off and an additional three with a half-inning break. Even with the break and a few games off during the season, he is "utterly exhausted at the end of the season."

Not all games are the same. Some move quickly with considerable action or a compelling narrative: the wild-card race is tight, a slugger goes for sixty home runs, a pitcher is nearing two hundred strikeouts, or a runner is looking for his fortieth bag. But there are also the long late-season games when the team is out of it. Steiner knows the announcer must rise to the challenge during "those interminable games that are five hours and nothing is going on": "Those are exhausting. It's August, your club is twenty games out, and they've had nine pitching changes. Players don't seem to care; listeners, if there are any, probably don't care. But that's when we have to work the hardest; we have to be the best."

For Hughes, difficult games often feature too many walks. Too many bases on balls can produce four-hour games, and when combined with a rain delay or two, the contest can go well into the night. He recalled one late-season game that, because of rain delays, started after 10:30 p.m.; Hughes was still broadcasting at 1:20 a.m. The Cubs at the time were about forty games under .500. Any losing season is going to be full of challenges: "You are going to have games that are frankly meaningless in August, September, and maybe even July." Losing also produces anxiety for players, coaches, and the manager. "There is a bunch of paranoia that just seems to ripple through the traveling party from ballplayers thinking they're going to get traded or released to managers and coaches thinking they're going to get fired." Most announcers develop at least a professional working relationship and often a friendship with team members. In bad times, the announcer stays, but he or she likely will be losing friends and confidants as a bad season spirals down.

Barber extended his passion for impartiality to his relationships with players. He believed that the broadcaster should not develop strong personal friendships with players. "I never visited in a ballplayer's house, nor had a ballplayer come to my house." Barber thought he "should be on good, friendly, working terms with them all—speak to them all, be interested in them and their work, but no more interested in one of them than in the other."[29] Scully took Barber's advice "not to get too close to the players": "Very early I found that it was easier for me to be objective, to remain unemotional. Then I saw things with my eyes instead of with my heart, and I cut down on a lot of mistakes."[30]

All sports feature extralong contests and meaningless late-season games for losing teams. Announcers in these sports also can lose friends overnight through trades or termination. But baseball, the national pastime, also requires announcers to fill time. Hughes feels that "the real craft of doing baseball on the radio is filling in between plays; that's the job. . . . Other announcers in other sports have no idea how difficult that is." Most other sports have continuous action, but baseball announcers face some games with limited action and long gaps between those acts. For Hughes, who has broadcast most major sports, the slow pace and breaks in the action make "baseball on the radio . . . the most difficult job to do well." To stick as a baseball announcer, you had better be a good storyteller. The longtime *Los Angeles Times* sports columnist the late Jim Murray saw Scully as a master story weaver: "Baseball is a game of long, lagging periods, and Vinnie distracts you from them. He paints clear word-pictures, he'll segue into a story about Duke Snider that happened thirty years ago, and he'll do it so smoothly you'd swear Duke was still playing now. He's almost like a Celtic poet—he keeps your attention."[31]

Another reality faced by the modern broadcaster that makes the long season even longer is the travel schedule for Major League teams. As the jet age replaced train travel, the transit time decreased, but at the same time, travel distances increased as MLB added West Coast franchises. The shift to predominantly night games also meant that much of the travel takes place in the wee hours of the morning. As the announcer ages, it becomes harder to manage the effects of late-night travel. Barber, for most of his radio career, rarely traveled with his team after spring training. Road games were handled by re-creations from telegraph reports (see chapter 7). For most of the season, the announcer could sleep in his own bed and see his family every morning. The contemporary announcer must take care of much of his personal business in the off-season because travel and the daily grind leave little time for personal concerns.

The most challenging travel scenarios happen when the team concludes a series with a night game and then has a game the next night in another city. Hughes recounts the team's schedule after a Sunday-night game in St. Louis followed by a Monday-night game in Pittsburgh.

> Everyone thinks [Sunday-night games] are so exciting, except people who are actually in the game. They think they're a complete pain because they delay you getting to the next city. The game starts at 7 o'clock; it goes to 10 to 10:30. You don't leave Bush Stadium until 11:30. You take two buses to the airport; it's midnight until you get there. By the time they load up all of the baggage, it's going to be 12:30 to 12:45. You leave St. Louis about 1 in the morning. . . . You land in Pittsburgh at 4 a.m. eastern time; it's a long bus ride. . . . It's a lovely trip unless you are making it at 4 in the morning. It's 4:30 by the time you get to the hotel. . . . You wait for the luggage to arrive from the airport; now its 5 a.m. By the time you [unpack], it's going to be 5:30 in the morning; 5:30—you haven't been to sleep yet, and, oh, by the way, there is a game tonight. . . . You finally fall asleep; you are cross-eyed with fatigue.

The experienced announcer will force himself to get up by noon, or his sleep cycle will be off for several days.[32] With a long tenure and stature, announcers can negotiate for reduced road travel. Barber did it, and Scully followed his lead in the early 1970s.

What Makes for Great Announcing?

While there is a considerable subjectivity in codifying greatness in the craft of baseball announcing, many people have offered their opinions. In *The Voices of Summer*, Curt Smith ranked the one hundred best baseball announcers of all time. Smith used ten criteria: longevity, continuity, network coverage, kudos, language, popularity, persona, voice, knowledge, and miscellany. For each criterion, he rated each announcer on each criterion on a ten-point scale. His rank started with baseball's longest-running announcer, Vin Scully (100 points), then Mel Allen (99), Ernie Harwell (97), Jack Buck (96), Red Barber (95), Harry Caray (94), and so on. The list ends with Major League Baseball's first regular-season-game radio announcer, Harold Arlin (60 points), who also had the shortest career by far. Although television announcers were included, all of the top sixteen announcers started on radio.[33]

For the baseball scholars Anna R. Newton and Jean Hastings Ardell, the "five-tool announcer" has knowledge of baseball fundamentals, is truthful, understands baseball's historical place in American culture, has an appealing voice, and has a style that is "compatible with the rhythm of the game."[34] They also note that, while many announcers have written about their craft, "only Red Barber writes an instruction manual for baseball broadcasters with unequivocal advice for how to be a professional."[35]

My colleague Rob Bellamy and I also attempted to answer what makes for announcing greatness, in an earlier volume on the history of baseball on television.[36] Our MAT theory (medium, announcer, team) includes two factors, medium and team, that appear to influence just how far an announcer will rise in the ranks. While the announcer's individual talent is clearly the most important factor, great announcers are also often fortunate to be affiliated with great franchises, featuring winning teams and an extensive fan base. The all-time greats are also able to take advantage of shifts in the media environment. Red Barber and Mel Allen exploited the opening of the New York market to radio. Gordon McLendon capitalized on the growing need for radio programming after World War II. Dizzy Dean profited from the development of the television *Game of the Week* in the 1950s. Vin Scully's considerable talents blossomed when the Dodgers limited local TV coverage after they moved to Los Angeles. Trapped in a cavernous LA Coliseum, Dodgers fans used their transistor radios and Scully's artful calls to help them "see" more clearly what was happening on the field. Harry Caray was helped by media transformations twice: first by the development of an extensive Cardinals radio network after World War II and then by the creation of WGN's national cable superstation in the 1980s.

None of announcers cited in this chapter offered their own theory of announcing greatness, but they all have opinions about what makes for an excellent gamecast. While Barber offers "six serving-men for the radio-television sports broadcaster," his reflections in *The Broadcasters* clearly privilege preparation, concentration, and impartiality. Broadcasters are, above all else, professionals who take pride in their work and understand that, in radio, they are the eyes of the fan. They must be accurate, detailed, and fair in their calls. Scully, taking his mentor's advice, celebrated the unique characteristics of each broadcaster. Scully relates what Barber told him to "bring into the booth one precious ingredient that no one else could bring there—me, and whatever qualities made me a human being." Barber also reminded Scully not to talk all of time. "Red taught me that dead air wasn't the worst thing, that people liked to hear the crowd once in a while."[37]

Hughes believes that the principles of good radio work are manifold and timeless. They include "good solid accurate reporting, a smooth play-by-play, a little bit of a sense of humor, a little personality, the command of the language, the use of the vocabulary, developing a home run call, creating drama in a broadcast, [and] working with your partner [and] tapping into the best he has to offer." He also acknowledges that good teams make their broadcasters better; the most challenging times are often when the team and the season are in the tank. Steiner believes that the greatest calls come from simply telling the listener what is right in front of him. Years ago he internalized his announcer friend Jon Miller's succinct advice: "Just tell them everything you see." The one constant is the need for an announcer. "Somebody still has to paint the picture." While the technology for delivering the broadcasts has changed and will change more in the future, the best announcers, says Steiner, will have "the ability to describe and tell the truth."

This chapter has reviewed some of the techniques, approaches, and challenges of announcing baseball on the radio. It is a voice craft that, at its best, becomes verbal artistry. Commencing in the golden age of the early 1950s, the conversation documented in this chapter has spun out over three generations of announcers: from the legendary Red Barber to the ageless master Vin Scully to contemporary, award-winning professionals Pat Hughes and Charley Steiner. As we explore some of the most recent developments of the digital age in the next chapter, it is important to remember that the need for a competent professional to describe the action on the field instantly, accurately, and colorfully is unchanged since the craft of baseball broadcasting was born in the 1920s.

12 Baseball Broadcasts in the Digital Era

Baseball has always engendered nostalgia, and baseball on the radio is a major source of that affection. As we saw in chapter 10, the boomer generation, raised on radio, was a cheerleader for the broadcast medium. But as with all mass media starting in the 1980s, the transformation from analog to digital technology impacted baseball on the radio. Even so, traditional analog media continue to offer every game of every Major League team. Today many stations use the same AM frequencies as the broadcast game's pioneers in the 1920s and 1930s. A receiver manufactured in the 1920s can still receive AM transmissions carrying Major League Baseball games. From the announcer's perspective, baseball broadcasting has changed very little since the golden age of radio. What digital media have transformed, however, is the fan's aural access to the game.

While a detailed technical discussion of analog and digital media is beyond the scope of this book, the practical differences should be noted. First, digital information can be compressed by removing redundant information from digitized audio material. That is why an MP3 player such as an iPod can store hundreds of songs, while a compact disc—digital but not compressed—can store only eighty-four minutes of voice or music. The first practical consequence of the digital age is that much more information can be carried over the networks. In broadcast television, the channel width necessary to carry one analog television signal can carry six digital signals of the same quality. Compressed digital audio makes even more efficient use of networks. Also, during the transformation to digital, the Internet's capacity to carry information expanded rapidly, making the World Wide Web revolution of the 1990s possible. Even greater Internet capacity in the twenty-first century transformed the web from a text, graphics, and still-photo medium into an audio and video medium.

One practical effect on radio was that the cost of radio networking plummeted. In the 1970s AT&T charged the St. Louis Cardinals $30,000 a month for the landlines needed to connect the team's broadcast to its vast mid-America network.[1] Currently, the Internet transmission of a digital signal of equivalent quality costs next to nothing and can be managed from a simple netbook computer. The cost became so modest that Internet companies such as Live365.com began offering modestly priced, or even free, Internet radio access to anyone. Soon recorded and live audio podcasts became the AM radio of the digital generation. Anyone with a microphone, a computer, and Internet access could become a radio producer.

The traditional analog radio and television environment privileged distribution channels and production resources. There was a limited number of national networks and local stations in any one market. The new digital realities have made audio and video production and distribution available to the masses. Anyone with a contemporary smart phone can capture video of his or her cat's antics and use YouTube to deliver it to a worldwide audience. Of course, the world can only welcome so many cute cat videos. When anyone can make and distribute audio and video content over the Internet, compelling content becomes even more valuable, and Major League Baseball has compelling content. As Bob Bowman, the chief executive of Major League Baseball Advance Media, put it, "Baseball is uniquely situated for the Internet. It's lively, local, every day, with endings Hollywood can't write."[2]

The Internet: MLB Pounces

Throughout the analog era of broadcast radio and television, Major League Baseball had fought the emerging media. As extensively documented in this book, the battle over broadcast radio lasted nearly twenty years. Broadcast television was initially welcomed by owners but quickly was scapegoated for declining Major League attendance and Minor League contraction in the early 1950s. Television coverage for most teams was restricted to weekend games. West Coast owners quickly embraced pay television in the late 1950s, but that industry never got off the ground because of movie-industry resistance. As the 1960s and 1970s unfolded, baseball's popularity eroded as the television-ready NFL became the glamour sport for networks and advertisers. But as the Internet evolved from a text and graphics medium in the mid-1990s to one that could transmit lower-quality audio signals, MLB seized the day.

Starting in the mid-1990s, a few radio stations originating MLB games were offering their radio feed on the World Wide Web. A 1998 *Chicago Tribune* article documented the enthusiastic reception of Internet transmissions of WGN's Cubs games from a Montreal student and a Cubs fan in Southeast Asia at the Myanmar-Thailand border. WGN reported as many as 28,500 Internet listeners for a single Cubs contest. At the time, only about 5 percent of U.S. radio stations were on the web, only 43 percent of U.S. households had computers, and virtually all consumer Internet connections used dial-up modems. Internet broadcast services such as Yahoo, RealNetworks, and Mark Cuban's AudioNet (later Broadcast.com) were starting to offer music, concerts, and sports on the web. The Internet later made Cuban a billionaire, giving him the resources to purchase the NBA's Dallas Mavericks. But at this stage, most Internet content, including baseball, was free. Even the web enthusiast Cuban thought, "It'll probably be another two or three years before it [Internet radio] makes big money."[3] In three years, the web grew dramatically in scope and capacity, and the potential for people offering the right type of content was clearer. In May 2001, MLB became one of the content providers to buck the "web should be free" mantra of the net generation. Internet baseball fans were not happy.

MLB was not the first major sports league to charge for Internet radio. The NBA had a four-year head start, charging listeners $29.95 per year. In contrast, MLB charged a modest $9.95 for a full season of games on its Gameday Audio, including a $10 gift certificate for the MLB.com store. Clearly, MLB was sensitive to listeners' resistance in an era when there was very little subscription-based content. MLB Advanced Media (MLBAM) also signed a three-year contract with RealNetworks to carry the games. Although competing with MLB.com, Real Networks' higher charge of $4.95 per month made MLB.com's radio offering more appealing. Bob Bowman, the chief executive of MLBAM, saw a shifting Internet landscaping where displaced fans would be willing to pay a modest fee for access to their favorite team's broadcasts. Other analysts saw the free-to-fee Internet transition as mirroring the earlier shift from broadcast to cable television. Jim Reynolds, an analyst with the Seattle-based Ragen MacKenzie, opined, "People think the Internet is free, but if you are going to get really quality stuff, it's just like any other media distribution. You will end up paying for high-quality content."[4]

But a 2001 Consumer Electronics Association survey found that over three-quarters of consumers objected to paying for web-based information.[5] Even Bowman recognized that paying for the Internet was not a popular idea. Offering a baseball metaphor, Bowman told the *New York Times*, "We're trampling down a newly lined first-base path here."[6] The new deal forced local stations to pull games from the web. To deflect criticism, stations told their former Internet listeners to complain to MLB about the removal of the baseball webcasts from station websites. The new MLB.com pay audio service also included the commercials in the broadcast radio feed. Digital listeners "paid twice": once with their seasonal fee and every time they listened to commercials. Bob Agnew, the program director for KNBR, which had carried San Francisco Giants games for many years, summed up the distress of many fans, raised on ad-supported broadcast radio: "The magic of radio is that it is free, charging, even on the Internet, is un-American"[7] Alien or not, MLB's Internet-for-a-fee movement already had its foot in the door.

In 2002 the yearly fee was raised to $14.95, a 50 percent increase, and the $10 MLB.com gift certificate was nowhere to be found. Despite the grumbling, MLB's Internet-based service continued to grow. MLB.com signed up 115,000 Gameday Audio subscribers in its first year.[8] For many fans, slightly less than $15 for access to twenty-four hundred games seemed a reasonable fee, especially as more Internet content providers began to charge.

Internet service providers also began to use sports to improve their subscription rate. In April 2004, EarthLink, at the time the nation's fourth-largest ISP, offered its subscribers a sports bundle, including MLB's audio feeds and eight other subscription-only sports websites. The package cost $9.95 a month. MLB.com saw it as a means of broadening its audience and drawing new subscribers to its other services, including its more expensive video service. MLB.com's Jim Gallagher speculated, "Somebody might buy this EarthLink product and listen to the games and then say to themselves, 'I wish I could actually watch this.'"[9]

MLB.com's push into subscriber services was beginning to pay off. The website, including its audio and video subscription services, generated $36 million in 2001. By 2004, with projected subscriptions of 750,000, MLB.com brought $140 million into MLB's coffers. As broadband developed and the webcasting of video became more common, MLB.com's revenues expanded rapidly. In 2005 MLB.com's revenues jumped to $236 million and in 2006 to $380 million. In late 2007, MLBAM was streaming nearly twelve thousand live events, including the NCAA basketball tournament and the World Baseball Classic—more than any other website. MLBAM's stock was valued at nearly $5 billion, or more than $150 million per team.[10]

In September 2006, MLBAM flexed its expanding new-media muscle by removing all its podcast materials from Apple's iTunes, indicating that it no longer needed Apple's massive distribution system. At the time, three-quarters of MLB's forty- to fifty-thousand-per-day podcast downloads were coming from its own website.[11] In 2011 Business Insider ranked MLBAM's value as eighth among the world's top one hundred private tech companies, predicting revenues of $620 million in 2012.[12] That $620 million would represent about 8.3 percent of MLB's $7.5 billion 2012 revenues.[13]

Unlike local radio and television revenues, the MLB.com bounty was shared equally among the thirty Major League clubs. After decades in which first radio and then television had increased the revenue disparity between "large market" and "small market" clubs, a new media product was helping to close the gap. In the media age, the distinction between small and large market had more to do with media-market size than overall population. On the owners' side, the 1994 baseball lockout had been pushed by the small-media-market teams' perceived need to restrict players' salaries so they could compete with large-media-market clubs. The lockout canceled the 1994 World Series and was a public-relations nightmare for MLB. Fighting with the players' union was a losing strategy for all. Growing the media-revenue pie, so that all teams would make profit, despite market limitations, was a winning call for all. MLB's shared revenues continued to expand throughout the decade. By 2012 MLBAM produced about $20 million in revenue for each Major League franchise. While only a small part of that came from Gameday Audio, MLB.com's Internet radio service led the way, helping lower the barriers to fee-based Internet services. The Internet was no longer free, but for those who could afford to pay, the baseball product continued to improve.

Satellite Radio

By the early 2000s, MLB.com had found an audience for out-of-market radio broadcasts on the Internet. But Internet radio was just developing, and access to streaming audio was restricted to those who had personal computers with a wired connection to the Internet. By 2004 MLB's Internet-radio package had grown to only 850,000 subscribers, despite several years of incubation.[14] Most Americans accessed the Internet through dial-up modems with modest bandwidth that limited the quality of audio transmissions. At the time, only about 25 percent of U.S. households had broadband connections. Wi-Fi connections were rare, and cell phones were used to make voice calls and receive text, not to access the Internet. Most Americans were unable to access the baseball cornucopia that MLB.com offered for only a few dollars a year.

Since the 1950s, radio had been a medium on the go. The time periods with highest listening levels were morning and afternoon drive time, when suburban commuters, trapped on freeways in their cars, spent time with the radio. For the digital revolution to have full impact on baseball broadcasts, it would need to become mobile. In October 2004, mobility came to digital baseball in the form of satellite radio.

During 2004, the nation's two competing satellite radio services, XM and Sirius, were engaged in a content arms race. XM held a major subscriber advantage, with 2.5 million to Sirius's 700,000. As is often the case in an oligopoly, the weaker player made the biggest initial play. In 1939 the fledgling Mutual Broadcasting System outmaneuvered the much more powerful NBC and CBS networks by obtaining exclusive rights to the World Series from Commissioner Landis. In 2004 Sirius began a seven-year, $220 million contract with the NFL for exclusive satellite-radio coverage of its games. Sirius had already signed exclusive satellite deals with the NBA and the NHL. With three major sports in its pocket, Sirius next signed the most popular shock jock in the country, Howard Stern, to a five-year, $500 million deal. Initially, satellite radio had marketed itself as a national, commercial-free music alternative to traditional local broadcast radio. But in signing Stern, the NFL, the NBA, and the NHL, Sirius was changing the game plan, embracing the "content is king" philosophy of media competition. XM needed to reply in kind. To match Stern, XM signed its own shock jocks, Opie and Anthony, who began their XM show four days after Stern signed with Sirius. Existing contracts with NASCAR, the Big Ten for basketball games, and the Pac-10 for football and basketball contests gave XM some sports programming. But XM's biggest haul was Major League Baseball.

Two weeks after Sirius signed Howard Stern, XM signed a contract with MLB that could reach eleven years and $650 million. The contract called for $10 million up front, $40 million in the first year, and then $60 million per year through 2012. MLB had an option to continue the contract for three more years at $60 million a year.[15] The difference between the NFL and MLB deals was striking, $220 million versus $650 million. But football and baseball on the radio are also very different. Sirius was buying only 256 NFL regular-season games per year, while XM was purchasing rights for about twenty-four hundred MLB games.

Baseball was also more of a radio sport. Professional football is appointment television. Fans make time in their schedules to watch the games. But many baseball fans still follow the game on radio, listening when it is convenient to do so. As one industry analyst put it, baseball "will help differentiate [XM's] services at the retail distribution level. . . . The difference between the NFL and the MLB is that baseball already has a very large audience that listens to it on the radio." For XM's chief executive, Hugh Panero, Major League Baseball was "the fastest way" for the company to increase "credibility."[16] As with radio in the early 1920s and television in the late 1940s, the national pastime was the lure to attract paying customers to a new communication technology.

The initial response to XM's baseball play was mildly negative. Some critics believed that the wide coverage of baseball on broadcast radio stations, some with far-reaching, high-powered AM signals, would blunt any positive impact on XM's subscriber count. If fans only wanted out-of-market baseball broadcasts, MLB.com offered the same games on the Internet at a fraction of the price of XM's monthly $9.95 fee for its full channel lineup that included baseball. Other analysts felt that there just were not enough out-of-market fans for the deal to benefit XM.

Despite these skeptical predictions, the short-term results were encouraging for XM. By the end of July 2005, the middle of XM's first baseball summer, subscribership had jumped to 4.4 million, and XM was raising its end-of-the-year subscriber forecast to 6 million. XM credited the "gains in part to customer interest in its comprehensive broadcasts of Major League Baseball games."[17] Indeed, a survey of new XM subscribers in May and June 2005 found that 23 percent were drawn to the satellite service by the MLB games.[18]

The analysts had failed to see the value of the service for hardcore baseball fans, especially boomer-generation radio lovers. While out-of-market fans were limited in number, there was a niche audience of baseball-on-the-radio fans who were ecstatic about the new service. Many of them made a connection between the new XM service and their own youthful experience of listing to distant baseball broadcasts delivered via nighttime AM sky-wave signals. The superstar sports broadcaster

Bob Costas, a lifelong fan of baseball on the radio, saw XM's radio baseball buffet as a wonderful blending of the past and present: "What you have here is cutting-edge technology that brings in the past."[19] The *Chicago Tribune*'s Bob Verdi, a self-professed "baseball nut," wrote, "XM radio is not a service, it is a narcotic." Verdi recalled asking his father years ago for the car keys so he could "work the dial in search of a static-ridden transmission from some faraway ballpark."[20] Now XM's MLB service brought him every Major League game in a wallet-sized radio. That small satellite radio gave voice to a pantheon of big league announcers, including Vin Scully, Harry Kalas, Marty Brennaman, Jerry Coleman, Herb Carneal, Denny Matthews, Bob Uecker, Mike Shannon, Skip Caray, and Jon Miller. Costas and Verdi were not the only XM baseball enthusiasts.

Displaced fans appreciated the ability to follow their favorite teams. Some fans in remote areas were happy to finally get baseball on the radio. Many enjoyed the variety of announcers. The early adopters of XM's baseball service were also great fans of the radio game. A computer programmer from Columbia, South Carolina, said, "Baseball is one of the only sports where it is better to hear it on the radio than see it on TV . . . . There is something about hearing the call and developing a mental picture of the situation as it is happening." Another radio fan, an art museum administrator, gushed about "the pure joy and freedom that the combination of baseball and the radio can provide": "Baseball on the radio is the background to my life. . . . It has the ability to transform tedious and boring chores into a wonderful escape to the ballpark while hand and body are busy on autopilot."[21] One delivery driver built his work schedule around Cardinals games, starting his day early to catch a day game or in the late afternoon to hear a West Coast night game. "It makes me feel at home even when I'm a long way away."[22] The early adopters clearly loved their new access to the national pastime, but satellite radio was gaining competitors even as XM was just embracing Major League Baseball.

In 2005 one industry analyst estimated that the two satellite services would corral 46.7 million subscribers by 2011.[23] Some prognosticators even ventured that satellite radio would surpass cable television in popularity, capturing more than 90 million subscribers. Subscribership was expected to take off after satellite radios became standard in automobiles. For the 2005 model year, GM offered XM radios as options in more than fifty vehicle models, while Ford had already signed a deal with Sirius to equip one million 2006–7 cars with its receivers. At that point, XM and Sirius began to pose a major threat to traditional broadcast stations.

A Changing Radio Industry

The Telecommunications Act of 1996 removed national ownership limits on radio stations, producing a radical consolidation of the industry. Corporate owners such as Clear Channel and Infinity paid dearly for their new stations. To reduce costs, staff was cut, formats standardized, and commercial load increased.[24] Many radio-industry critics saw satellite radio as the antidote to broadcast radio's creative contraction. But neither X M nor Sirius anticipated the explosive growth in cellular data transmission and the smart-phone revolution.

The iPhone/smart-phone revolution transformed a voice and text device into a portable audio, video, and Internet center. The development of apps made it even easier to use data services. As early as 2002, MLB was working with its RealNetworks partner to transmit M L B games over cell phones. Over the Internet, RealNetworks sent the game broadcasts to cellular providers, which then retransmitted the games to their customers. RealNetworks saw the M L B broadcasts as part of its strategy "to take the Internet off the PC and onto other devices." AT&T Wireless signed onto the service in early September, offering its twenty-million users an unlimited number of MLB games for the remainder of the 2002 season for $19.95.[25] By 2005 M L B was selling its audio feeds directly to cell-phone providers.[26] While the initial charge of $9.99 a month was steep, the pioneering service showed that the cell phone could give baseball fans the same universal exposure to Major League games that XM was just beginning to offer. The growth of smart phones dramatically altered the prospects for satellite radio, just as the big bird in the sky appeared to be taking flight.

Although cellular competition hurt, satellite radio's extravagant spending and the explosive growth of digital music players, starting with the iPod, hurt even more. Two years after the MLB, NFL, and Howard Stern deals, as well as other expensive contracts, XM and Sirius announced plans to merge. Together their subscribers totaled fourteen million, well below early, more optimistic forecasts. The merger of the only two satellite-radio companies in the United States created an industry monopoly. Both the Department of Justice and the FCC expressed reservations despite the two companies' shaky financial state. Together they had $6 billion in accumulated losses and both faced declining share value.[27] In May 2008, with seventeen million combined subscribers, the Department of Justice approved the merger. The FCC came on board later that summer. Both government watchdogs had bought XM and Sirius's argument that broadcast radio, iPods, nascent HD radio, and Internet audio on cell phones provided consumers with enough audio choices. However, the merger relief was not enough to prevent the new Sirius/XM merged service from considering bankruptcy protection in early 2009. That scenario was avoided by a cash influx from Liberty Media. By 2012 Sirius XM's CEO, Mel Karmazin, was gone after conflicts with Liberty Media's chairman, John Malone. In early 2013, Liberty Media took control of Sirius XM after approval by the FCC.

While the service continues, the future of satellite radio remains cloudy, even after the company's bloated contracts with content providers come off the books. As smart phones become as universal as cell phones, the Internet will become fully portable and integrated into automobile sound systems. Satellite radio's last protected space, the family car, will be open to all web-based audio services. However, MLB will remain in a strong position as long as it maintains control of is audio and video content.

New technologies and new service providers will come and go, but all will need attractive content. Bob Bowman, the chief executive of MLBAM, reflected on the sport's web virtues: "The Internet probably works for baseball more than any other sport. We have 15 games a day and tons of content."[28] In the old broadcast-television environment of three major networks, baseball had too much content. Weekly NFL games were appointment television. Daily regular-season baseball games were only occasionally critical. In the 1950s, radio, not television, had the stations to exploit the everydayness of baseball. In the twenty-first century, the Internet now has the distribution capacity to maximize the value of MLB's content, which includes audio and video webcasts, feature stories and analysis, breaking news, scores and statistics, and fantasy games. Since 1921, Major League Baseball has provided audio content that draws customers to various media platforms. In the twenty-first century, the value of Major League Baseball to media companies is one of the few constants in a rapidly altering media environment.

Traditional Radio in the Information Age

As more alternative distribution channels multiplied, baseball on traditional broadcast radio experienced the demassification. As early as 2001, broadcasters were worried that websites running video and audio clips were diluting the value of their television and radio rights. MLB instituted new rules to limit what news organizations could do with photographs taken at games. Photos could be used only in connection with stories about the games. Harking back to baseball-radio battles of the 1930s, the new rules also restricted play-by-play coverage of the games. MLB saw "a baseball game as a private performance whose information they totally control, rather than a public news event which ought to be in the public domain."[29] In the 1930s, baseball owners tried to protect attendance at their games, which provided them almost all of their revenues. Unauthorized radio re-creations of the games based on play-by-play reports were the main concern. In the twenty-first century, MLB wanted to protect its television and radio partners from the poaching of their exclusive rights by websites.

But MLB's radio partners were more concerned about poaching by MLB's Internet presence and XM contracts than competition from the working press. The first years of the twenty-first century represented the final period in which broadcast radio rights were protected. During the remainder of the decade, the growth of satellite radio and Internet audio, delivered online or on cell phones, eroded the value of local radio rights, while MLB gained new revenues from these digital platforms. For a time, broadcast rights also continued to grow. In late 2001, the Yankees sold their radio rights to WCBS-AM for five years for a record $9.75 million yearly. CBS saw Yankees radio as a "blue-ribbon" property and was willing to pay for it.[30] The fee was more than double what WGN paid for Chicago Cubs radio rights, although those fees were likely suppressed because the Tribune Company owned both WGN and the Cubs.[31]

In 2002 KOMO in Seattle won a bidding war with KIRO for rights to Mariners broadcasts. The team was selling at just the right time, having won 116 games in 2001. Despite a market only a fraction the size of New York, KOMO paid just under $10 million for each year of the six-year deal. Baseball was especially attractive because it drew a sizable audience in the evenings and weekends, when radio listenership declines. It also provides a promotable product that brings to a station listeners who would otherwise ignore it. For a team's fans, the local baseball station occupies one of the memory buttons on the car radio.

Despite siphoning by digital outlets, broadcast rights fees continued to grow. By 2005 the Atlanta Braves earned $13 million annually from their radio rights, and the next year the Red Sox signed a ten-year deal with Entercom (WEEI-AM, WRKO-AM) for about $16 million per year.[32] Still, broadcast executives were not happy.

CBS Radio chairman Joel Hollander complained that MLB.com's Gameday and XM's MLB coverage were rapidly diluting the value of broadcast radio rights. Each additional distribution channel made the local rights less valuable. Blackout strategies protected local television-rights holders, but radio was open to competition. One radio consultant believed that stations lost money on ten out of every eleven deals.[33] In late 2006, Hollander acted on his concerns when CBS's radio rights for the Detroit Tigers games came up for renewal. Michigan was entering a deep recession, and the advertising market was in decline. CBS Radio would no longer pay $5 million in rights fees to the Tigers. Instead it offered a revenue-sharing arrangement to the team. In Minneapolis, CBS Radio ended a four-decade bond with the Twins. Despite winning the World Series in 2005, the Chicago White Sox took $1 million less per year in their next radio contract. While flush-market franchises were still bringing in rights increases (the Yankees expected a 17 percent increase in their new CBS Radio deal), baseball's small- and medium-market teams were looking at a new reality.[34] The broadcast industry's resistance forced teams to look for new radio-rights arrangements.

In 2004 the St. Louis Cardinals ended a decades-long relationship with KMOX, transferring their radio rights to Simmons Media Group (KSLG, WFFX). In addition to rights, the Cardinals were given an equity stake in the radio group. The new stations lacked KMOX's powerful fifty thousand watts, prompting complaints that reception, even in the St. Louis area, was poor at night.[35] By 2010 the Cardinals were back on KMOX. The bottom-feeding Tama Bay Rays were forced to take their radio rights in house, selling their own advertising. The team paid a fee to WHNZ to air the games. The technique was a return to the 1930s, when some teams bought time and found their own sponsors.

The Tampa Bay Rays exploited the new arrangement by offering free publicity to prospective and current advertisers during game broadcasts. The slow pace of baseball allows for considerable extraneous talk time and promotion during the gamecasts, a practice that goes at least as far back as WGN's promotion of *Sam 'n' Henry*, forerunner of *Amos 'n' Andy*, in the 1920s.[36] In Boston, Entercom's WEEI/WRKO sold naming rights to its network, further commercializing its product. Asking "several million dollars a year," Entercom offered to tell listeners at least twenty-one times per game over its sixty-six-station network, "We'll be right back on the WEEI/WRKO (Your Company Name) Red Sox Radio Network."[37]

The Current State of Baseball on the Radio

Although the digital age is now well entrenched, baseball on the radio still originates in the over-the-air broadcast. The local flagship station and team network structure produces the game broadcast that is then offered by MLBAM over the Internet or Sirius XM by satellite. The technology of AM radio transmission has remained the same. Receivers built in 1923 that could receive Graham McNamee's call of the Yankee-Giants

World Series could bring in Pat Hughes's daily call of the Chicago Cubs' uneven fortunes. As of 2012, the top-ten flagship stations in audience size were all on the AM side of the dial, including several stations that started broadcasting baseball in the 1920s (e.g., WGN in Chicago, WLW in Cincinnati, KMOX in St. Louis).

As additional television and Internet connections have replaced many radios in the home and workplace, the automobile has become the primary venue for listening to baseball on the radio. In the auto-intense Los Angeles market, Dodgers broadcaster Charley Steiner cherishes his one-on-one relationship with the captive car audience. "When you're on the radio as opposed to calling a game on television, you know you've got a captive audience. They're driving by and large. . . . So radio means you really have a one-to-one relationship with your audience, and that is what I think about when calling a game. I'm talking to one person; it could be one times a million, but it is one person."[38] Although Steiner is rarely talking to a million listeners, his broadcasts do reach many men aged twenty-five to fifty-four, an elusive demographic group targeted by many advertisers.

Recent Arbitron data shows that MLB's radio audience can be substantial. On opening day 2012, the top-five-rated MLB teams captured an average share of 34.7 (percentage of people listening to radio) for men aged twenty-five to fifty-four. The total number of listeners averaged 466,000 for those top-rated teams. Although large-market teams such as the Yankees, Mets, Cubs, Phillies, and Red Sox produced the largest audiences, small-market clubs such as the Indians, Reds, and Brewers cracked the top ten. Indeed, the Detroit Tigers had 510,000 listeners, second only to the Yankees. Of historical interest, five clubs that most aggressively used radio in the 1920s—the Cubs, Red Sox, Indians, Reds, Tigers—were all in the top ten.[39]

But opening-day radio ratings, like opening-day attendance, can be deceiving. As the season wears on and as a team's fortunes change, the audience drops off considerably. For the 2012 season, the average number of listeners to the top-ten-rated MLB teams was substantially less than on opening day. Additionally, the three-year trend showed a decline from 192,000 in 2010 to 183,000 in 2011 and 172,000 in 2012 for the same teams. As with opening-day listening, MLB teams with the longest history of radio broadcasts did the best job of capturing their targeted adult-male listeners. From 2010 to 2012, the top two teams in radio shares of men aged twenty-five to fifty-four were the Cincinnati Reds, reaching 24.6 percent of that audience, and the Detroit Tigers, reaching 22.7 percent.

The Arbitron ratings also reflect the impact of a team's success on radio ratings. For example, the Milwaukee Brewers' share jumped from 13.1 in 2010 to 22 in 2011 after they improved from seventy-seven wins in 2010 to ninety-six wins with a National League Central Division title in 2011. The Pittsburgh Pirates' share of men aged twenty-five to fifty-four more than doubled from 7.2 during their fifty-seven-win 2010 season to 15.5 in their seventy-nine-win 2012 season.[40] Clearly, fair-weather fans want to tune in when the team is winning, but a substantial number of die-hard fans listen even when their team struggles.

The digital-age challengers, Internet and satellite radio, have provided the daily, predominantly AM, baseball broadcasts some serious competition. While the three-year decline in listening among the top-ten-rated MLB teams reveals that broadcast stations are losing some listeners, the substantial rights fees paid by sponsors in the new millennium suggest that the old baseball broadcast warrior is far from finished. Baseball on the radio no longer has a distribution monopoly, but it still provides the product that feeds all the other distribution channels.

In the digital era, the major threat for baseball on the radio may come not from digital competitors but from an advertising glut spawned by inflated rights fees. With current radio rights to the Chicago Cubs in the $10 million range and to the top-of-the-heap Yankees estimated to be $15–20 million,[41] broadcasters are forced to pack more advertising into the games. Since the 1930s, critics have lamented the use of "drop-in" announcements, in which game action is tied to a particular sponsor. But in the twenty-first century, the number of drop-ins has exploded. In the contemporary baseball broadcast, they can take many forms.

A recent *New York Times* article offered many examples from Yankees broadcasts:

1. When the Yankees pitcher paints the corner with a strike, "painting at the corners is sponsored by CertaPro Painters. Because painting is personal."
2. The first Yankees walk brings an invitation to "just walk into any of CityMD's six convenient locations."
3. Yankees calls to the bullpen have three different sponsors.
4. The Bronx Bombers' postgame wrap-up is branded by Reynolds Wrap.
5. The otherwise-unremarkable fifteenth out of Yankees games prompts the announcer to tell listeners that "a 15-minute call to Geico can help them save 15 percent on their auto insurance."
6. The umpires' lineup and the broadcast copyright policy are sponsored by two different law firms.

Ironically, the Yankees, one of the final franchises to embrace radio, appear to be leading the charge into a hypercommercialized era of baseball on the radio. By the *Times'* accounting, the July 4, 2013, Yankees-Twins contest had sixty-one drop-ins, while the Independence Day Mets-Pirates game had twenty-one.[42] This advertising is in addition to traditional commercial breaks before and after each game and during every half inning. The drop-ins do not necessary generate additional revenue. In many cases, the drop-ins are bonus plugs offered to spot advertisers to help justify the soaring cost of bringing fans MLB broadcasts. Because teams are focused on maximizing their rights fees, radio groups that invest in baseball must find ways to generate more revenue. In the twenty-first century, drop-ins have become a popular approach. While drop-ins are hardly a new marketing strategy, their increased use may seriously compromise the radio product. After all, baseball fans did not tune in to the Home Shopping Network!

Epilogue

The history of baseball on the radio is a temporally protracted version of the history of electronic media. The first wireless medium was the creation of a technology that had been refined during the First World War and was activated by a new application of that technology. No longer focused on providing point-to-point communication where telephone or telegraph lines dare not go, wireless became radio by "broadcasting" its signal to as many takers as possible. Radio broadcasting grew rapidly in the 1920s as many new stations offered the expanding audience of radio listeners whatever programming they could obtain at little cost. Like television in the 1950s and the Internet in the 1990s, radio exploded on the American scene. In less than a decade, it became an essential new expression of popular culture.

Radio's growth was aided by an open system. Broadcast licenses were granted to virtually every applicant, with few government restrictions. While the result was technological chaos until the creation of the Federal Radio Commission in 1927, open licensure triggered an abundance of experimentation and participation. But the fertile ground of radio broadcasting did not extend to baseball on the radio. Major League Baseball was a cartel that evaluated the potential benefits or harms of the medium on the basis of its own interests. There were plenty of stations but only a limited number of sources of Major League Baseball in the nation.

Baseball on the radio originated as a publicity stunt. First KDKA in Pittsburgh and then WJZ in Newark used Major League Baseball to draw listeners and the press to their new stations. These nascent ether trickles were produced with little input or forethought by the baseball owners. The World Series was a national institution controlled by one man, Commissioner Kenesaw Mountain Landis. If the judge could be co-opted, Series coverage would expand and help promote both baseball and the new medium. He was, and it did. By 1927 Series coverage reached coast-to-coast, offering an avalanche of publicity that helped solidify Major League Baseball's position as the acme of the national pastime.

The Series' prominence put it on the same time line as radio itself. But the universal broadcasting of regular-season games was delayed. Owners slowly split into pro- and antiradio camps, and the universal coverage of regular-season games by the medium took nearly two decades to unfold. Only after the three New York teams joined the rest of the cartel in offering all of their home games in 1939 did Major League Baseball finally enter the radio age.

A second medium delay occurred after World War II. After a brief honeymoon in the late 1940s, owners once again split over the benefits of television. Many saw overexposure on television in New York, Philadelphia, and Boston as a major catalyst for the relocation of the Dodgers, Giants, Athletics, and Braves in the 1950s. The relocated franchises all had restrictive television policies; some telecast no games at all or only the home opener. Most other franchises limited television to weekend games or just road games. Most owners offered their fans some televised contests, but the only daily access to Major League Baseball was on the aural medium.

While the golden age of network radio ended in the 1950s, the golden age of baseball on the radio lasted another two decades. Only the emergence of cable television, including ESPN and regional sports networks in the 1980s, opened the doors to extensive visual coverage of regular-season games outside of a few franchises. That shift moved baseball on the radio from a primary to a secondary media tier for most baseball fans. Those aging fans who had been raised on the radio version of the game cherished it and waxed poetically about it for decades, but the next generation of fans watched rather than listened to the national pastime.

The third delay was far briefer but once again favored the aural medium over the visual. The limited data-transmission capacity of the Internet made video transmission of MLB games difficult but enabled clear audio signals. In 2001 MLB repackaged its radio broadcasts as Gameday Audio, making its universal aural coverage available to the emerging Internet generation.

MLB created Major League Baseball Advanced Media (MLBAM) to exploit the newest electronic medium, pooling revenues and equally dividing them among its franchises. The financial structure, modeled on the national television contract, tempered the vast disparities in local media revenues. MLBAM's "audio only" period was brief, but it did establish a new digital revenue stream shared equally among large- and small-market teams. Local television contracts still contribute mightily to MLB's revenue disparities, but MLBAM's piece of the pie provides hope for a more equitable future.

While MLB's future might feature greater parity, the future of baseball on the radio is far from clear, simply because the future of radio is far from clear. AM and FM radio is still viable, but it may prove an analog dinosaur in the digital age. The car radio, long the captive-audience savior of the medium, has become a digital-audio arcade. Traditional radio competes for the driver's attention with satellite and HD radio, Internet-based digital audio services (e.g., Pandora, Spotify), CD players, MP3 devices featuring music and podcasts, and cell-phone calls (no texting, please). The primary aural delivery system for MLB's seasonal product is still traditional radio, but the "digital native" generation has learned to find its sounds elsewhere.

In the digital age, distribution can take many forms, but captivating content will find an audience. Major League Baseball offers such content. Baseball is still, in the words of the Hall of Fame baseball writer Roger Angell, "The Summer Game."[1] So long as the seasons still change, so long as we need to hear the ball games we cannot see, so long as we want soulful sessions with the voices of the game, the "crack of the bat" will still sustain this summer game for its passionate listeners.

APPENDIX

Number of Team Radio Stations by Year, 1936–2001

Statistics for the years 1936–58 are from the *Sporting News*; statistics for 1960 and 1962–2001 are from *Broadcasting* and *Broadcasting & Cable*; statistics for 1959 and 1961 are from *Sponsor*. These data include stations that carried any portion of the team's games. An asterisk (*) indicates missing information. A blank cell indicates the team was not part of MLB in that season.

Table 1. 1936–44

	1936	1937	1938	1939	1940	1941	1942	1943	1944
AMERICAN LEAGUE									
Athletics	2	2	11	11	11	11	12	12	12
Browns	2	2	2	2	3	2	2	16	5
Indians	2	1	1	1	2	2	2	2	*
Red Sox	11	13	14	14	18	18	19	23	20
Senators	0	0	1	1	1	1	2	1	2
Tigers	8	10	10	10	9	9	9	7	14
Yankees	0	0	0	1	1	0	2	0	1
White Sox	4	5	4	3	4	3	3	4	1

Table 1 (*continued*)

	1936	1937	1938	1939	1940	1941	1942	1943	1944
NATIONAL LEAGUE									
Braves	11	13	14	14	18	18	19	21	20
Cardinals	2	2	2	2	3	2	2	16	5
Cubs	4	5	4	3	4	3	3	3	1
Dodgers	0	0	0	2	1	1	1	1	1
Giants	0	0	0	1	1	0	2	0	1
Phillies	2	2	1	11	11	11	12	14	12
Pirates	0	0	1	2	2	2	6	9	9
Reds	1	2	2	2	2	2	1	4	2
Average	3	4	4	5	6	5	6	8	7

Table 2. 1945–53

	1945	1946	1947	1948	1949	1950	1951	1952	1953
AMERICAN LEAGUE									
Athletics	5	7	11	14	9	19	17	20	19
Browns/ Orioles	12	8	1	2	2	*	26	25	17
Indians	*	*	1	1	24	26	29	26	32
Red Sox	16	19	12	20	29	36	28	34	37
Senators	2	2	2	4	4	2	1	9	27
Tigers	17	21	23	24	32	33	37	36	37
White Sox	1	1	1	2	2	8	4	14	17
Yankees	1	1	2	1	1	16	20	27	30
NATIONAL LEAGUE									
Braves	15	19	12	20	29	36	27	27	15
Cardinals	12	7	20	43	46	73	72	74	76
Cubs	1	1	13	22	30	34	36	42	40
Dodgers	1	1	1	1	2	9	2	2	2
Giants	1	1	1	1	2	13	19	8	8
Phillies	5	7	11	14	9	19	18	20	19
Pirates	8	8	14	16	20	22	22	31	26
Reds	2	12	14	14	19	32	32	34	42
Average	7	8	9	12	16	25	24	27	28

Table 3. 1954–62

	1954	1955	1956	1957	1958	1959	1960	1961	1962
AMERICAN LEAGUE									
Athletics	18	34	48	49	36	7	*	7	8
Orioles	7	14	10	40	14	13	*	7	53
Indians	33	33	41	54	48	48	36	36	37
Red Sox	42	43	46	47	49	48	41	45	46
Senators/ Twins	32	37	40	10	14	13	*	8	41
Tigers	35	39	38	46	44	41	51	51	61
White Sox	27	18	26	36	39	51	61	61	83
Yankees	32	34	37	37	39	41	41	41	41
Angels								23	17
Senators								*	*
NATIONAL LEAGUE									
Braves	45	43	41	41	40	41	51	43	32
Cardinals	92	90	86	69	88	71	81	61	61
Cubs	26	25	28	21	1	1	1	1	1
Dodgers	1	1	20	20	12	11	20	17	22
Giants	11	10	7	8	9	9	*	11	17
Phillies	18	22	19	17	21	20	28	21	23
Pirates	21	22	27	20	17	22	*	34	31
Reds	37	41	42	48	52	51	*	51	51
Astros									15
Mets									18
Average	30	32	35	35	33	31	41	30	35

Table 4. 1963–71

	1963	1964	1965	1966	1967	1968	1969	1970	1971
AMERICAN LEAGUE									
Athletics	11	*	13	*	16	10	9	11	8
Orioles	24	31	31	61	61	68	76	61	64
Indians	37	41	19	26	26	26	26	26	25
Red Sox	46	46	46	46	45	44	41	48	48
Twins	32	31	45	45	101	101	101	101	101
Tigers	49	50	21	21	29	32	33	33	25
White Sox	83	81	76	81	86	91	91	91	11
Yankees	41	41	41	41	41	39	39	39	31
Angels	17	20	20	19	21	23	22	21	21
Senators	1	1	8	16	1	1	*	*	2
Royals							49	51	39
Pilots/Brewers							51	51	51
NATIONAL LEAGUE									
Braves	32	63	*	35	41	48	48	*	*
Cardinals	61	101	101	101	101	101	101	101	101
Cubs	1	1	1	1	1	1	9	25	*
Dodgers	11	10	19	17	11	11	13	13	9
Giants	17	17	17	18	19	19	15	15	15
Phillies	24	25	25	25	25	24	24	25	25
Pirates	22	27	28	28	29	31	29	*	*
Reds	51	81	61	51	92	101	75	101	61
Astros	19	26	27	30	31	33	33	*	33
Mets	16	13	10	10	3	32	33	33	43
Expos							*	13	20
Padres							7	5	4
Average	30	37	32	35	39	42	42	43	35

Table 5. 1972–80

	1972	1973	1974	1975	1976	1977	1978	1979	1980
AMERICAN LEAGUE									
Athletics	18	19	*	19	*	*	*	*	*
Orioles	53	41	41	26	36	51	51	51	57
Indians	21	21	21	19	24	27	27	31	28
Red Sox	48	51	53	51	53	55	67	80	81
Twins	46	46	46	36	31	21	21	26	21
Tigers	32	39	40	51	51	54	55	51	51
White Sox	16	*	3	1	1	1	1	1	1
Yankees	33	31	31	41	36	31	41	61	87
Angels	20	21	19	18	20	19	20	20	20
Rangers	26	17	13	22	25	25	21	21	16
Royals	31	51	51	51	51	71	93	93	116
Brewers	46	41	51	25	53	58	58	58	61
Blue Jays						19	21	21	23
Mariners						25	8	12	10
NATIONAL LEAGUE									
Braves	64	56	56	61	56	66	61	61	61
Cardinals	121	114	119	119	119	119	121	91	96
Cubs	11	21	25	25	*	16	11	*	*
Dodgers	11	11	11	16	20	21	21	25	24
Giants	15	15	16	16	14	17	24	9	10
Phillies	21	17	20	20	22	27	26	34	34
Pirates	21	43	44	50	49	41	41	41	51
Reds	85	81	113	113	125	101	104	116	111
Astros	33	33	34	33	26	29	21	28	36
Mets	31	26	26	26	26	26	21	*	11
Expos	38	29	27	30	27	22	25	28	40
Padres	3	1	1	1	1	1	1	1	1
Average	35	36	37	36	39	38	38	42	44

Table 6. 1981–89

	1981	1982	1983	1984	1985	1986	1987	1988	1989
AMERICAN LEAGUE									
Athletics	11	12	15	16	15	16	15	17	15
Orioles	58	58	61	61	61	64	85	41	41
Indians	31	31	41	36	31	29	34	29	29
Red Sox	81	85	74	78	76	66	76	82	82
Twins	23	31	31	31	41	61	63	66	66
Tigers	61	61	36	31	46	38	38	38	41
White Sox	1	15	15	23	23	15	22	27	31
Yankees	63	61	61	61	61	61	46	40	51
Angels	17	16	21	21	16	30	24	23	23
Rangers	16	13	15	13	11	15	16	19	19
Royals	119	111	111	109	114	118	118	121	133
Brewers	53	61	73	51	51	65	62	61	68
Blue Jays	31	32	32	27	27	53	51	66	66
Mariners	13	15	21	18	23	21	31	31	31
NATIONAL LEAGUE									
Braves	61	71	71	101	101	101	101	108	94
Cardinals	101	101	101	109	116	116	116	116	131
Cubs	*	21	27	47	47	64	68	75	84
Dodgers	24	30	32	29	29	29	5	32	37
Giants	10	5	7	9	9	9	43	44	11
Phillies	35	35	27	26	27	26	25	30	24
Pirates	45	46	37	36	40	37	21	41	45
Reds	118	118	118	99	87	82	101	73	76
Astros	37	41	41	35	31	12	44	44	46
Mets	21	21	26	11	18	23	43	111	23
Expos	60	66	80	79	79	82	73	41	40
Padres	23	12	35	21	38	38	44	34	31
Average	45	45	47	45	47	49	53	54	51

Table 7. 1990–97

	1990	1991	1992	1993	1994	1995	1996	1997
AMERICAN LEAGUE								
Athletics	23	*	13	24	23	21	19	19
Orioles	41	*	31	31	21	*	30	30
Indians	31	*	36	36	31	33	36	36
Red Sox	66	*	64	58	61	*	61	61
Twins	81	*	66	69	71	71	60	67
Tigers	48	*	38	36	33	36	33	31
White Sox	31	*	28	29	29	29	29	34
Yankees	*	*	38	21	21	21	16	14
Angels	23	*	29	24	24	11	14	16
Rangers	26	*	33	34	34	52	57	61
Royals	136	*	125	125	116	116	107	107
Brewers	64	*	49	49	49	49	58	47
Blue Jays	51	*	46	46	49	49	46	41
Mariners	34	*	31	27	27	31	31	36
NATIONAL LEAGUE								
Braves	107	*	151	176	163	151	165	182
Cardinals	131	*	131	121	126	121	121	102
Cubs	72	*	58	64	65	54	55	51
Dodgers	30	*	36	33	30	32	27	25
Giants	15	*	18	15	15	17	18	13
Phillies	27	*	31	31	22	22	21	20
Pirates	*	*	51	51	51	53	52	49
Reds	81	*	83	83	71	71	74	61
Astros	44	*	51	51	47	51	51	51
Mets	9	*	21	21	21	21	24	16
Expos	54	*	55	54	49	51	33	35
Padres	*	*	14	14	15	*	3	3
Rockies				51	51	61	55	58
Marlins				22	19	23	25	*
Average	53	*	55	50	48	50	47	47

Table 8. 1998–2001

	1998	1999	2000	2001
AMERICAN LEAGUE				
Athletics	16	16	21	26
Orioles	26	26	26	24
Indians	36	36	39	39
Red Sox	59	57	57	52
Twins	71	70	49	49
Tigers	33	50	31	35
White Sox	36	40	38	38
Yankees	29	31	34	34
Angels	9	6	6	11
Rangers	71	69	71	71
Royals	101	85	96	86
Blue Jays	33	36	31	31
Mariners	39	31	36	41
Rays	18	17	17	12
NATIONAL LEAGUE				
Braves	176	166	174	176
Cardinals	108	108	108	108
Cubs	47	39	39	39
Dodgers	26	27	27	29
Giants	16	18	18	14
Phillies	20	19	19	16
Pirates	46	41	36	36
Reds	51	46	61	61
Astros	51	51	51	51
Mets	16	16	7	11
Expos	33	33	*	21
Padres	7	7	2	2
Brewers	53	53	53	53
Rockies	63	66	66	66
Marlins	21	16	16	16
Diamondbacks	17	21	21	18
Average	44	43	43	42

NOTES

INTRODUCTION

1. Curt Smith, *Voices of the Game: The Acclaimed Chronicle of Baseball Radio and Television Broadcasting—from 1921 to the Present*, updated ed. (New York: Fireside, 1992); Eldon L. Ham, *Broadcasting Baseball: A History of the National Pastime on Radio and Television* (Jefferson NC: McFarland, 2011); Tony Silvia, *Baseball over the Air: The National Pastime on the Radio and in the Imagination* (Jefferson NC: McFarland, 2007).
2. James R. Walker and Robert V. Bellamy, Jr., *Center Field Shot: A History of Baseball on Television* (Lincoln: University of Nebraska Press, 2008), 49–51.
3. Pat Hughes, telephone interview by the author, January 23, 2013, Chicago IL.
4. "Frick Asks for Curbs on Radio Blurbs," *Sporting News*, January 14, 1953, 4.
5. Charley Steiner, interview by the author, March 30, 2012, International Association for Communication and Sport Symposium, Peoria IL.
6. "MLB Salaries," CBSSports.com, http://www.cbssports.com/mlb/salaries/avg salaries; Garrett Broshuis, "Playing for Peanuts," Baseball America, March 31, 2010, http://www.baseballamerica.com/today/minors/season-preview /2010/269689.html.
7. G. William Domhoff, "Wealth, Income, and Power," Who Rules America?, posted September 2005, updated February 2013, http://www2.ucsc.edu/who rulesamerica/power/wealth.html.

1. EARLY WORLD SERIES COVERAGE

1. The "faith of fifty million" reference comes from chapter 4 of F. Scott Fitzgerald's *The Great Gatsby*. The fictional gambler Meyer Wolfsheim, a stand-in for Arnold Rothstein, is identified as "the man who fixed the World's Series back in 1919" and someone who could "start to play with the faith of fifty million people—with the single-mindedness of a burglar blowing a safe." F. Scott Fitzgerald, *The Great Gatsby* (New York: Charles Scribner's Sons, 1925), 74.

2. Erik Barnouw, *The Golden Web: A History of Broadcasting in the United States 1933–1953* (New York: Oxford University Press, 1968).

3. Wayne M. Towers, "World Series Coverage in the 1920s," *Journalism Monographs*, February 1981, 5; Homer Coy, "The Newspaper That Comes through Your Walls," *Popular Radio*, September 1922, 13.

4. "Voice-Broadcasting the Stirring Progress of the 'Battle of the Century,'" *Wireless Age*, August 1921, 14.

5. Thomas H. Cowan, "Reminiscences of Thomas H. Cowan," 1951, 14, Columbia Center for Oral History Collection, Columbia University, New York NY.

6. Cowan, "Reminiscences of Thomas H. Cowan," 16–17.

7. John Dunning, *On the Air: The Encyclopedia of Old-Time Radio* (New York: Oxford University Press, 1998), 628; William Peck Banning, *Commercial Broadcast Pioneer: The WEAF Experiment, 1922–1926* (Cambridge MA: Harvard University Press, 1946), 49; "Ships to Get World's Series by Wireless," *Telegraph-Herald*, October 5, 1920, 2.

8. "Ten Triumphant Days of Radio at the Electrical Show, *Wireless Age*, November 1921, 19; "N.A.W.A. Radio Station and 'Ku Kux' Call," *Wireless Age*, November 1921, 13–14.

9. Curt Smith, *Voices of the Game: The Acclaimed Chronicle of Baseball Radio and Television Broadcasting—from 1921 to the Present*, updated ed. (New York: Fireside, 1992), 8.

10. Ted Patterson, "First Series Aircaster—Writer Grantland Rice," *Sporting News*, October 28, 1972, 11.

11. Joseph Durso, *The Days of Mr. McGraw* (Englewood Cliffs NJ: Prentice-Hall, 1969), 155–56; Sam J. Slate and Joe Cook, *It Sounds Impossible* (New York: Macmillan, 1963), 51.

12. Grantland Rice, *The Tumult and the Shouting: My Life in Sport* (New York: A. S. Barnes, 1954), xv; William A. Harper, *How You Played the Game: The Life of Grantland Rice* (Columbia MO: University of Missouri Press, 1999), 312; Charles Fountain, *Sportswriter: The Life and Times of Grantland Rice* (New York: Oxford University Press, 1993), 192.

13. "KDKA," *Wireless Age*, August 1922, 40–41, 44; "Radio Broadcasting Started at KDKA Four Years Ago Today," *New York Times*, November 2, 1924, 16.

14. Towers, "World Series Coverage in the 1920s," 5.

15. Red Barber, *The Broadcasters* (New York: Dial, 1970), 24.

16. Towers, "World Series Coverage in the 1920s," 6.

17. Glenn Scott, "'Seeing' a World's Series by Radio," *Wireless Age*, November, 1922, 32.

18. Scott, "'Seeing' a World's Series by Radio," 31.

19. Scott, "'Seeing' a World's Series by Radio," 32.

20. Scott, "'Seeing' a World's Series by Radio," 46.

21. Gleason L. Archer, *History of Radio to 1926* (New York: American Historical Society, 1938), 279.

22. Scott, "'Seeing' a World's Series by Radio," 46.

23. "Trans-Atlantic Broadcasting Now Looms Up," *New York Tribune*, October 8, 1922, 4; "World's Series Radio Tuned for 'Play Ball,'" *New York Tribune*, October 3, 1922, 1.

24. "3 Million Hear Tribune Radio Despite Storm," *New York Tribune*, October 8, 1922, 7.

25. "3 Million Hear Tribune Radio Despite Storm," 7.

26. "Another Radio Victory Scored in Third Game," *New York Tribune*, October 7, 1922, 20.

27. "Tribune's Radio 'Clear as a Bell' for Game To-day," *New York Tribune*, October 4, 1922, 11.

28. "Hear the Crowd Roar!," *New York Tribune*, October 4, 1922, 13.

29. "Never Mind Those World Series Tickets," *New York Times*, October 4, 1922, 4.

30. "Radio Makes East Vast Grand Stand," *New York Times*, October 5, 1922, 29.

31. Raymond Francis Yates, "Reporting Baseball Series to Millions," *Wireless Age*, November 1923, 25.

32. Towers, "World Series Coverage in the 1920s," 12.

33. "To Broadcast Series," *New York Times*, October 9, 1923, 18.

34. "Robinson to Install Radio during World Series Week," *St. Joseph Gazette*, September 21, 1923, 3.

35. Graham McNamee, *You're on the Air* (New York: Harper & Brothers, 1926), 54.

36. Yates, "Reporting Baseball Series," 26.

37. "Today's Radio Program," *New York Times*, October 10, 1923, 24.

38. Yates, "Reporting Baseball Series," 25, 27.

39. "WNYC to Broadcast World's Series Today," *New York Times*, October 5, 1924, 17; "World Series Broadcast," *Boston Daily Globe*, October 3, 1924, 22.

40. "Broadcasting the World Series," *New York Times*, October 12, 1924, 14.

41. Christopher H. Sterling and John Michael Kittross, *Stay Tuned: A History of American Broadcasting*, 3rd ed. (Mahwah NJ: Erlbaum, 2002), 827.

42. Stuart Hyde Hawkins, "Sports: Polo-Racing-Tennis-Baseball-Football," *Wireless Age*, November, 1924, 24.

43. "Need for National Radio System Outlined by Hoover," *New York Times*, October 12, 1924, 14.

44. Hawkins, "Sports," 25.

45. "Capital Fans Still Hoping," *St. Petersburg Times*, October 7, 1924, 4.

46. Roger N. Batchelder, "Curiosity Led McNamee, Singer into Radio Announcing and Fame," *Boston Daily Globe*, March 29, 1925, B7.

47. "1925 Pennant Race Ends as Pirates Beat Phillies, 2–1," *New York Times*, September 24, 1925, 19.

48. "Millions to Hear Series on Radio," *New York Times*, October 7, 1925, 23.
49. "Coolidges Stay by Radio until Nats' Final Play," *Chicago Tribune*, October 14, 1925, 29.
50. "Radio Bears Scores to Macmillan Party," *New York Times*, October 9, 1925, 19.
51. McNamee, *You're on the Air*, 64.
52. Barber, *Broadcasters*, 25.
53. "Every Corner of U.S. to Hear World's Series," *Boston Daily Globe*, October 2, 1925, 23A.
54. Slate and Cook, *It Sounds Impossible*, 44. "Players Wear Radio Sets in Mimic Series Games," *New York Times*, October 10, 1925, 12.
55. Slate and Cook, *It Sounds Impossible*, 45.
56. Slate and Cook, *It Sounds Impossible*, 44.
57. "Broadcasting Company to Cover World Series," *Boston Daily Globe*, September 25, 1926, 8.
58. "Yankees Win, 2 to 1, While 63,00 Watch, 15,000,000 Listen In," *New York Times*, October 3, 1926, 1; "Station WJZ Linked with Stations Which Will Radiate Play by Play Description of Today's Game, Beginning at 1:45 O'Clock," *New York Times*, October 3, 1926, 15; "Chain Broadcast of World Series," *Boston Daily Globe*, October 1, 1926, A20.
59. "Series Score-Board No Longer Big Lure," *New York Times*, October 6, 1926, 17.
60. "Play in Final Game as Told over Radio," *New York Times*, October 11, 1926, 26.
61. "Boy Regains Health as Ruth Hits Homers," *New York Times*, October 8, 1926, 17.
62. "Sick Boy Expecting Ruth 'Homer' Today," *New York Times*, October 9, 1926, 19.
63. "Pacific Coast Stations Will Join with East on Thursday Night to Radiate Blow by Blow Description of Bout," *New York Times*, July 17, 1927, 12.
64. "Radio Will Report Baseball Series," *New York Times*, October 4, 1927, 34.
65. "N.Y. Cranes Its Neck to Follow Yankees' Fight," *New York Times*, October 6, 1927, 15.
66. "Greenland Fans Listen to World's Series Game," *New York Times*, October 9, 1927, 7.
67. "Marconi Will Open Beam Radio Here," *New York Times*, September 13, 1927, 34.
68. "M'Namee's Eye Not on the Ball," *New York Sun*, October 5, 1927.
69. "Globe Gives News to Crowd of 1000," *Boston Daily Globe*, October 6, 1927, 15.
70. "World Series on Radio," *New York Times*, September 28, 1928, 30; "Radio Chains Ready for World's Series," *New York Times*, October 4, 1928, 32; "Radio Relays Game to Nation's Millions," *New York Times*, October 2, 1931, 29; "Millions to Hear World Series," *Boston Daily Globe*, September 25, 1932, A58.
71. "Athletics Express Elation over Radio," *New York Times*, October 15, 1929, 34.
72. "Wide Radio Hook-Up for World Series," *New York Times*, September 28, 1932, 23.

73. Sterling and Kittross, *Stay Tuned*, 862.
74. "Will Rogers, Out in California, Listens to the World Series," *New York Times*, October 2, 1930, 27.

2. THE LOCAL GAME BEGINS

1. "First Program Broadcast by KDKA Six Years Ago," *New York Times*, October 31, 1926, 16.
2. John Thorn, Pete Palmer, Michael Gershman, and David Pietrusza, *Total Baseball*, 6th ed. (New York: Total Sports, 1999), 106–7.
3. "This Our Latest Problem," *Sporting News*, April 27, 1922, 4.
4. John B. Sheridan, "Back of Home Plate," *Sporting News*, August 17, 1922, 4.
5. Francis C. Richter, "Casual Comment," *Sporting News*, June 21, 1923, 4.
6. "Radio and the Printed Word," *Sporting News*, June 7, 1923, 4.
7. Ted Patterson, "The Big Broadcast," *Sporting News*, April 5, 1969, 55.
8. "Inside Corner," *Sporting News*, September 25, 1965, 2.
9. Curt Smith, *Voices of Summer* (New York: Carroll & Graf, 2005), 7.
10. Patterson, "Big Broadcast," 55.
11. Michael K. Bohn, "Sports on the Radio, 1921: The First Wireless Revolution," McClatchy Tribune Information Services, April 17, 2011, available online at Michael K. Bohn's website, http://www.bohnbooks.com/2011/04/17/sports-on-the-radio-1921-the-first-wireless-revolution/.
12. Curt Smith, *Voices of the Game: The Acclaimed Chronicle of Baseball Radio and Television Broadcasting—from 1921 to the Present*, updated ed. (New York: Fireside, 1992), 8.
13. Christopher H. Sterling and John Michael Kittross, *Stay Tuned: A History of American Broadcasting*, 3rd ed. (Mahwah NJ: Erlbaum, 2002), 827.
14. "The Herald Flashes Score of Game by Radio," *Washington Herald*, April 14, 1922.
15. "Baseball Returns by Radio Monday," *Washington Herald*, April 16, 1922.
16. Kirk Miller, "Finn, Esq.," *Washington Times*, April 14, 1922, 1.
17. Charles Sloan, "High Schools May Give Radio as New Course," *Chicago Tribune*, April 24, 1922, 7.
18. "Radio Fans to Get Details of Cubs-Pirates Opener," *Chicago Tribune*, April 17, 1923, 25.
19. "K.Y.W. at Bat," *Chicago Tribune*, October 5, 1924, A3.
20. Red Barber, *The Broadcasters* (New York: Dial, 1970), 74; Speed Johnson, *Who's Who in Major League Baseball* (Chicago: Buxton, 1933), 514.
21. Barber, *Broadcasters*, 74.
22. Johnson, *Who's Who in Major League Baseball*, 517; Smith, *Voices of the Game*, 15; Robert Remount, *The Red Sox Encyclopedia* (Champaign IL: Sports Publishing, 2002), 226.

23. Judith Waller, interviewed by Frank Ernest Hill on June 1, 1951, at NBC, Merchandise Mart, Chicago IL. Transcript accessed at the Wisconsin Historical Society, Madison WS.

24. Thorn et al., *Total Baseball*, 106–7, 2091, 2095.

25. WMAQ, *The Story of WMAQ* (Chicago: WMAQ, 1931).

26. "Public Cheers Broadcasting Achievements of W-G-N," *Chicago Tribune*, November 2, 1924, E9.

27. "Radio Programs for Today," *Chicago Tribune*, April 14, 1925, 10; "Tune In on W-G-N," *Chicago Tribune*, April 14, 1925, 21; "Tribune's 1926 Radio Program Calls for Many Features," *Chicago Tribune*, January 10, 1926, E1.

28. "Cubs' Opening Game to Be Put on Air for Fans," *Chicago Tribune*, April 18, 1926, E11.

29. "Tune In on W-G-N Today for Fight and Ball Game," *Chicago Tribune*, July 3, 1926, 15.

30. "W-G-N to Broadcast All Home Games of Cubs and White Sox," *Chicago Tribune*, April 3, 1927, H8.

31. Quin A. Ryan, "Inside the Loud Speaker," *Chicago Tribune*, June 12, 1927, G4.

32. "Radio Wins in Daylight Fight of Summertime," *Chicago Tribune*, June 21, 1925, D6.

33. Ford C. Frick, *Games, Asterisks, and People: Memoirs of a Lucky Fan* (New York: Crown, 1973), 107.

34. National League Owners Meeting, July 9, 1923, 26–27, National Baseball Hall of Fame Library, Cooperstown NY (hereafter cited as Hall of Fame Library).

35. "Radio Station Loses New Permit," *New York Times*, April 12, 1927, 23.

36. Baseball, Opening Game of the 1931 Major League New York Yankees vs. the Boston Red Sox, April 14, 1931, and Giants Opening Game New York Giants vs. Philadelphia, NBC program log, Recorded Sound Center, Library of Congress, Washington DC; Baseball, Opening Game of the National League: Giants vs. Philadelphia Phillies, April 12, 1932, Opening Game of the American League: Yankees vs. Philadelphia Athletics, April 20, 1932, NBC program log, Recorded Sound Center, Library of Congress, Washington DC.

37. Frick, *Games, Asterisks, and People*, 109.

38. David J. Halberstam, *Sports on New York Radio: A Play-by-Play History* (Chicago: Masters, 1999), 225.

39. N. J. Abodaher, "Baseball via the Ether Waves," *Baseball Magazine*, November 1929, 551.

40. "Tigers Opener to Go on Air: WWJ to Broadcast All Home Games Play by Play," *Detroit News*, April 19, 1927.

41. Smith, *Voices of the Game*, 16.

42. Smith, *Voices of the Game*, 15.

43. Smith, *Voices of the Game*, 19.

44. Abodaher, "Baseball via the Ether Waves," 551.

45. Abodaher, "Baseball via the Ether Waves," 552.

46. William Evans, General Manager of the Cleveland Baseball Company, to John F. Royal, VP and GM, WTAM and WEAR, April 18, 1930, NBC Archives, Wisconsin Historical Society, Madison WI (hereafter cited as NBC Archives).

47. Niles Trammell to John F. Royal, March 5, 1932, NBC Archives.

48. John F. Royal to Niles Trammell, March 7, 1932, NBC Archives.

49. John F. Royal to William Evans, General Manager of the Cleveland Baseball Company, March 4, 1931, NBC Archives.

50. Smith, *Voices of the Game*, 14.

3. INVENTING A NEW CRAFT

1. Christopher H. Sterling and John Michael Kittross, *Stay Tuned: A History of American Broadcasting*, 3rd ed. (Mahwah NJ: Erlbaum, 2002), 116.

2. Sterling and Kittross, *Stay Tuned*, 86.

3. Curt Smith, *Voices of Summer* (New York: Carroll & Graf, 2005), 10.

4. Smith, *Voices of Summer*, 12.

5. Jim Bowman, "The Way We Were," *Chicago Tribune*, May 1, 1983, G11.

6. Red Barber, *The Broadcasters* (New York: Dial, 1970), 91.

7. Mrs. L. A. Wood to National Broadcasting Co., August 29, 1934, NBC Archives, Wisconsin Historical Society, Madison WI (hereafter cited as NBC Archives).

8. Bowman, "Way We Were," G11.

9. "Pick Three-I's Hal Totten to Top Southern," *Chicago Tribune*, April 7, 1960, D3.

10. William Currie, "Quin Ryan, Dies at 79; Chicago Radio Pioneer," *Chicago Tribune*, October 8, 1978, C23.

11. Ann Lord, "Chicago Broadcasts," *Wireless Age*, April, 1925, 40.

12. Bowman, "Way We Were," G11.

13. Quin A. Ryan, "Inside the Loud Speaker," *Chicago Tribune*, May 1, 1927, H10.

14. Eldon L. Ham, *Broadcasting Baseball: A History of the National Pastime on Radio and Television* (Jefferson NC: McFarland, 2011), 55.

15. "Quin Ryan Set to Broadcast World Series," *Chicago Tribune*, October 6, 1929, I10.

16. Barber, *Broadcasters*, 91.

17. "Program Notes," *Broadcasting*, December 15, 1931, 23.

18. "Fred Hoey Moved to the Radio Booth from Usher, Player, Reporter Roles," *Sporting News*, May 7, 1936, 2.

19. "Fred Hoey Moved to the Radio Booth," 2.

20. "Fred Hoey Moved to the Radio Booth," 2.

21. "Hoey and Bingham in Lead in Radio Popularity Voting," *Sporting News*, September 17, 1936, 2.

22. "Fred Hoey Day at Wigwam Great Tribute to Radio Announcer," *Boston Globe*, June 21, 1931, A25.

23. "Announcer Hoey Wins Vote," *Sporting News*, December 17, 1931, 6.

24. Curt Smith, *Voices of the Game: The Acclaimed Chronicle of Baseball Radio and Television Broadcasting—from 1921 to the Present*, updated ed. (New York: Fireside, 1992), 21.

25. "On the Air Lines," *Sporting News*, December 31, 1936, 2.

26. Barber, *Broadcasters*, 96.

27. "On the Airlines," *Sporting News*, January 7, 1937, 8.

28. "Ball Fans!," *Boston Globe*, April 30, 1937, 27.

29. "Fred Hoey Suffers from Bad Cold, and His Voice Fails Him," *Boston Globe*, October 4, 1933, 1.

30. Barber, *Broadcasters*, 96.

31. Hy Hurwitz, "Frankie Frisch Signs to Broadcast Local Ball Games," *Boston Globe*, March 16, 1939, 9.

32. Hurwitz, "Frankie Frisch Signs," 9.

33. "Attention Baseball Fans of New England," *Boston Globe*, March 27, 1939, 5.

34. "Ex-Sportscaster Fred Hoey Dead," *Boston Globe*, November 18, 1949, 26.

35. Radio Staff of the Detroit News, *WWJ—The Detroit News* (Detroit MI: Evening News Association, 1922), 7.

36. Radio Staff of the Detroit News, *WWJ—The Detroit News*, 9.

37. Smith, *Voices of the Game*, 17.

38. Smith, *Voices of the Game*, 35.

39. "Tiger Opener to Go on Air: WWJ to Broadcast All Home Games Play by Play," *Detroit News*, April 19, 1927.

40. "We Pay Our Respects to—," *Broadcasting*, September 1, 1932, 17.

41. Speed Johnson, *Who's Who in Major League Baseball* (Chicago: Buxton, 1933), 516.

42. Smith, *Voices of Summer*, 25.

43. "Pat Flanagan," *Broadcasting*, June 15, 1939, 64; Larry Wolters, "Coolidge Story Bobs Up in Wake of Broadcast," *Chicago Tribune*, October 18, 1931, D6.

44. Smith, *Voices of Summer*, 14.

45. "Pat Flanagan, Sportscaster 15 Years, Dies," *Chicago Tribune*, July 3, 1963, C2.

46. Smith, *Voices of Summer*, 15.

47. Edward Burns, "You Have to Be Air Minded to Try It, but Mr M'Evoy Can't Complain That He's Lonely," *Chicago Tribune*, February 21, 1937, B3.

48. F. P. Wagener, "Consistency Pays Prima Beer," *Broadcasting*, April 1, 1934, 16.

49. Smith, *Voices of Summer*, 13.

50. Wagener, "Consistency Pays Prima Beer," 16.

51. "Sports Experience Qualifies France Laux for Radio Role," *Sporting News*, January 14, 1932, 6; "World's Series Broadcasters," *Sporting News*, October 5,

1933, 3; "France Laux," *New York Times*, November 18, 1978, 45; "113 Stations Join in Salute to Laux," *Sporting News*, January 27, 1938, 6.

52. "113 Stations Join in Salute to Laux," 6.

53. "France Laux and Tom Manning to Give All-Star Game on Air," *Sporting News*, July 5, 1934, 2.

54. "Sports Experience Qualifies France Laux for Radio Role," 6.

55. "Youngest Baseball Announcers," *Broadcasting*, July 1, 1938, 30.

56. Smith, *Voices of the Game*, 97.

57. Smith, *Voices of the Game*, 97.

58. John Husar, "Cub Field Announcer Pieper Dead at 88," *Chicago Tribune*, October 23, 1974, E1.

59. John Thorn, Pete Palmer, Gershman, and David Pietrusza, *Total Baseball*, 6th ed. (New York: Total Sports, 1999), 2508.

60. Ted Patterson, *Golden Voices of Baseball* (Champaign IL: Sports Publishing, 2002), CD 1, track 4.

61. Patterson, *Golden Voices of Baseball*, 104.

62. Patterson, *Golden Voices of Baseball*, CD 1, track 4.

63. Billy Evans, General Manager, the Cleveland Baseball Company, to John F. Royal, VP and GM, WTAM, April 18, 1930, NBC Archives.

64. "Manning Named as Game's Outstanding Announcer," *Sporting News*, November 24, 1938, 9.

65. Smith, *Voices of the Game*, 15.

66. Barber, *Broadcasters*, 74.

67. "Voice of the Fan," *Sporting News*, February 11, 1932, 4.

68. "On the Air Lines," *Sporting News*, October 12, 1933, 2.

69. Wood to National Broadcasting Co., August 29, 1934.

70. "Honeymooning Hartmans," *Sporting News*, March 23, 1939, 6.

71. "Fans Vote Leadership to Harry Hartman and Harry Johnson in Air Popularity Poll," *Sporting News*, October 5, 1936, 2.

72. Smith, *Voices of the Game*, 19.

73. Barber, *Broadcasters*, 69.

74. Smith, *Voices of the Game*, 20.

75. Smith, *Voices of the Game*, 20.

76. Patterson, *Golden Voices of Baseball*, 112.

77. Ring Lardner, "Opening Game Seemed Like Double-Header to Lardner," *Boston Globe*, October 6, 1927, 15.

78. Ring Lardner, "Col. Ruppert Nominated by Lardner to Pitch Game Today," *Boston Globe*, October 8, 1927, 11.

79. "Quin Ryan Set to Broadcast World Series," *Chicago Tribune*, October 6, 1929, I10.

80. James. M. Gould, "Is the Radio Good for Baseball?," *Baseball Magazine*, June 1930, 341–42.

81. Edward Burns, "Now It's Glib Radio Announcers Who Embarrass Ye Baseball Scribe," *Chicago Tribune*, August 31, 1930, A3.

82. Burns, "Now It's Glib Radio Announcers," A3.

83. "Floyd P. Gibbons, War Reporter, 52," *New York Times*, September 25, 1939, 24.

84. *Floyd Gibbons School of Broadcasting, Lesson No. 26, Sports Broadcasting*, no date, 4, accessed at the Library of American Broadcasting, Hornbake Library, University of Maryland, College Park MD.

85. *Gibbons School, Sports Broadcasting*, 5.

86. *Gibbons School, Sports Broadcasting*, 5.

87. *Gibbons School, Sports Broadcasting*, 9.

88. Johnson, *Who's Who in Major League Baseball*, 513.

89. Johnson, *Who's Who in Major League Baseball*, 513.

4. THE BASEBALL-RADIO WAR

1. Erik Barnouw, *The Golden Web: A History of Broadcasting in the United States 1933–1953* (New York: Oxford University Press, 1968), 20–22.

2. N. J. Abodaher, "Baseball via the Ether Waves," *Baseball Magazine*, November 1929, 551–52.

3. Abodaher, "Baseball via the Ether Waves," 552.

4. Reconvened and Scheduled Meeting of the National League of Professional Baseball Clubs, New York NY, February 8, 1927, 7, National Baseball Hall of Fame Library, Cooperstown NY (hereafter cited as Hall of Fame Library).

5. Special Meeting of the National League of Professional Baseball Clubs, New York NY, December 10, 1929, 103, Hall of Fame Library.

6. Special Meeting of the National League of Professional Baseball Clubs, December 10, 1929, 104.

7. Annual Meeting of the National League of Professional Baseball Clubs, December 10 and 11, 1929, 129, Hall of Fame Library.

8. Annual Meeting of the National League, December 10 and 11, 1929, 130–46; "Big Leagues Will Not Ban Baseball Broadcasts," *Broadcast Advertising*, December 1929, 12–13.

9. Joint Meeting of American Baseball League and National Baseball League, Chicago, December 10, 1931, 121, Hall of Fame Library.

10. Joint American League and National League Meeting, December 10, 1931, 123.

11. Joint American League and National League Meeting, December 10, 1931, 123.

12. Joint American League and National League Meeting, December 10, 1931, 126–28.

13. Joint American League and National League Meeting, December 10, 1931, 126–27.

14. Joint American League and National League Meeting, December 10, 1931, 127.

15. Joint American League and National League Meeting, December 10, 1931, 128.
16. Joint American League and National League Meeting, December 10, 1931, 132.
17. Joint Meeting of the National League of Professional Baseball Clubs and the American League of Professional Baseball Clubs, New York NY, December 15, 1932, 9, Hall of Fame Library.
18. Joint National League and American League Meeting, December 15, 1932, 10.
19. Joint National League and American League Meeting, December 15, 1932, 15.
20. Joint National League and American League Meeting, December 15, 1932, 16.
21. Joint National League and American League Meeting, December 15, 1932, 46.
22. Joint National League and American League Meeting, December 15, 1932, 47.
23. "On the Air Lines," *Sporting News*, February 15, 1934, 3.
24. "On the Air Lines," *Sporting News*, February 22, 1934, 5.
25. Annual Meeting of the American League of Professional Baseball Clubs, New York NY, December 11 and 13, 1934, 11–12.
26. Meeting of the American League, December 11 and 13, 1934, 13.
27. Meeting of the American League, December 11 and 13, 1934, 15.
28. "On the Radio Airlines," *Sporting News*, March 28, 1935, 6.
29. John Thorn, Pete Palmer, Michael Gershman, and David Pietrusza, *Total Baseball*, 6th ed. (New York: Total Sports, 1999), 107.
30. Charles C. Alexander, *Breaking the Slump: Baseball in the Depression Era* (New York: Columbia University Press, 2002), 48–49.
31. Alexander, *Breaking the Slump*, 52.
32. Alexander, *Breaking the Slump*, 37.
33. J. Roy Stockton, "The Pros and Cons of Night Baseball," *Baseball Magazine*, August 1930, 391–92.
34. John K. Davis, "The First Night Baseball Games: Early Major League Games Were Few and Far Between," Suite101.com, June 21, 2008, http://baseballhistory .suite101.com/article.cfm/first_night_baseball_games#ixzz09AtazoE4.
35. "General Mills Sponsors Baseball on WOC-WHO," *Broadcasting*, April 15, 1934, 45; Michael Chamberlain, "Baseball on the Air: Reinterpretations of the History of Radio Baseball" (master's thesis, Concordia University, Montreal, 1996), 53.
36. "Parkview Pharmacies Report on Radio Survey," Kansas City MO, September 17, 1936, available at the Broadcast Pioneers Library, University of Maryland, College Park MD.
37. "Opportunity of the Majors," *Sporting News*, December 7, 1933, 4.

5. THE WORLD SERIES TRIGGERS A NATIONAL OBSESSION

1. "TV's 10 Highest-Rated World Series Games," MarketWatch, October 24, 2012, http://www.marketwatch.com/story/tvs-10-highest-rated-world -series-games-2012-10-24.

2. Associated Press, "World Series Has Record-Low Rating," ESPN.go.com, October 30, 2012, http://espn.go.com/mlb/playoffs/2012/story/_/id/8570950/world -series-finishes-record-low-rating.

3. Anthony Crupi, "Nielsen: Cable Commands 70 Percent of Prime-Time GRPs: Cord-Cutting Not Eating into Pay-TV Deliveries," *Adweek*, June 21, 2012, http://www.adweek.com/news/television/nielsen-cable-commands -70-percent-prime-time-grps-141286.

4. "357 Stations to Broadcast World Series," *Chicago Daily Tribune*, October 5, 1938, 20; Christopher H. Sterling and John Michael Kittross, *Stay Tuned: A History of American Broadcasting*, 3rd ed. (Mahwah NJ: Erlbaum, 2002), 827.

5. Niles Trammell to L. R. Lohr, NBC President, August 29, 1938, NBC Archives, Wisconsin Historical Society, Madison WI (hereafter cited as NBC Archives).

6. Graham McNamee to Judge Kenesaw Mountain Landis, September 17, 1931, NBC Archives.

7. Niles Trammell to L. R. Lohr, "Resume of Discussion with Judge Landis," August 29 1938, NBC Archives.

8. Kenesaw M. Landis to Niles Trammell, July 26, 1938, NBC Archives.

9. A. A. Schechter to Niles Trammell, July 29, 1938, NBC Archives.

10. Niles Trammell to E. P. H. James, August 1, 1938, NBC Archives.

11. P. G. Parker to John Royal, October 25, 1933, NBC Archives.

12. John F. Royal to P. G. Parker, October 27, 1933, NBC Archives.

13. Phillips Carlin to P. G. Parker, September 26, 1932, NBC Archives.

14. P. G. Parker to John Royal, September 19, 1932, NBC Archives.

15. Red Barber, *The Broadcasters* (New York: Dial, 1970), 82–83.

16. Telegram from Niles Trammell to John Royal, June 9, 1938, NBC Archives.

17. Barber, *Broadcasters*, 80.

18. D. U. Bathrick to John Royal, August 28, 1934, NBC Archives.

19. E. H. Jacobson to Merle H. Aylesworth, August 31, 1934, NBC Archives.

20. John F. Royal to P. G. Parker, August 31, 1934, NBC Archives.

21. P. G. Parker to Messrs. Morton and Kobak, September 26, 1934, NBC Archives.

22. Jefferson B. Webb to John Royal, September 15, 1934, NBC Archives.

23. Philip Sawyer to National Broadcasting Company, Attention: John F. Royal, September 17, 1934, NBC Archives.

24. Commissioner Landis to Frank J. Nevin, September 26, 1934, NBC Archives.

25. P. G. Parker to Roy C. Witmer, May 23, 1934, NBC Archives.

26. Wm. Burke Miller to John F. Royal, July 7, 1934, NBC Archives.

27. John F. Royal to Edgar Kobak, September 1, 1934, NBC Archives.

28. Edgar Kobak to Messrs Witmer, Shaw, Withycomb, Hedges, Myers, Hager, Hasenbalg, Russell, Trammell Carpenter, Gilman, Anderson, Smith, Nelson, Bathrick, September 13, 1934, NBC Archives.

29. E. R. Hitz to B. Brainard, May 10, 1934, NBC Archives.

30. D. U. Bathrick to John F. Royal, August 10, 1934, NBC Archives.
31. John F. Royal to Niles Trammell, September 14, 1934, NBC Archives.
32. Kobak to Shaw, September 14, 1934.
33. John F. Royal to Edgar Kobak, September 17, 1934, NBC Archives.
34. Kobak to Shaw, September 14, 1934.
35. Royal to Trammell, September 14, 1934.
36. Mark Woods to Richard C. Patterson Jr., October 15, 1934, NBC Archives.
37. H. L. McClinton to R. H. White, April 3, 1936, NBC Archives.
38. Merle H. Alysesworth to Richard C. Patterson Jr., November 28, 1934, NBC Archives.
39. Richard C. Patterson Jr. to John F. Royal, December 26, 1934, NBC Archives.
40. John F. Royal to Richard C. Patterson Jr., April 15, 1935, NBC Archives.
41. John F. Royal to Richard C. Patterson Jr., October 1, 1935, NBC Archives.
42. John F. Royal to Richard C. Patterson Jr., April 15, 1935, NBC Archives.
43. David Rosenblum to Roy C. Witmer, October 19, 1935, NBC Archives.
44. Mark J. Woods to Lenox R. Lohr, September 8, 1936, NBC Archives.
45. "Ford's Forfeiture," *Broadcasting*, November 15, 1937, 59.
46. "World Series Covered as Sustaining Program," *Broadcasting*, October 15, 1937, 71.
47. Niles Trammell to L. R. Lohr, "Resume of Discussion with Judge Landis," August 29, 1938, NBC Archives.
48. "Gillette Sponsors Baseball on MBS," *Broadcasting*, September 1, 1939, 14.
49. "Special Baseball Announcement of World Series on WOR Sponsored by Gillette," August 17, 1939, audio recording, RWA 3883, Recorded Sound Reference Center, Library of Congress, Washington DC.
50. "Staff for World Series Is Complete; Controversy on Rights Still Simmers," *Broadcasting*, October 1, 1939, 16.
51. National Broadcasting Company, Inc., to Federal Communications Commission, November 14, 1939, NBC Archives.
52. National Broadcasting Company to Federal Communications Commission, November 14, 1939.
53. "Baseball Carried by 238 Stations," *Broadcasting*, October 15, 1939, 16.
54. "FCC Stirs Network Issue by Request for World Series Data from Stations," *Broadcasting*, November 15, 1939, 26.
55. "FCC Stirs Network Issue," 26.
56. Major League Baseball annual reports 1934–1946, National Baseball Hall of Fame Library, Cooperstown NY.
57. Albert B. Chandler to Warren C. Giles, June 4, 1951, National Baseball Hall of Fame Library, Cooperstown NY.

6. ADVERTISERS EXPAND BASEBALL COVERAGE

1. Erik Barnouw, *The Sponsor: Notes on a Modern Potentate* (New York: Oxford University Press, 1978), 14.
2. Barnouw, *Sponsor*, 16.
3. Barnouw, *Sponsor*, 15.
4. Susan Smulyan, *Selling Radio: The Commercialization of American Broadcasting 1920–1934* (Washington DC: Smithsonian Institution Press, 1994), 1.
5. Smulyan, *Selling Radio*, 8–9.
6. Erik Barnouw, *The Golden Web: A History of Broadcasting in the United States 1933–1953* (New York: Oxford University Press, 1968).
7. Roy C. Witmer to G. F. McClelland, May 3, 1933, NBC Archives, Wisconsin Historical Society, Madison WI (hereafter cited as NBC Archives).
8. Roy C. Witmer to John F. Royal, July 27, 1933, NBC Archives.
9. Witmer to McClelland, May 3, 1933.
10. Niles Trammell to R. C. Patterson Jr., March 24, 1933, NBC Archives.
11. Witmer to Royal, July 27, 1933.
12. P. G. Parker to Bill Hay, January 17, 1934, NBC Archives.
13. Lloyd C. Thomas to Edgar Kobak, April 3, 1934, NBC Archives.
14. Lloyd C. Thomas to Edgar Kobak, March 30, 1934, NBC Archives.
15. Roy C. Witmer to P. G. Parker, February 9, 1934, NBC Archives.
16. P. G. Parker to Roy C. Witmer, February 14, 1934, NBC Archives.
17. Telegram from Showerman to J. Shaw, December 8, 1934, NBC Archives.
18. Larry Wolters, "News of the Radio Stations," *Chicago Tribune*, April 22, 1935, 12.
19. Mark Woods to R. C. Patterson Jr., November 13, 1933, NBC Archives.
20. Edgar Kobak to Mark Woods, November 18, 1935, NBC Archives.
21. David Rosenblum, Vice President and Treasurer, NBC, to W. S. Booth, Treasurer, WWJ, November 22, 1935, NBC Archives.
22. Frank E. Mason to Lenox R. Lohr, March 4, 1937, NBC Archives.
23. William S. Hedges to Roy C. Witmer, May 12, 1938, NBC Archives; William S. Hedges to Roy C. Witmer, July 5, 1938, NBC Archives.
24. Roy C. Witmer to William S. Hedges, July 7, 1938, NBC Archives.
25. Roy C. Witmer to Albert H. Morton, August 9, 1938, NBC Archives.
26. Niles Trammell to Lenox R. Lohr, September 13, 1938, NBC Archives.
27. Alfred H. Morton to Lenox R. Lohr, September 14, 1938, NBC Archives.
28. Frank M. Russell to Lenox R. Lohr, September 17, 1938, NBC Archives.
29. "General Mills Sponsors Baseball on WOC-WHO," *Broadcasting*, April 15, 1934, 4.
30. "General Mills Sponsors Base Ball in Cleveland, *Broadcasting*, April 1, 1935, 46.
31. "Baseball Openings Attract Sponsors," *Broadcasting*, April 15, 1936, 20.

32. Meeting of the National League of Baseball Clubs, July 6, 1936, 34–35, National Baseball Hall of Fame Library, Cooperstown NY (hereafter cited as Hall of Fame Library).

33. Meeting of the American League of Baseball Clubs, Boston MA, July 6, 1936, 5–13, Hall of Fame Library.

34. Meeting of the American League, July 6, 1936, 44.

35. Meeting of the American League, July 6, 1936, 14.

36. "Baseball Trophies Will Be Awarded by General Mills," *Broadcasting*, May 1, 1936, 20.

37. Donald D. Davis to Powel Crosley Jr., July 2, 1936, Hall of Fame Library, 118.

38. H. A. Bellows to D. D. Davis, "General Mills, Inc. Report, Broadcasting Increases Baseball Attendance," July 1, 1936, Hall of Fame Library, 1.

39. Bellows, "Broadcasting Increases Baseball Attendance," 2.

40. Bellows, "Broadcasting Increases Baseball Attendance," 4.

41. Meeting of the American League, July 6, 1936, 55.

42. Hal Tate, "General Mills Spends Million on Baseball," *Broadcasting*, April 15, 1937, 13.

43. Tate, "General Mills Spends Million," 27.

44. H. G. Salsinger, "A Sock from Salsinger," *Broadcasting*, September 1, 1937, 22.

45. "Sponsors Sign for Baseball Season," *Broadcasting*, April 1, 1937, 15.

46. "Guest Announcers," *Broadcasting*, September 1, 1937, 60.

47. "Summer Sport Schedule of Atlantic Refine Co. to Include 400 Games," *Broadcasting*, May 15, 1937, 18.

48. "Sponsors Sign for Baseball Season," 15.

49. "Kellogg Sports Series on WJJD Will Entail $130,000 Expenditure," *Broadcasting*, April 15, 1937, 67.

50. "Kellogg Promotes Baseball Schedule," *Broadcasting*, May 1, 1937, 14.

51. "General Mills to Use 75 for Baseball," *Broadcasting*, April 15, 1938, 16–17, 72; "General Mills Adds Four to Season's Baseball List," *Broadcasting*, June 1, 1938, 26.

52. "Kellogg Sponsoring Baseball on 60 Stations This Season," *Broadcasting*, May 1, 1938, 23.

53. Meeting of the American League, July 6, 1936, 51.

54. "Lorillard Tours," *Broadcasting*, May 1, 1939, 37.

55. "Three to Sponsor Gotham Baseball," *Broadcasting*, February 1, 1939, 84.

56. "Gotham Baseball Eyed by Sponsors," *Broadcasting*, January 1, 1939, 14.

57. "Summer Baseball Sponsorship Doubled by Atlantic Refining," *Broadcasting*, March 15, 1939, 14.

58. "General Mills Baseball on 67 Stations," *Broadcasting*, April 1, 1939, 14.

59. "General Mills, Goodrich Hold Baseball Session on the Coast," *Broadcasting*, April 1, 1939, 15.

60. Meeting of the National League of Baseball Clubs, July 6, 1936, 34.

61. "Frick Asks for Cubs on Radio Blurbs," *Sporting News*, January 14, 1953, 4.

7. RE-CREATING BASEBALL

1. J. Steven Smethers and Lee Jolliffe, "The Partnership of Telegraphy and Radio in 'Re-Creating' Events for Broadcast," *Journal of Radio Studies* 1 (1993): 83–96.

2. Red Barber, *The Broadcasters* (New York: Dial, 1970), 110.

3. Curt Smith, *Voices of the Game: The Acclaimed Chronicle of Baseball Radio and Television Broadcasting—from 1921 to the Present*, updated ed. (New York: Fireside, 1992), 28.

4. Barber, *Broadcasters*, 108.

5. Barber, *Broadcasters*, 110.

6. "Inside Corner," *Sporting News*, September 25, 1965, 2.

7. Smethers and Jolliffe, "Partnership of Telegraphy and Radio," 87.

8. Smith, *Voices of the Game*, 335.

9. Larry Wolters, "Cubs Plan to Rebroadcast Home Games," *Chicago Daily Tribune*, April 4, 1936.

10. Dave Henley, "It Sounded Nutty, This Idea," *Broadcasting*, December 15, 1937, 4.

11. Smethers and Jolliffe, "Partnership of Telegraphy and Radio," 84.

12. Joint Meeting of the American League of Professional Baseball Clubs and the National League of Professional Baseball Clubs, Chicago IL, December 13, 1928, National Baseball Hall of Fame Library, Cooperstown NY (hereafter cited as Hall of Fame Library).

13. Joint Meeting of the American League and National League, December 13, 1928.

14. American League Meeting, Boston MA, July 6, 1936, 19–20, Hall of Fame Library.

15. American League Meeting, July 6, 1936, 21.

16. "Cannon Baseball Monopoly Bill Seeks Data on Western Union WJBK Case," *Broadcasting*, May 15, 1937, 69; "FCC Asked to Act in Baseball Case," *Broadcasting*, July 15, 1937, 28.

17. "FCC Gets League Baseball Complaint," *Broadcasting*, August 1, 1937, 24.

18. "WJBK Drops Its Case against Western Union," *Broadcasting*, September 15, 1937, 36.

19. Hubert Mitzell, "Re-Creating Ball Games Was Rare Radio Art," *Sporting News*, October 18, 1975, 45.

20. Ron Morris, "An Old Concept Is Revived in Durham," *Sporting News*, July 5, 1980, 45.

21. Mitzell, "Re-Creating Ball Games," 46.

22. Smethers and Jolliffe, "Partnership of Telegraphy and Radio."

23. Barber, *Broadcasters*, 108.

24. Smethers and Jolliffe, "Partnership of Telegraphy and Radio," 89.
25. Smith, *Voices of the Game*, 215.
26. Smith, *Voices of the Game*, 27.
27. Ted Patterson, *The Golden Voices of Baseball* (Champaign IL: Sports Publishing, 2002), 164.
28. Smith, *Voices of the Game*, 32.
29. Patterson, *Golden Voices of Baseball*, 64.
30. Smith, *Voices of the Game*, 32–33.
31. Julian W. Pollard, "'Peoples' on the Air—People in the Stores," *Broadcasting*, November 1, 1935, 15.

8. BASEBALL RELUCTANTLY EMBRACES RADIO

1. Meeting of the National League of Professional Baseball Clubs, New York NY, December 8 and 9, 1936, 62, National Baseball Hall of Fame Library, Cooperstown NY (hereafter cited as Hall of Fame Library).
2. Meeting of the American League of Professional Baseball Clubs, Boston MA, July 6, 1936, 36–37, Hall of Fame Library.
3. Meeting of the American League, Boston, July 6, 1936, 16.
4. Meeting of the American League, Boston, July 6, 1936, 49.
5. Meeting of the American League, Boston, July 6, 1936, 50.
6. Meeting of the American League, Boston, July 6, 1936, 34.
7. Meeting of the American League of Professional Baseball Clubs, November 12, 1936, 99, Hall of Fame Library.
8. Meeting of the American League, November 12, 1936, 102.
9. Meeting of the American League, November 12, 1936, 103–4.
10. Annual Meeting of the American League of Professional Baseball Clubs, December 8 and 9, 1936, 68–69, Hall of Fame Library.
11. Annual Meeting of the National League of Professional Baseball Clubs, New York NY, December 8 and 9, 1936, 67, 94–98, Hall of Fame Library.
12. Annual Meeting of the National League of Baseball Clubs, December 6 and 7, 1937, 204, Hall of Fame Library.
13. "Silent Paul Waner Makes Flag Noise," *Sporting News*, July 21, 1938, 2.
14. "On the Radio Airlines," *Sporting News*, July 21, 1938, 14.
15. "Baseball Pickups Are Basis of Suit," *Broadcasting*, July 15, 1938.
16. "Alleged Pirating of Pirates' Contests Argued in Pittsburgh Injunction Plea," *Broadcasting*, August 1, 1938, 18.
17. "KQV's Broadcasts of Pirate Games Enjoined by Court," *Broadcasting*, August 15, 1938, 82.
18. "Federal Court Enjoins KQV in Baseball Case," *Broadcasting*, October 15, 1938.
19. Opinion, Findings of Fact and Conclusions of Law, and Preliminary Injunction in Pittsburgh Athletic Company et al. v. KQV Broadcasting Company, No.

3415, In Equity, in the District Court of the United States for the Western District of Pennsylvania, August 1938, 21.

20. "American League Base-Ball Club of New York, Inc. Estimated Net Income for 1943," October 1, 1943, Yankee Baseball Collection, 1913–50, New York Public Library, New York NY.

21. "Package Plan Next for Baseball?," *Broadcasting*, February 24, 1964, 32; "Baseball 1983," *Broadcasting*, February 28, 1983, 51; Kim McAvoy, "Baseball Gets the Bucks," *Broadcasting & Cable*, April 2, 2001, 26.

22. Bob Nightengale, "TV deals for Angels and Rangers Open Door for Other Teams," *USA Today*, February 6, 2012, last updated February 10, 2012, http://usatoday30. usatoday.com/sports/baseball/story/2012-02-06/MLB-teams-using-lucrative -TV-deals-to-sign-talent/53032284/1.

23. Red Barber, *The Broadcasters* (New York: Dial, 1970), 127.

24. "Brooklyn Grants Baseball Pickups," *Broadcasting*, December 15, 1938, 16.

25. "Gotham Baseball Eyed by Sponsors," *Broadcasting*, January 1, 1939.

26. "Baseball Pickups Start in New York," *Broadcasting*, March 15, 1939, 14.

27. Barber, *Broadcasters*, 106.

28. "Radio and the Game," *Sporting News*, May 4, 1939, 4.

29. "Gotham Baseball to Include WNEW," *Broadcasting*, April 15, 1939, 56.

30. Material on the Yankee and Colonial Networks was drawn from Alexander Russo, *Points on the Dial: Golden Age Radio beyond the Networks* (Durham NC: Duke University Press, 2010).

31. Russo, *Points on the Dial*, 47.

32. The stations and locations were: WNAC (Boston), WEAN (Providence), WLBZ (Bangor, Maine), WNBH (New Bedford, Massachusetts), WORC (Worcester, Massachusetts), WICC (Bridgeport, Connecticut), WAAB (Boston), WPRO (Providence), WDRC (Hartford, Connecticut), WFEA (Manchester, New Hampshire), and WMAS (Springfield, Massachusetts). "We Pay Our Respects to John Shepard, III," *Broadcasting*, August 15, 1932, 17.

33. "Radio Broadens Baseball Broadcasts," *Sporting News*, April 21, 1938, 5.

34. "On the Air Line," *Sporting News*, April 2, 1942, 13.

35. "Broadcasts of Games Blanket America," *Sporting News*, April 23, 1936, 2.

36. "Broadcasts at All Major Parks Put Radio at New Peak," *Sporting News*, May 4, 1939, 5.

37. "Radio Broadens Baseball Broadcasts," 5.

38. Christopher H. Sterling and John Michael Kittross, *Stay Tuned: A History of American Broadcasting*, 3rd ed. (Mahwah NJ: Erlbaum, 2002), 232–33.

39. Franklin D. Roosevelt to Kenesaw M. Landis, January 15, 1942, available online at "President Franklin Roosevelt Green Light Letter—Baseball Can Be Played during the War," Baseball Almanac, http://www.baseball-almanac.com/prz_lfr. shtml.

40. David J. Halberstam, *Sports on New York Radio: A Play-by-Play History* (Chicago: Masters, 1999), 249.

41. "American League Broadcast Program," *Sporting News*, May 3, 1945, 21; "National League Broadcast Program," *Sporting News*, May 10, 1945, 11.

42. "Radio Log of Daily Play-by-Play Broadcasts," *Sporting News*, April 13, 1944, 4.

43. "On the Air Lines," 13.

44. "On the Radio Airlines," *Sporting News*, May 13, 1943, 2.

45. Roosevelt to Landis, January 15, 1942.

46. John Thorn, Pete Palmer, Michael Gershman, and David Pietrusza, *Total Baseball*, 6th ed. (New York: Total Sports, 1999), 107.

47. Meeting of the National League of Professional Baseball Clubs, February 4, 1930, 90–97, Hall of Fame Library.

48. Daniel M. Daniel, "Night Baseball Nothing New," *Baseball Magazine*, February 1935, 389.

49. Clifford Bloodgood, "1931, a Test for Night Baseball," *Baseball Magazine*, April 1931, 509.

50. F. C. Lane, "The Sweeping Success of Night Baseball in the Minors," *Baseball Magazine*, January 1937, 369.

51. Charles C. Alexander, *Breaking the Slump: Baseball in the Depression Era* (New York: Columbia University Press, 2002), 106.

52. Alexander, *Breaking the Slump*, 106; Thorn et al., *Total Baseball*, 107.

53. Meeting of American League, July 6, 1936, 63; According to *Baseball Magazine*, Barrow's distaste for night baseball dated back to his experience with the 1896 Wilmington night game. Barrow told the publication, "My experience that night no doubt has colored my views about night baseball since then. It is a game of daylight, a game of sunshine. It has no place in the dark." Daniel, "Night Baseball Nothing New," 389–90.

54. Barber, *Broadcasters*, 128.

55. Daniel M. Daniel, "Mr. Bradley Gazes at the Stars," *Baseball Magazine*, February 1939, 391.

56. Daniel, "Mr. Bradley Gazes at the Stars," 391.

57. David Pietrusza, *Lights On! The Wild Century-Long Saga of Night Baseball* (Lanham MD: Scarecrow, 1997), 193.

9. AN EXPLOSION IN NATIONAL COVERAGE

1. Data on the number of stations carrying MLB games in this chapter comes from three sources. For the years 1936 to 1958, annual reports on radio and television published in the *Sporting News*, often called "Radio Log" or "Log of Play-by-Play Broadcasts, Telecasts," provided the data. For 1960 and 1962 to 2000, annual reports of radio and television coverage of baseball published in *Broadcasting* or *Broadcasting & Cable* were consulted. For 1959 and 1961,

Sponsor was the source. The figures incorporate all originating and network stations, including Spanish-language stations. When a range was given (e.g., 96–100 stations), the midpoint was used (98). No information on team networks was available from these sources for the 1991 season. Years with missing data were not used in calculating averages.

2. "Baseball Sponsors Show Increase," *Radio Daily*, April 26, 1949, 1.

3. "The Sponsor Hits a Home Run," *Sponsor*, May 9, 1949, 66.

4. "Baseball Sponsors Show Increase," *Radio Daily*, April 26, 1949, 8.

5. "Sponsor Hits a Home Run," 30.

6. Data on the radio industry are from Christopher H. Sterling and John Michael Kittross, *Stay Tuned: A History of American Broadcasting*, 3rd ed. (Mahwah NJ: Erlbaum, 2002), 827–28.

7. Sterling and Kittross, *Stay Tuned*, 830.

8. Sterling and Kittross, *Stay Tuned*, 285.

9. Sterling and Kittross, *Stay Tuned*, 210.

10. Sterling and Kittross, *Stay Tuned*, 296.

11. "Majors, Minors to Operate under Two Five-Year Pacts," *Sporting News*, December 11, 1946, 3.

12. Albert B. Chandler to All Major League Clubs, Notice No. 61, May 12, 1949, Radio and Television File, *Sporting News* Research Center, St. Louis MO.

13. Department of Justice press release, October 27, 1949, 2, Radio and Television File, *Sporting News* Research Center, St. Louis MO.

14. Minutes of a Special Meeting of the Board of Directors of American League Baseball Club of New York, Inc., October 24, 1939, Yankee Baseball Collection, 1913–50, New York Public Library.

15. "Baseball Probe: Justice Suspends Action; Eyes New Major Rules," *Broadcasting*, October 31, 1949, 23, 81.

16. The *Sporting News'* listing of Brooklyn Dodgers stations includes only those broadcasting live. But according to Curt Smith, in late 1950, the Dodgers developed a vast network of stations to broadcast re-creations of their games. At the peak of the Dodgers network in 1953, it numbered 117 outlets concentrated in the South. The region had no MLB teams of its own and a large African American population interested in the team's many black stars. The franchise's relocation to the West Coast in 1958 meant its games would start late in the East, leading to smaller audiences. The network was discontinued in 1962. Curt Smith, *Voices of the Game: The Acclaimed Chronicle of Baseball Radio and Television Broadcasting—From 1921 to the Present*, updated ed. (New York: Fireside, 1992), 136–37.

17. James R. Walker and Robert V. Bellamy, "Did Radio Grow the Game? An Analysis of the Relationship between the Size of Team Radio Networks and Attendance from 1936–1959" (paper presented at the *NINE* Spring Training Conference, Tempe AZ, March 2013).

18. Ronald Garay, *Gordon McLendon: The Maverick of Radio* (Westport CT: Greenwood, 1992), 14–18.

19. Garay, *Gordon McLendon*, 19.

20. Val Adams, "'Just Like Topsy': The Saga of the Liberty Broadcasting System," *New York Times*, September 17, 1950, sec. 2, p. 11.

21. Garay, *Gordon McLendon*, 21.

22. Garay, *Gordon McLendon*, 19.

23. Garay, *Gordon McLendon*, 29.

24. Smith, *Voices of the Game*, 112.

25. Garay, *Gordon McLendon*, 29.

26. "Baseball Ban Prompts WARL to Ask for Anti-trust Action," *Broadcasting*, October 6, 1947, 6.

27. Garay, *Gordon McLendon*, 28.

28. Department of Justice press release, October 27, 1949, 5.

29. Albert B. Chandler to All Major League Clubs, Notice No. 61, May 12, 1949, 1, Radio and Television File, *Sporting News* Research Center, St. Louis MO.

30. Chandler to All Major League Clubs, May 12, 1949, 5.

31. Department of Justice press release, October 27, 1949, 1.

32. Albert B. Chandler to All Major League Clubs and the President of the National Association, Notice No. 85, October 1949, 3, Radio and Television File, *Sporting News* Research Center, St. Louis MO.

33. Chandler to All Major League Clubs, October 1949, 3.

34. Albert B. Chandler to All Major and Minor League Clubs, Ruling No. R-3, June 6, 1950, Radio and Television File, *Sporting News* Research Center, St. Louis MO.

35. Albert B. Chandler to All Major League Clubs and the President of the National Association, Notice No. 86, November 3, 1949, 3, Radio and Television File, *Sporting News* Research Center, St. Louis MO.

36. Department of Justice press release, October 27, 1949, 3.

37. Garay, *Gordon McLendon*, 34.

38. Garay, *Gordon McLendon*, 34–35.

39. Garay, *Gordon McLendon*, 35–36.

40. Garay, *Gordon McLendon*, 38.

41. Smith, *Voices of the Game*, 113.

42. Garay, *Gordon McLendon*, 30.

43. Garay, *Gordon McLendon*, 30.

44. Gordon McLendon, address to National Association of Broadcasters, 3, Library of American Broadcasting, University of Maryland, College Park MD.

45. McLendon, address to National Association of Broadcasters, 4–6.

46. McLendon, address to National Association of Broadcasters, 7.

47. Smith, *Voices of the Game*, 117.

48. Garay, *Gordon McLendon*, 54.

49. Garay, *Gordon McLendon*, 55.

50. Garay, *Gordon McLendon*, 56.

51. Smith, *Voices of the Game*, 134.

52. Garay, *Gordon McLendon*, 47, 57.

53. Gordon McLendon, speech over the Liberty Broadcasting System, May 15, 1952, McLendon Papers, Southwest Collection of Texas Tech University, Lubbock TX.

54. Garay, *Gordon McLendon*, 57–58.

55. American League Press release, January 10, 1955, Radio and Television File, *Sporting News* Research Center, St. Louis MO.

56. Garay, *Gordon McLendon*, 60–61.

57. "Baseball Swings Hard for Rule 1(d) Comeback," *Broadcasting*, May 11, 1953, 56.

58. "Baseball's Frick Says Justice Dept. Reneged on 'Test Case' for Radio-TV," *Broadcasting*, December 12, 1955, 58.

59. Smith, *Voices of the Game*, 118.

60. Robert Cole, "Al Helfer and the Game of the Day," *SABR Research Journal* 10 (1981), available online at *SABR Research Journal* Archive, http://research.sabr .org/journals/al-helfer.

61. Smith, *Voices of the Game*, 119.

62. Cole, "Al Helfer and the Game of the Day."

63. Curt Smith, *Voices of Summer* (New York: Carroll & Graf, 2005), 68.

64. Smith, *Voices of Summer*, 68.

65. Cole, "Al Helfer and the Game of the Day."

10. RADIO IN THE AGE OF TELEVISION

1. Albert B. Chandler to Warren C. Giles, June 4, 1951, National Baseball Hall of Fame Library, Cooperstown NY.

2. While cable television, know at the time as community antenna television (CATV) did exist, it was limited to isolated communities with poor over-the-air reception.

3. James R. Walker and Robert V. Bellamy, Jr., *Center Field Shot: A History of Baseball on Television* (Lincoln: University of Nebraska Press, 2008), 334.

4. The coastal San Diego Padres expanded their geographic territory by extending their Spanish-language radio coverage into Mexico. The extent of their Mexican presence was irregularly documented in *Broadcasting & Cable*. In some years the number of Mexican stations was included, and in others it was not.

5. "Champion Plugs Radio in Baseball Buy," *Broadcasting*, March 14, 1977, 51.

6. "Baseball '92," *Broadcasting*, March 16, 1992, 22–23.

7. Curt Smith, *Voices of the Game: The Acclaimed Chronicle of Baseball Radio and Television Broadcasting—From 1921 to the Present*, updated ed. (New York: Fireside, 1992), 1.

8. Eldon L. Ham, *Broadcasting Baseball: A History of the National Pastime on Radio and Television* (Jefferson NC: McFarland, 2011), 155.

9. J. Anthony Lukas, "In Indiana, Radio Is a Young Cub Fan's Best Friend," *New York Times*, September 22, 1969, 22.

10. Tony Silvia, *Baseball over the Air: The National Pastime on the Radio and in the Imagination* (Jefferson NC: McFarland, 2007), 5.

11. Jonathan Schwartz, "TV View: Why Radio Plays Baseball Better than TV," *New York Times*, October 14, 1990, sec. 2, p. 35.

12. Schwartz, "TV View," 35.

13. John Grisham, *A Painted House* (New York: Random House, 2001), 36–37.

14. Willie Morris, *North toward Home* (Boston: Houghton Mifflin, 1967), 108.

15. Morris, *North toward Home*, 111.

16. Smith, *Voices of the Game*, 438.

17. Smith, *Voices of the Game*, 438.

18. Smith, *Voices of the Game*, 441.

19. "Majors Close 4-Year Deal with CBS Radio," *Sporting News*, May 24, 1975, 46.

20. "A Big Hit for the Old Ball Game," *Broadcasting*, March 8, 1976, 50.

21. Smith, *Voices of the Game*, 439.

22. "Majors Close 4-Year Deal with CBS Radio," 46.

23. "Baseball Rights Inch Up in '78 for Broadcasting," *Broadcasting*, March 6, 1978, 73.

24. "Major Radio-TV Tab Climbs to $54.5 Million," *Sporting News*, April 7, 1979, 10.

25. "Baseball Rights: A Slow, Rising Curve," *Broadcasting*, March 12, 1979, 116.

26. "Baseball! Rights Go Out of the Park," *Broadcasting*, March 10, 1980, 34.

27. Smith, *Voices of the Game*, 440.

28. Gary Deeb, "Cosell on Monday Night Baseball, Despite Kuhn," *Chicago Tribune*, February 8, 1977.

29. Barry Lorge, "Drysdale Pleasant, but Not ABC Coverage," *Washington Post*, April 14, 1978.

30. Deeb, "Cosell on Monday Night Baseball."

31. "Voice of the Fan," *Sporting News*, January 6, 1979, 4.

32. Jack Craig, "A Feast for College Fans," *Sporting News*, September 3, 1984, 12.

33. "Baseball! Rights Go Out of the Park," 34.

34. "Baseball 1981," *Broadcasting*, March 2, 1981, 46.

35. "Baseball 1982," *Broadcasting*, March 1, 1982, 47.

36. "Riding Gain," *Broadcasting*, December 19, 1983, 76.

37. "Riding Gain," *Broadcasting*, November 19, 1984, 70.

38. Smith, *Voices of the Game*, 440.

39. "Baseball's Back on Network Radio," *Broadcasting*, March 4, 1985, 46.

40. Smith, *Voices of the Game*, 294.

41. "Rep Stats on Baseball Fans Show Good Jobs and Incomes," *Television/Radio Age*, March 20, 1989, 21.
42. "CBS Radio's Final Baseball Season?," *Broadcasting*, March 6, 1989, 43.
43. "CBS Radio Signs Four-Year Baseball Contract," *Broadcasting*, March 13, 1989, 56.
44. "MLB Hits Long Ball to ESPN," *Daily Variety*, September 10, 1993, 1.
45. T. Tyler, "New Deal Reshapes Baseball on TV," *Electronic Media*, June 7, 1993, 10.
46. Walker and Bellamy, *Center Field Shot*, 156.

11. THE MODERN BASEBALL ANNOUNCER

1. Milton Jerome Bergstein, "A Study of the Techniques and Principles of Radio Broadcasting of Sports" (master's thesis, Pennsylvania State College, 1950).
2. Bergstein, "Study of the Techniques and Principles," 52.
3. Bergstein, "Study of the Techniques and Principles," 56.
4. Bergstein, "Study of the Techniques and Principles," 59.
5. Bergstein, "Study of the Techniques and Principles," 61.
6. Bergstein, "Study of the Techniques and Principles," 63.
7. Bill James, *The Bill James Guide to Baseball Managers from 1870 to Today* (New York: Scribner, 1997).
8. Quotations from Pat Hughes and Charley Steiner in this chapter come from Pat Hughes, telephone interview by the author, January 23, 2013, Chicago; and Charley Steiner, interview by the author, March 30, 2012, International Association for Communication and Sport Symposium, Peoria IL.
9. John F. Royal to A. H. Morton, October 6, 1936, NBC Archives, Wisconsin Historical Society, Madison WI.
10. Red Barber, *The Broadcasters* (New York: Dial, 1970), 187.
11. Curt Smith, *Voices of the Game: The Acclaimed Chronicle of Baseball Radio and Television Broadcasting—from 1921 to the Present*, updated ed. (New York: Fireside, 1992), 486.
12. Vin Scully to Red Barber, June 25, 1971, Walter Lanier "Red" Barber Papers and Book Collection, Smathers Libraries, University of Florida, Gainesville FL.
13. "Around the Horn," *Chicago Tribune*, August 24, 2013, sec. 2, p. 4.
14. Barber, *Broadcasters*, 228.
15. Barber, *Broadcasters*, 225.
16. Barber, *Broadcasters*, 228.
17. Barber, *Broadcasters*, 229.
18. Smith, *Voices of the Game*, 494.
19. Barber, *Broadcasters*, 229.
20. Barber, *Broadcasters*, 230.
21. Barber, *Broadcasters*, 232.

22. Barber, *Broadcasters*, 232.

23. Barber, *Broadcasters*, 234.

24. Barber, *Broadcasters*, 234.

25. Barber, *Broadcasters*, 235.

26. Barber, *Broadcasters*, 116.

27. Scully to Barber, June 25, 1971. To be fair to "JOCKS," in the 1971 letter to Barber, Scully was also even "less of a fan of the bored super announcer who does everything from Super Bowl to Series with All Star game thrown in," a clear reference to NBC's reigning "super announcer" Curt Gowdy.

28. Pat Hughes and Rich Wolfe, *Ron Santo: A Perfect 10* (Chicago: Lone Wolfe, 2011).

29. Barber, *Broadcasters*, 234.

30. Smith, *Voices of the Game*, 487.

31. Smith, *Voices of the Game*, 490.

32. While the travel challenges faced by contemporary announcers are substantial, Mutual's *Game of the Day* announcers in the 1950s, including Al Helfer, faced daily flights during most of the baseball season. Their nationally broadcast games originated from a different ballpark almost every day. These announcers were kings of both the airwaves and the airport (see chapter 9).

33. Smith, *Voices of Summer*, 391–93.

34. Anna R. Newton and Jean Hastings Ardell, "Taking the Measure of Baseball Broadcasters: What It Takes to Be a Five-Tool Announcer," *NINE: A Journal of Baseball History and Culture* 15, no. 2 (2007): 85.

35. Newton and Ardell, "Taking the Measure of Baseball Broadcasters," 80.

36. James R. Walker and Robert V. Bellamy Jr., *Center Field Shot: A History of Baseball on Television* (Lincoln: University of Nebraska Press, 2008), 257–59.

37. Smith, *Voices of the Game*, 487.

12. BASEBALL BROADCASTS IN THE DIGITAL ERA

1. Charles Haddad, "KMOX Brings Baseball into the Space Age," *St. Louis Post-Dispatch*, undated article, radio clippings file, National Baseball Hall of Fame Library, Cooperstown NY.

2. Richard Sandomir, "Baseball's Web Site Is Big Business," *New York Times*, April 2, 2006, B10.

3. Tim Jones, "A Radio with No Boundaries," *Chicago Tribune*, May 11, 1998, 1.

4. Tricia Duryee, "Seattle-Based RealNetworks Scores Exclusive Major League Baseball Contract," *Seattle Times*, March 28, 2001, http://community.seattle times.nwsource.com/archive/?date=20010328&slug=realmlb28.

5. Chris Gaither, "Major League Baseball to Charge for Web Broadcasts," *New York Times*, March 27, 2001, C4.

6. Gaither, "Major League Baseball to Charge for Web Broadcasts," C4.

7. "Baseball Swings for Online Profits with RealNetworks Deal for Game Broadcasts," *San Jose Mercury News*, March 29, 2001. Accessed in Newspaper Source database.

8. "It's a Baseball-Lover's Dream, but It Will Cost You," *Saint Paul Pioneer Press*, April 14, 2002, A6.

9. Alan Krauss, "Earthlink Bundles Subscription-Only Sports Features from Popular Web Sites," *New York Times*, April 12, 2004, C6.

10. Jorge L. Ortiz, "MLB's Advanced Media Arm Pulls in Profits," *USA Today*, December 5, 2007, http://usatoday30.usatoday.com/sports/baseball/2007-12 -04-baseball-online_N.htm.

11. "Major League Baseball Pulls Podcast Clips from Apple's iTunes," *Wall Street Journal*, September 27, 2006, B2.

12. Alyson Shontell, "THE DIGITAL 100: The World's Most Valuable Private Tech Companies," *Business Insider*, October 3, 2012, http://www.businessinsider .com/2012-digital-100?op=1.

13. Matt Snyder, "Report: MLB Revenues in 2012 Were $7.5 Billion," CBSSports. com, December 9, 2012, http://www.cbssports.com/mlb/blog/eye-on-base ball/21335810/report-mlb-revenues-in-2012-were-75-billion.

14. Alan Robinson, "New Audience for Old Voices," *Chicago Tribune*, May 15, 2005, 6.

15. "Baseball Joins Satellite Radio," *New York Times*, October 21, 2004, D6.

16. "XM Adds Baseball Broadcasts to Lineup," *Chicago Tribune*, October 21, 2004, 3.

17. "XM Radio Raises Subscriber Forecast," *New York Times*, July 29, 2005, C14.

18. Jeffrey Tomich and Tim McLaughlin, "What Happened to the Mighty 'MOX'?," *St. Louis Post-Dispatch*, August 7, 2005, A1.

19. Lee Jenkins, "Baseball Rediscovers Its Radio Days," *New York Times*, July 12, 2005, D2.

20. Bob Verdi, "It's Wall-to-Wall Baseball via Satellite," *Chicago Tribune*, August 7, 2005, sec. 3, p. 2.

21. Robinson, "New Audience for Old Voices," 6.

22. Jenkins, "Baseball Rediscovers Its Radio Days," D2.

23. Tomich and McLaughlin, "What Happened to the Mighty 'MOX'?," A1.

24. Lorne Manly, "As Satellite Radio Takes Off, It Is Altering the Airwaves," *New York Times*, April 5, 2005, A1.

25. Nick Wingfield, "Health & Technology: RealNetworks, Baseball Unite to Broadcast via Cellphone," *Wall Street Journal*, September 6, 2002, B5.

26. Mike Conklin, "Play-by-Play over Cellphones," *Chicago Tribune*, May 1, 2005, 9.

27. Richard Siklos and Andrew Ross Sorkin, "Satellite Radio in Plan to Merge," *New York Times*, February 20, 2007, A1.

28. Ashlee Vance, "For a Fee, a Stream of Tunes, Talk and Video," *New York Times*, September 9, 2004, G8.
29. Felicity Barringer, "Baseball Is Trying to Limit How News Coverage Is Used," *New York Times*, March 31, 2001.
30. Richard Sandomir, "WCBS Wins the Rights to Yanks on the Radio," *New York Times*, S3.
31. Teddy Greenstein, "Cubs' Bottom Line: Is It Out of Line?," *Chicago Tribune*, February 4, 2001, sec. 3, p. 1.
32. Sasha Talcott, "Sox Radio Pact May Top $12M per Year," *Boston Globe*, April 13, 2006, D1; Andrew Grossman, "Red Sox Radio: $16M a Year," *Sports Business Weekly*, May 15, 2006, http://www.sportsbusinessdaily.com/Journal/Issues/2006/05/20060515/This-Weeks-News/Red-Sox-Radio-$16M-A-Year.aspx?hl=red%20sox%20radio%20%2416M%20a%20year&sc=0.
33. Talcott, "Sox Radio Pact May Top $12M per Year."
34. Andrew Zimbalist, "Tigers Considering No-Rights-Fee Radio Deal," *Sports Business Journal*, December 18, 2006, http://www.sportsbusinessdaily.com/Journal/Issues/2006/12/20061218/Media/Tigers-Considering-No-Rights-Fee-Radio-Deal.aspx?hl=tigers%20considering%20no-rights-fee&sc=0.
35. Dan Caesar, "Where, Oh Where, Is Baseball on the Radio?," *St. Louis Post-Dispatch*, October 6, 2007, B7.
36. Alan Snel, "Old-Time Technique Gets New Airing," *Tampa Tribune*, May 5, 2006, 1.
37. Sasha Talcott, "Firm Seeks Sox Radio Network Name Deal," *Boston Globe*, June 28, 2006, C1.
38. Charley Steiner, interview by the author, March 30, 2012, International Association for Communication and Sport Symposium, Peoria IL.
39. David Broughton, "Arbitron Data Shows CBS Radio Led MLB Opening Day Radio Broadcasts," *Sports Business Journal*, May 18, 2012, http://www.sportsbusinessdaily.com/Daily/Issues/2012/05/18/Research-and-Ratings/MLB-arbitron.aspx?hl=radio%20ratings%20baseball&sc=0.
40. David Broughton, "Radio Roundup: Yanks Lead Way Despite Drop," *Sports Business Journal*, December 17, 2012, http://www.sportsbusinessdaily.com/Journal/Issues/2012/12/17/Media/MLB-radio.aspx.
41. Ed Sherman, "WGN Tuning Out Cubs?," *Chicago Tribune*, October 17, 2013, sec. 3, p. 2.
42. Richard Sandomir, "Here's the Pitch. But First, One from Our Sponsor," *New York Times*, August 18, 2013, http://www.nytimes.com/2013/08/19/sports/baseball/radio-broadcasts-balance-baseball-with-advertising.html.

EPILOGUE
1. Roger Angell, *The Summer Game* (Lincoln: University of Nebraska Press, 2004).

INDEX

Chicago Cardinals, 185

Chicago Cubs, ix–x, 5, 7–8, 11, 13–15, 39, 56, 59, 98, 134, 157, 182–83, 208, 223, 232–33, 241; arguing for MLB broadcasts, 82, 86–89, 91, 148; early broadcasts, 47–52; evening re-creations, 146; first baseball announcers, 61–63, 68–70; first broadcast booth, 76; General Mills sponsorship, 125–26, 132; NBC conflicts over local broadcasts, 120–21; recent rights fees, 251, 253–54; rights fees, 162; World War II reduction in station coverage, 173

Chicago Daily News, 48–49, 60–61

Chicago Tribune, 47, 50, 60–63, 77–78, 214, 241, 247

Chicago Tribune Magazine, 214

Chicago White Sox, 86, 125, 132, 134, 173, 182, 195, 251; baseball announcers, 59, 61, 69; early broadcasts, 48, 51; support for broadcasts, 91–92

Cincinnati Reds, 15, 94, 111, 132, 143, 166, 171, 179, 182, 195, 207, 223; early broadcasts, 55–56; early rights fees, 162–63; night baseball, 175–76, recent ratings, 253–54

Clear Channel, 248

Cleveland Indians, 9, 24, 39, 101, 121, 126, 132, 154, 176, 182, 253; early baseball announcer, 73–74; early broadcasts, 48, 55; early rights fees 57; first baseball announcer, 72–73; support for broadcasts, 86, 89, 92

Coca-Cola, 108, 135

Coleman, Jerry, 213, 217, 231, 247

"College Football Roundup," 223–24

Collins, Edward T., 159–60

Colonial Network, 9, 169–71

Comiskey, Charles A., 51

Communications Act of 1934, 112, 117, 150, 165; Rule 177, 150

Coolidge, Mrs. Calvin, 33–34

Cosell, Howard, 214–15

Costas, Bob, 247

Cowan, Thomas, 11, 22–25, 144

Craig, Jack, 215

Crosley Field, 55, 175

Crossley surveys of baseball audiences in 1938, 124

Dallas Rebels, 185

Davis, David. D., 126–27

Dean, Dizzy, 71, 183, 195, 198, 231, 236

Dempsey-Carpentier Heavyweight Fight, 22

Dempsey-Sharkey Heavyweight Fight, 37

Desmond, Connie, 224

Detroit Free Press, 68

Detroit Lions, 185

Detroit News, 5, 23, 55, 60, 67–68, 76, 102, 122, 131

Detroit Tigers, 10, 56, 76, 85, 169, 213, 251, 253–54; first baseball announcer, 67–68

digital media, 239–40, 242, 245, 249, 251–52, 254, 258

DiMaggio, Joe, 167, 173

"Disc Jockey Roundtable," 193

Dorsey, Tommy, 185

Doubleday, Abner, 141

drop-ins (in game commercials), 14, 254–55

Dudley, Jimmy, 73, 154

Dunphy, Don, 173

EarthLink, 243

Ebbets Field, 142, 192

satellite radio, 4–5, 244–49, 254, 258

Schacht, Al, 173

Schembechler, Bo, 213

Schoonmaker, F. P. (federal judge), 164–65

Schwartz, Jonathan, 209

Scully, Vin, x–xi, 1, 209, 213, 220, 227, 231, 234–38, 247; example of announcing skills, 209; mentoring by Red Barber, 222–25, 230

Seattle Mariners, 206, 251

Shannon, Mike, 247

Shepherd, John, III, 9, 106

Shibe, Ben, 129

Shibe, John, 129, 166

Silvia, Tony, 2, 208–9

Simmons, Lon, ix

Simmons Media Group, 252

Sinclair Refining, 132

Sirius, 245, 248–49, 252

Sirius XM, 4, 249, 252

Sixth Report and Order, 204

Skelton, Red, 224

Slater, Bill, 173

Smith, Curt, 2, 22, 24, 31, 61, 68, 74, 142, 198, 220; evaluating announcers, 61, 68, 73, 225, 235–36; on the beauty of baseball on the radio, 207–8

Smith, J. O., 24, 31

Smulyan, Susan, 116–17

Snider, Duke, 234

Socony-Vacuum Oil (later Mobil Oil), 65, 104, 115, 132, 164, 167

Sosa, Sammy, 231

Southern League (minor league), 126

Spang, J. P., 109–10

Speaker, Tris, 133

Sponsor, 178

Sporting News, (*TSN*), 14, 24, 46, 83, 150, 163, 212–15; on France Laux,

70–71; on Fred Hoey, 64–65; on gamecasts coming to NYC, 168; on Harry Hartman, 73–74; position on radio coverage of baseball, 43–44, 58, 95; on Tom Manning, 73

Sports Broadcasting Act of 1961, 187

Sports Illustrated, 212

Spotify, 258

Standard Brands, 119, 120

Steiner, Charley, 14, 253; on the announcing craft, 220, 222, 225, 227–28, 230, 233, 237–38

Stern, Bill, 220

Stern, Howard, 245, 249

St. Louis Browns, 8, 10, 67, 70–71, 75–77, 92, 131, 159, 161, 182

St. Louis Cardinals, 10, 15, 50, 54, 66, 68, 75, 96, 98, 102, 161, 171, 204, 213; early baseball announcer, 70–71; development of team network, 182–85, 205, 237, 240; John Grisham recalls broadcasts, 210; resistance to broadcasts, 86, 89–90; rights fees, 207; satellite radio listening, 246; switching from KMOX, 252

St. Louis Post-Dispatch, 71

Stockton, Dick, 217

Stoneham, Charles, 53, 176

Stram, Hank, 214

Street, Gabby, 71

Sunday Call (Newark), 23

superstations (cable television), 237

superstations (radio), 33, 118

Tampa Bay Rays, 206, 252

team networks, 3, 10, 15–16, 158, 195, 197, 199, 212, 252; during World War II, 173–74; first team networks 168–71; postwar expansion, 178–83; in TV age, 203–6

recent rights fees and ratings,
251–53
WGY, 25, 28, 30–32, 37–38, 40
Wheaties, 10, 71, 82, 94, 125–30, 133
White, Bill, 213
White, Major J. Andrew, 15, 22, 29, 37,
39, 54
WHK, 48, 57, 72, 121
WHNZ, 252
WHO, 125, 145
Williams, Ted, 173
Wilson, Bert, x
WIND, 146, 173
WINS, 173, 185
wired radio, 159
Wireless Age, 25–27, 29, 31, 33, 62
Witmer, Roy C., 119–21, 123
WJAR, 30–32
WJBK, 149–50
WJSV, 167
WLS "The Prairie Farmer Station,"
168
WLW, 55, 73, 107, 167, 223, 253
WMAF, 32
WMAQ, 11, 39, 48–51, 52, 60–62, 69, 75,
87, 119–22
WMCA, 5, 54, 126–27, 149, 158, 160, 173
WMFF, 123
WMGM, 193
WNAC, 48, 169–70
WNEW, 168
WOC, 69, 125
Wolff, Bob, 198

Woods, Jim, 231
WOR, 34, 54, 107, 110, 167, 173
World Baseball Classic, 243
World Series radio coverage, 1920, 5,
23–24; 1921, 22–25; 1922, 25–29; 1923,
29–31; 1924, 31–33; 1925, 33–35; 1926,
35–36; 1927–33, 36–41; 1934, 101–3;
1935–36, 106–8; 1937, 108; 1938,
108–9; 1939, 109–12
World Series radio rights fees, 104–9,
113–14, 206, 212–13, 215–18
World Wide Web, 240–41
Wrigley Field, 11, 47, 63, 75, 88, 133, 198
Wrigley, Philip K., 56, 146, 162
Wrigley, William, Jr., x, 49, 56, 68, 76,
86, 89, 183
WRKO, 252
WRUF, 223
WSAI, 163, 167, 171, 223
WTAM, 39, 48, 55, 57, 72–73
WTMV, 71
WWJ, 5, 11, 23, 55, 60, 67–68, 76, 101–2,
122–23, 131, 170
WWSW, 164
WXYZ, 107, 131, 170–71

XM, 245–51

Yankee Network, 63, 65, 106, 124, 126,
159, 169–70
Yankee Stadium, 21, 29, 36, 52, 98, 198

Zeldis, Malcah, 1

www.ingramcontent.com/pod-product-compliance
Lightning Source LLC
Chambersburg PA
CBHW030939150426
42812CB00064B/3062/J